I0823054

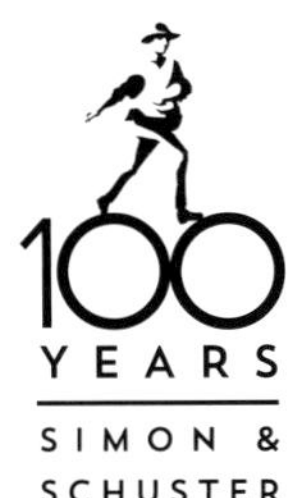
100
YEARS
SIMON &
SCHUSTER

KAMALA

Her HISTORIC, JOYFUL and AUSPICIOUS Sprint to the White House

DEBORAH WILLIS and KEVIN MERIDA

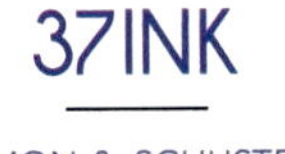

SIMON & SCHUSTER

NEW YORK AMSTERDAM/ANTWERP LONDON TORONTO SYDNEY NEW DELHI

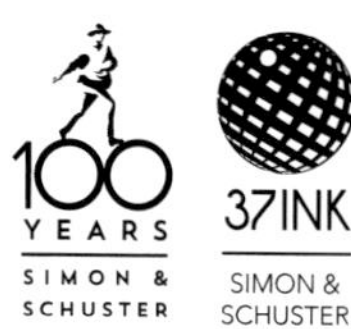

An Imprint of Simon & Schuster, LLC
1230 Avenue of the Americas
New York, NY 10020

First 37 INK/Simon & Schuster hardcover edition December 2024

37 INK/SIMON & SCHUSTER and colophon are trademarks of Simon & Schuster, LLC

Simon & Schuster: Celebrating 100 years of publishing in 2024.

For information about special discounts for bulk purchases, please contact Simon & Schuster Special Sales
at 1-866-506-1949 or business@simonandschuster.com.

The Simon & Schuster Speakers Bureau can bring authors to your live event.
For more information or to book an event, contact the Simon & Schuster Speakers Bureau
at 1-866-248-3049 or visit our website at www.simonspeakers.com.

Interior design by Ruth Lee-Mui

Manufactured in the United States of America

1 3 5 7 9 10 8 6 4 2

Library of Congress Cataloging-in-Publication Data has been applied for.

ISBN 978-1-6680-9554-6
ISBN 978-1-6680-9556-0 (ebook)

For my granddaughters Zenzele Ruth Hockley Thomas
and Kazuri Thandeka Hockley Thomas
—DEBORAH WILLIS

For my mom, Doris Hill,
and my grandson, Sydney Britt
—KEVIN MERIDA

"Photography is an art form that extends beyond place and time. It creates lasting impressions and sometimes challenges what you thought you knew for sure."

—KEVIN MERIDA

INTRODUCTION

Over a lightning-swift 107 days, Kamala Harris completely rewrote the American political playbook.

She took her perpetually underestimated self and sprinted across the 2024 presidential campaign landscape, giving voice to aspiration and ambition, bringing confidence to little girls, championing small businesses as part of her economic vision, and launching a Historically Black Colleges and Universities (HBCU) homecoming tour. She even ordered a slice of chocolate caramel cake—caramel's her favorite—at Dottie's Market in Savannah along the way.

Harris was the most sudden, improbable presidential nominee of a major political party in modern history, and she seized the opportunity as if the moment were made for her. Harris had been a loyal vice president living in the shadow of President Joe Biden, sometimes doubted and dissed, unable to pop out and show her value. Of course, vice presidents rarely stand out—they're background performers. Only once in 188 years had a sitting vice president—George H. W. Bush in 1988—been elected president. But one alarming debate performance by the then eighty-one-year-old Biden triggered a stunning sequence of actions that forced him to drop out of the race, and Harris to be catapulted to the main stage.

She became the one Democrats were waiting for, the one to shift the story. All of those potential voters who were feeling depressed about 2024, voters of different identities and allegiances dreading the choice of Biden versus a second Donald Trump presidency, were quickly in an unimaginably better mood.

Kamala: Her Historic, Joyful, and Auspicious Sprint to the White House is in some ways about that mood—the locomotion of new possibilities imagined. What Kamala Harris did in a few short months was popularize *joy*: A simple, sweet, infectious noun that became a kind of campaign anthem to rally around. The antidote to fear and hopelessness, and just maybe the inception of a saner kind of politics. The politics of decency.

Photography is the maker of memories, a visual concerto of unforgettable occasions and ordinary occurrences. Who doesn't love pictures? They capture our cherished times, preserve our recollections, make us wonder and sometimes just laugh at ourselves as we tell our unexpected stories. We owe the world's photographers our endless gratitude for hanging out in the background and documenting life as it unfolds, even when that life brings us heartache instead of pleasure, defeat instead of victory.

This book is a photographic biography of an extraordinary woman whose sprint for the presidency in 2024 is at the apex of a pioneering career. Hers is the life of a historic figure: the first woman, first Black American, and first Asian American to be elected district attorney in San Francisco (2003) and California attorney general (2010); the second Black woman and first South Asian American to be elected to the United States Senate (2016); the first woman, first Black American, and first Indian American to be sworn in as vice president of the United States (2021); and the first Black woman and first Asian American to become the presidential nominee of a major political party.

Her string of historic firsts reflects a combination of unshakable ambition, strategic savvy, preparation, and the ability to learn fast along the way. She also has bravery and intellect in her DNA, and a bit of luck on her side.

The photos in this collection tell the story of Kamala Harris's rise, her roots, and the village of family, friends, sorority sisters, and political supporters that got her here. We see her exuberant laughter and her solemnity, her confident stride across countless stages, and the way she lifts her eyebrows to convey empathy. We see moments of intensity—grilling Brett Kavanaugh and Jeff Sessions. These photos were curated by the esteemed visual historian Deborah Willis, chair of the Department of Photography and Imaging at New York University's Tisch School of the Arts. The photos come from a wide range of photographers, from decorated prizewinners to cell-phone-camera snappers who happened to be at the right place at the right time. Some of the images have never been published, and others are the creative result of digital imagination.

Photography is an art form that extends beyond place and time. It creates lasting impressions and sometimes challenges what you thought you knew for sure. Kamala Harris is just a shade over five foot, four inches tall, but she presents like she's much taller. In *Kamala: Her Historic, Joyful, and Auspicious Sprint to the White House*, the bigness of Harris's persona comes through. We see in her face the shifts from gravity to levity, from incredulity in listening to Trump's bluster on the debate stage to delight in taking a selfie with a little girl she must bend down to reach. She looks just as comfortable saluting military personnel stepping off her Marine Two helicopter as she does participating in the coin toss at the Howard–Hampton college football game.

We see through this collection of photos some of the issues and causes she is most passionate about: the fight to preserve a woman's right to make decisions about her body; the fights for marriage equality and LGBTQ+ rights. Harris officiated the first same-sex marriage after the ban against them was declared unconstitutional.

You notice her hugs have a warmth to them; that she often puts her hand over her heart when signaling approval or affirmation. Politicians are known to point to people in crowds, and Harris is expert at the specificity of gesturing, establishing a connection that makes it appear like her hands are speaking directly to you. We catch her staring longingly at her man, Second Gentleman Doug Emhoff, and then see her and running mate Tim Walz curiously reviewing the snack options at a Sheetz gas station in suburban Pittsburgh. Historic campaigns tend to attract all-star creativity in artistic expression. The 2024 run included a vivid mural by artist 4eene Vision in Los Angeles of Martin Luther King Jr., Barack Obama, and Kamala Harris side by side. And you know you're special when the artist Carrie Mae Weems designs a traveling billboard for you that accentuates your caring side. Its message: "Leading with Compassion, Not Complaint."

Harris's style is one of cool elegance, and she is the latest, most notable woman to make pantsuits—from Sergio Hudson to Chloé—a thing. In blues and grays, tans and whites, it's her uniform of power and poise. Sometimes she rocks Converse sneakers because that's how she rolls.

Hers has been a remarkable journey from the little girl who accompanied her mother to equal rights rallies and was taught by her father to run free to the self-assured political leader who changed people's minds about her and shook up electoral politics.

Born in Oakland in 1964, Kamala Devi Harris, a daughter of immigrants, grew up in a Bay Area home filled with music: the soulful R and B of Aretha Franklin, and the innovative jazz of John Coltrane.

Her mother, Shyamala Gopalan, was raised in southern India, graduating from the University of Delhi at age nineteen with a passion for science that brought her to California. Attending the University of California, Berkeley, she studied nutrition and endocrinology, received her doctorate, and later became widely recognized for her research in breast cancer, which she had long dreamed of curing. Harris's father, Donald Harris, was born in Jamaica and immigrated to the United States in 1961 to study economics at UC Berkeley, where he met his future wife. They fell in love during a time of fervent activism, both committed to the civil rights movement, both members of a Black study group. Donald Harris would go on to become a prominent, though unorthodox, economist, and the first Black scholar to achieve tenure at Stanford University's Department of Economics, where he is now an emeritus professor.

The Harris marriage didn't last long. The couple separated in 1969, when Kamala was five and her sister, Maya, was three; they filed for divorce three years later. As a result, Kamala and Maya grew up with their mother as the main influence in their lives. Their father has lamented his parental absence, attributing it to a contentious custody battle, and has been noticeably absent for key moments in her rise.

Though Kamala gives her father credit for teaching her to be fearless, she admitted to the *SF Weekly* in 2003, "My father is a good guy, but we are not close."

In her speeches and public appearances, she most often mentions her mother, who died in 2009 from colon cancer, as the guiding light for her and Maya. "She was the one most responsible for shaping us into the women we would become," Harris writes in her autobiography, *The Truths We Hold: An American Journey*. "My mother used to tell my sister and me, 'You may be the first to do many things. But make sure you're not the last.' "

She has, indeed, been the first to do many things. Struggle has often been in the backdrop of her achievement. She was motivated to become a prosecutor after her best friend in high school confided that she had been sexually abused by her stepfather; Harris wanted to protect young women like her friend. She landed a job out of law school as a deputy district attorney, but failed to pass the bar exam on her first try and had to begin in the Alameda County District Attorney's Office doing clerk duties. "I felt miserable and embarrassed," she wrote in her autobiography. "I wondered if people thought I was a fraud."

She passed the bar on her second try, proving that a setback would not stop her. She'd go on to be elected San Francisco district attorney, and next took on the challenge of seeking the top law enforcement job in the state. She was an underdog in that 2010 race for California attorney general. Her hometown paper, the *San Francisco Chronicle*, initially called the race on election night for her opponent. But after weeks of official vote tallies of mail-in and provisional ballots, Harris prevailed by less than a percentage point of the 9.6 million votes cast.

She was on her way to a new level of stature in California politics, and nationally. When Senator Barbara Boxer decided not to seek reelection in 2016, opening up a Senate seat that had been occupied for twenty-four years, Harris went for it. And won.

You know what came next: setting her eyes on the presidency.

Though she'd barely been in the Senate for two years, a bid against a stacked Democratic field for the chance to defeat Donald Trump in 2020 was irresistible. She was a rising star in the national party who had campaigned for candidates across the country in the 2018 midterm elections and had a strong base of Hollywood donors in the mecca of Democratic fundraising. (Indeed, as a senator she was one of the party's most influential fundraisers.) She had been tough on criminals while calling for criminal justice reforms, and her record on the environment included establishing one of the first environmental

"My mother used to tell my sister and me, 'You may be the first to do many things. But make sure you're not the last.'"

—KAMALA HARRIS

justice units of its kind as DA, holding polluters accountable as attorney general, and supporting the Green New Deal as a senator.

Her campaign brain trust believed her experience on these and other issues, from housing to college affordability to sexual assault, would make her a strong contender. From the outset, Harris was considered a top-tier candidate, but her 2020 campaign sputtered. With unclear messaging, difficulty raising money, challenges from progressives about her record as a prosecutor, and dissension within her inner circle, Harris left the race two months before the Iowa caucuses, the first nominating contest.

Her fast exit shocked some of the political cognoscenti; it might have been an insurmountable defeat for some politicians. Harris regrouped and went back to work as a senator. Biden went on to win the nomination, fueled by a landslide comeback in the South Carolina primary after his campaign was thought to be in deep trouble. Biden's victory there and his strong support among Black voters owed considerable thanks to the endorsement of Rep. James Clyburn (D-SC), one of the most influential Democrats in the House and one of the most prominent Black lawmakers in the nation. When Biden subsequently committed to picking a woman as his running mate, Clyburn privately and persuasively urged him to make it a Black woman.

Harris had already emerged as an early front-runner to be Biden's choice. But the drumbeat to name a Black woman took on life, and pressure mounted inside the Biden orbit that selecting a Black woman could galvanize the party and boost turnout among a critical Democratic constituency. Several other Black women were also considered strong possibilities, notably former National Security Advisor Susan Rice, then-Rep. Val Demings (D-FL), and then-Congressional Black Caucus Chairwoman Karen Bass (who was later elected the mayor of Los Angeles).

Harris became the clear and comfortable choice for Biden, who was drawn to her because she had already been tested on the national stage, because she represented generational change, because she had experience at various levels of government, and because she would be a historic pick. They also bonded over her friendship and close collaboration with Biden's late son, Beau, when they both were state attorneys general. The inordinate pressure and scrutiny Harris faced being the first woman, not to mention the first Black and first Indian American vice president, never abated. Almost as soon as she was selected, she was subject to racism, sexism, and questions about her identity that were driven by political opponents.

During her time at Biden's side, Harris spoke very little about her feelings that there was a double standard in how men and women were evaluated at that level. She took on the issues of gun violence, voting rights, reproductive health, and immigration—the latter issue causing her some problems as she was criticized by the Left and the Right for being slow to travel to the southern border, and later from progressives for telling Central American migrants not to come to the United States.

She suffered noticeable staff turnover within her senior ranks. Some top Democratic donors grumbled about whether she was an asset to Biden—let alone a future president—and whether she ought to be replaced on the 2024 ticket. When I was executive editor of the *Los Angeles Times*, it wasn't uncommon to hear from prominent California Democrats about their disappointment in and alienation from her. Many wondered where the remarkable woman whom they had stood beside for so many years was. Some no longer had the access they were accustomed to; some believed she didn't have the right organizational structure in place and wasn't receiving the kind of advice she deserved at critical moments.

But when Biden himself was under fire and his fitness for another term questioned, she was steadfast in her loyalty. Never wavering in her defense of him or taking an opportunistic tack, she demonstrated her toughness and how cool she was under duress.

When calls for Biden to leave the race reached a crescendo from notables as different as George Clooney and former House Speaker Nancy Pelosi, Biden knew he had no choice other than to exit. Some quickly made sure the party would not look past Harris; Clyburn and the Congressional Black Caucus foremost among them.

With Biden's endorsement, others quickly followed. Harris wasted no time consolidating support around her. She was ready.

Ashley Etienne, a former communications director for both Harris and Pelosi, reflected on what had primed Harris for a more triumphant second run at the presidency. "For four years, it was like spring training," said Etienne, who worked in both the Obama and Biden White Houses. "You have to build the muscle. Timing, opportunity, and preparation equal success."

Harris had to cultivate a broader range of relationships, learn to be less defensive, and become more confident in spaces she had not previously occupied. She was a quick study.

When Harris accepted her party's nomination in Chicago on August 22, 2024, she spoke of being "no stranger to unlikely journeys." She cited her mother's bravery crossing the world alone at nineteen with the dream of being the scientist who would cure breast cancer.

She acknowledged there were people of divergent political views watching.

"And I want you to know, I promise to be a president for all Americans," she said. "You can always trust me to put country above party and self. To hold sacred America's fundamental principles, from the

"When you lift up women,

you lift up families, you lift up

communities, you lift up economies—

and you lift up America."

—KAMALA HARRIS

rule of law to free and fair elections to the peaceful transfer of power. I will be a president who unites us around our highest aspirations. A president who leads and listens; who is realistic, practical, and has common sense, and always fights for the American people. From the courthouse to the White House, that has been my life's work."

Writing in *New York* magazine, Jonathan Chait described it as the best acceptance speech he had ever heard. "I could find nothing to criticize in this speech," he wrote.

Harris did not talk about gender identity that night. But she was motivated by the examples of many who came before her, daring to think they, too, could become president.

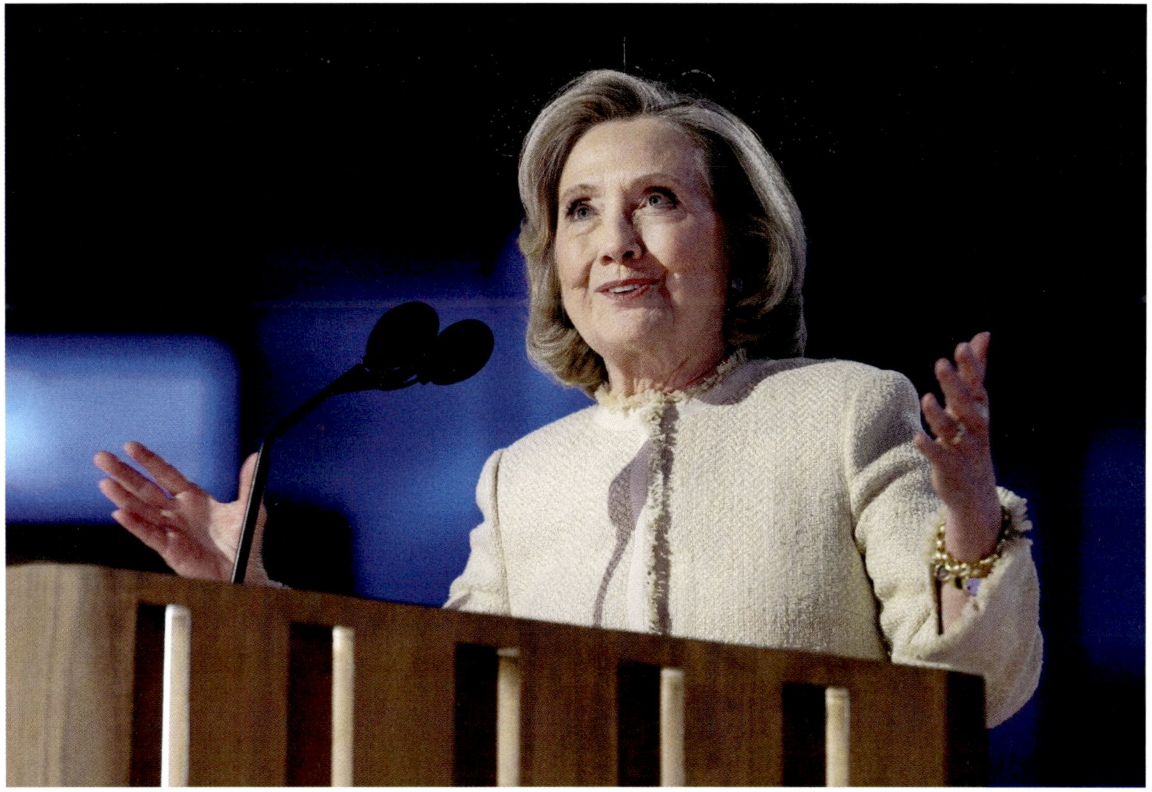

FORMER SECRETARY OF STATE HILLARY RODHAM CLINTON speaks during the 2024 Democratic National Convention. Clinton set the bar for what is possible for women and is often thought of as one of the most qualified presidential nominees in modern history. Many still can't believe she lost to Donald Trump in 2016, an upset few saw coming.

Hillary Clinton got closest to the goal—she beat Trump in 2016 by nearly 2.9 million popular votes nationwide but failed to get the required 270 Electoral College votes needed to win the presidency. Fewer than eighty thousand votes in three battleground states—Michigan, Pennsylvania, and Wisconsin—would've changed the outcome, and Donald Trump would never have been the ex-president Harris needed to beat.

There were many other women who broke down barriers, early pioneers who defied the expectations for what women could achieve in a presidential campaign. Some are buried in history. They include Victoria Claflin Woodhull, who accepted the National Equal Rights Party's call to run in 1872 even though she was thirty-three and did not meet the legal age requirement to become president. There was Senator Margaret Chase Smith (R-ME) in 1964, the first woman to have her name placed in nomination by a major party. There was Rep. Shirley Chisholm (D-NY) in 1972, "Unbought and Unbossed," the first African American woman to run for president under a major party's banner. There was Carol Moseley Braun, who preceded Harris as the first African American woman elected to the Senate and then ran for president in 2004. According to political scientist Jo Freeman, from 1964 to 2004, more than fifty women were on at least one ballot as presidential contenders, some of them minor party candidates who generated little national media attention. More major party candidates would follow in succeeding cycles.

Harris left the Democratic National Convention riding a spectacular wave of momentum. It had started earlier when Black women, forty-four thousand strong, hopped on a Zoom fundraiser and almost shut down the platform. What followed were Black men, white women, "white dudes," and ultimately more than one hundred other groups coalescing support around Harris's candidacy on virtual platforms—from Swifties for Kamala to Comics for Kamala. Her very candidacy had Trump perplexed. She was like a disciplined boxer, bobbing and weaving and toying with an opponent who seemed to be flailing. An undeniably dominant debate performance against Trump only added to her confidence.

She didn't adhere to campaign convention or respond to outside criticism. Exceedingly strategic about where she appeared and to whom she gave interviews, she did only six interviews in the first two months following Biden's withdrawal from the race. She prioritized local news outlets and forums like Stephanie "Chiquibaby" Himonidis's syndicated Spanish-language radio program, the *Chiquibaby Show*, and a National Association of Black Journalists' panel. She embraced British pop star Charli XCX, who started a whole neon lime meme explosion around her hit album, *Brat*, and transferred some of her youth cred to Harris when she tweeted: "kamala IS brat," which Charli explained as: "That girl who is a little messy and likes to party, and maybe says dumb things sometimes, who feels herself but then also maybe has a breakdown but parties through it."

The Harris campaign went with it, changing the backdrop of their official X page to *Brat* green. They were aggressive in turning viral memes to their advantage and creative with their messaging on social platforms, like TikTok.

And of course there was an Oprah "Unite for America" event, where Harris reiterated her support for the Second Amendment with this provocative quote: "If somebody breaks in my house, they're getting shot." Her point was clear: you can be a gun owner and also be for laws that would curb school shootings and other senseless gun violence.

As the campaign went on, she became more and more comfortable as the candidate poised to win the popular vote and capture enough battleground states to secure the 270 Electoral College votes needed to claim the presidency. Her blend of tenacity and compassion suited her. She knew she could be tough—she'd taken on big banks, exploitative for-profit colleges, transnational gangs, and child sexual predators

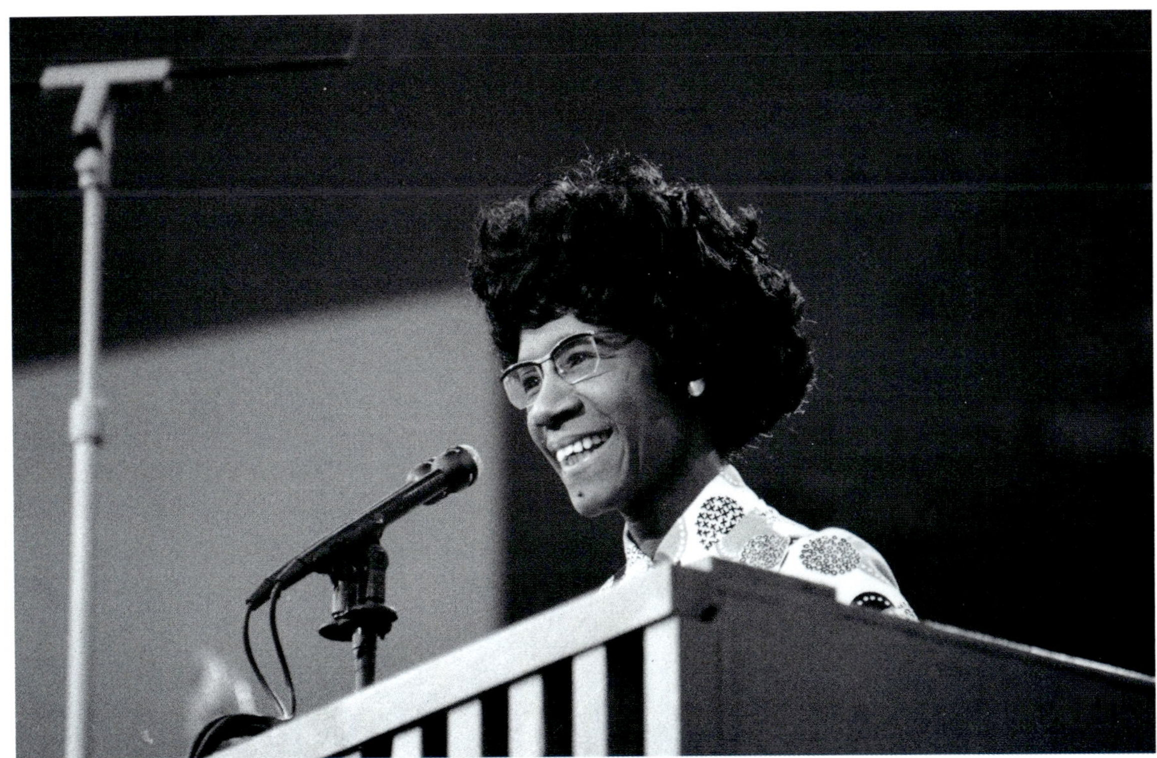

AFRICAN AMERICAN EDUCATOR AND U.S. CONGRESSWOMAN SHIRLEY CHISHOLM speaks at the Democratic National Convention in Miami Beach, Florida, in July 1972.

during her political career. Donald Trump? Not a problem. But she also related to women of color, like her mother, who'd been marginalized. She knew there were still people reeling economically and mentally from the pandemic. She wanted to speak to those suffering unseen in quiet spaces. So when her opponents mocked her for her laughter and her light touch, she shrugged it off. "I find joy in the American people," she said.

Millions have found joy in Harris—in her infectious enthusiasm, her intellect, her resolve, her elegance, and in the common touch reflected in her love of cooking Sunday dinners and her spontaneous onstage dance-offs. These characteristics are captured in this collection of images of a politician, devoted citizen, and remarkable woman coming into her own.

In June 2024, Kamala Harris posted on her Instagram account, "There is so much at stake in this election, and, ultimately, the question before us is: What kind of country do we want to live in?"

Kamala: Her Historic, Joyful, and Auspicious Sprint to the White House will undoubtedly appeal to many who would answer: "The kind that is led by you."

Kamala Harris's candidacy demonstrated that the unthinkable could happen. A woman, Black and Asian, with scant time to prepare for such an epic challenge, breathed hope into a deeply divided America, turning a moribund race for the presidency into a contest stocked with optimism and possibility.

—KEVIN MERIDA

"I find joy in the American people."

—KAMALA HARRIS

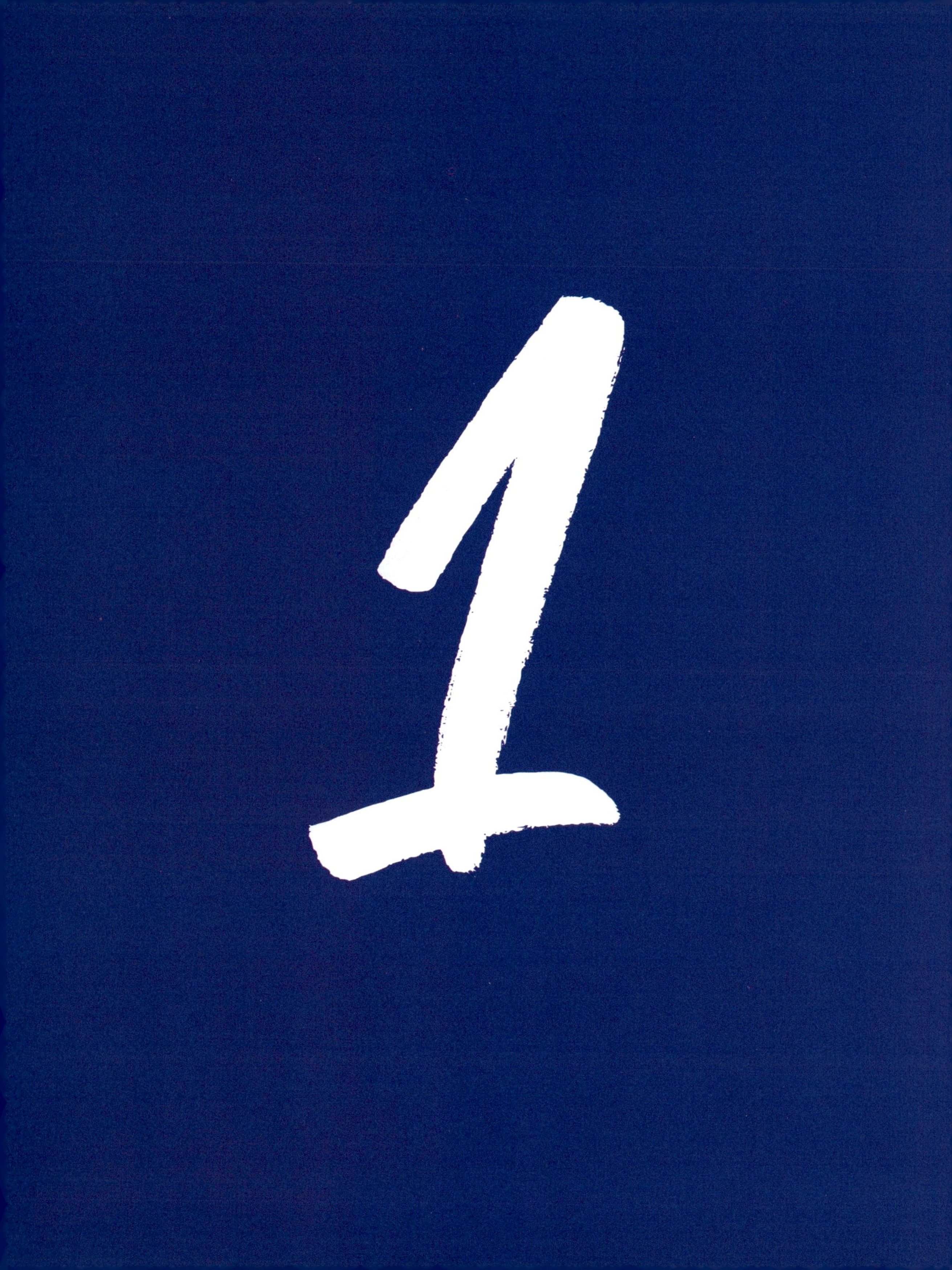
1

FAMILY AND EARLY LIFE

"My mother had always told me, 'Don't do anything half-assed,' and I had always taken that to heart."

—KAMALA HARRIS

In these photos, we see the young, adorable Kamala, the protective big sister, the Howard University graduate steeped in her Black identity. Kamala Harris's immediate family comes from Jamaica and southern India. The daughter of highly intellectual social activists, she developed a political consciousness that is embedded deep in her family tree: Her maternal grandfather, P. V. Gopalan, was involved in India's independence movement. Her mother, Shyamala Gopalan, was "born with a sense of justice imprinted on her soul," as Harris described her, and became a published scholar of more than one hundred research papers on breast cancer. Her sister, Maya, was a senior advisor to Hillary Clinton's 2016 presidential campaign and chaired Harris's own 2020 presidential run. As Harris noted in her autobiography about her parents' divorce when she and Maya were still in their formative years: "The only thing they fought about was who got the books." Though Harris did not have children of her own, her marriage to Doug Emhoff in 2014 resulted in a new blended family. She became "Momala" to Emhoff's children from a previous marriage, Cole and Ella, who were teenagers at the time Harris began dating their father. She and Emhoff's former wife, Kerstin, became friends who shared the responsibilities and pleasures of mothering.

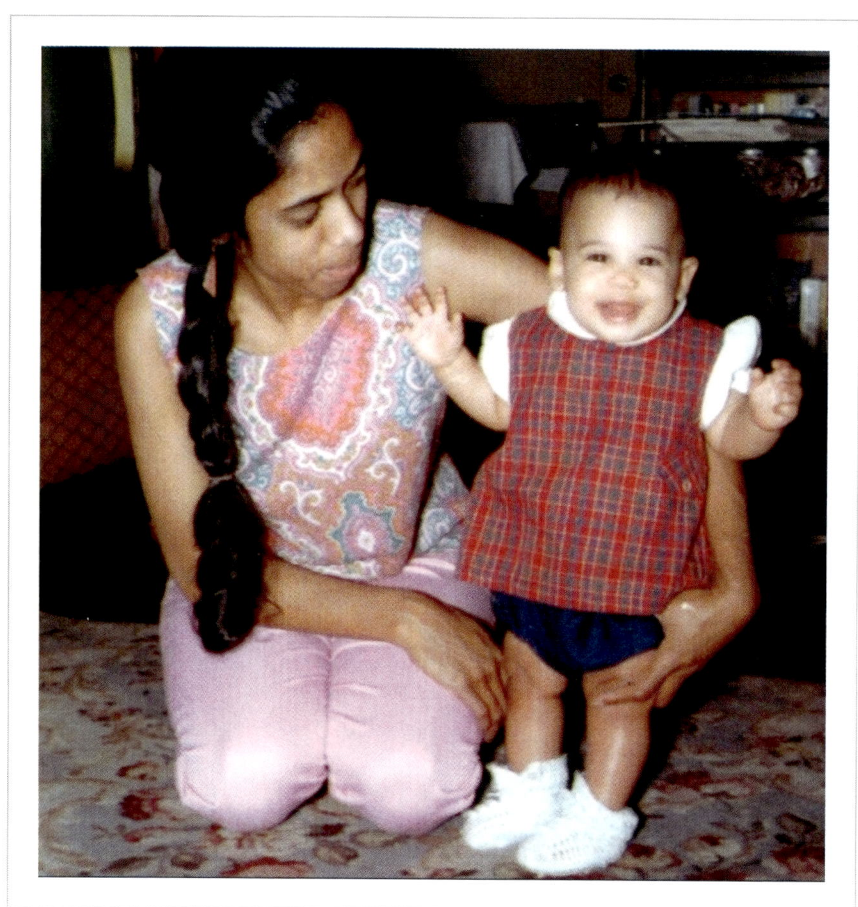

Above and opposite: Toddler Kamala with her mother, Shyamala, the most influential person in her life.

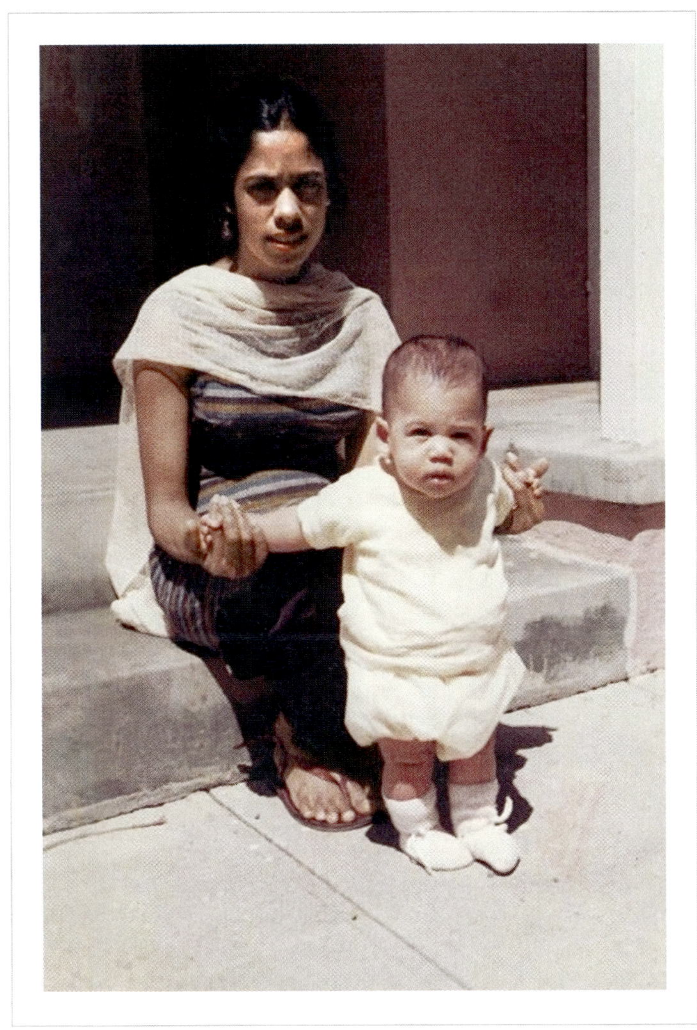

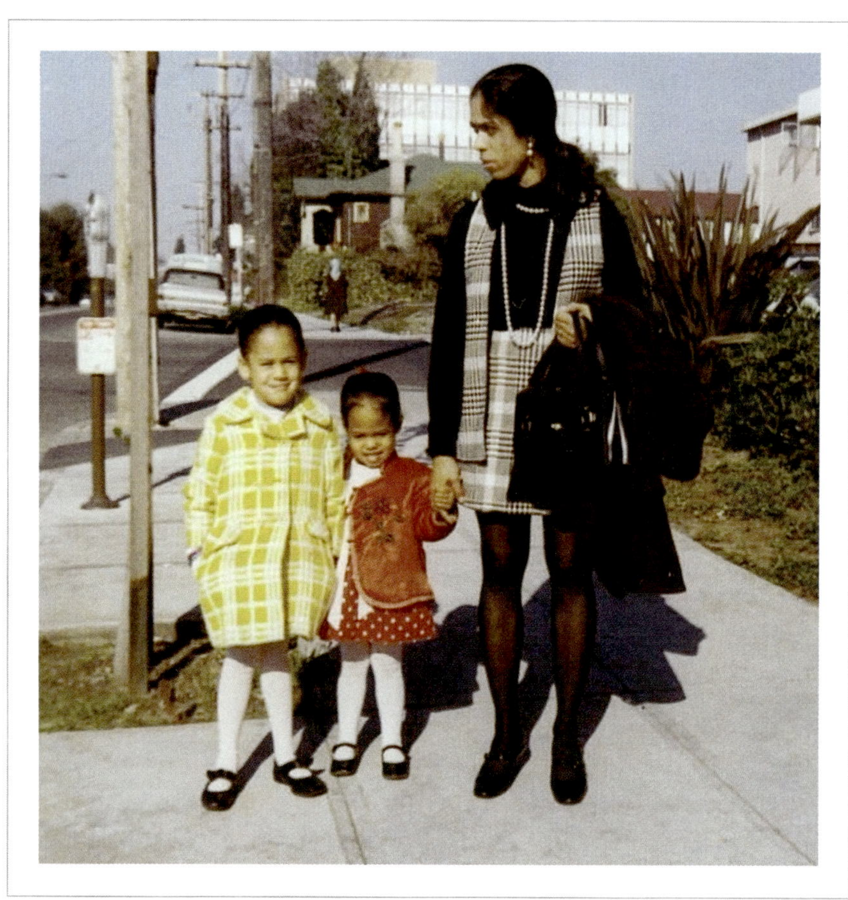

KAMALA HARRIS (*left*) with her sister, Maya, and mother outside their apartment in Berkeley, 1970.

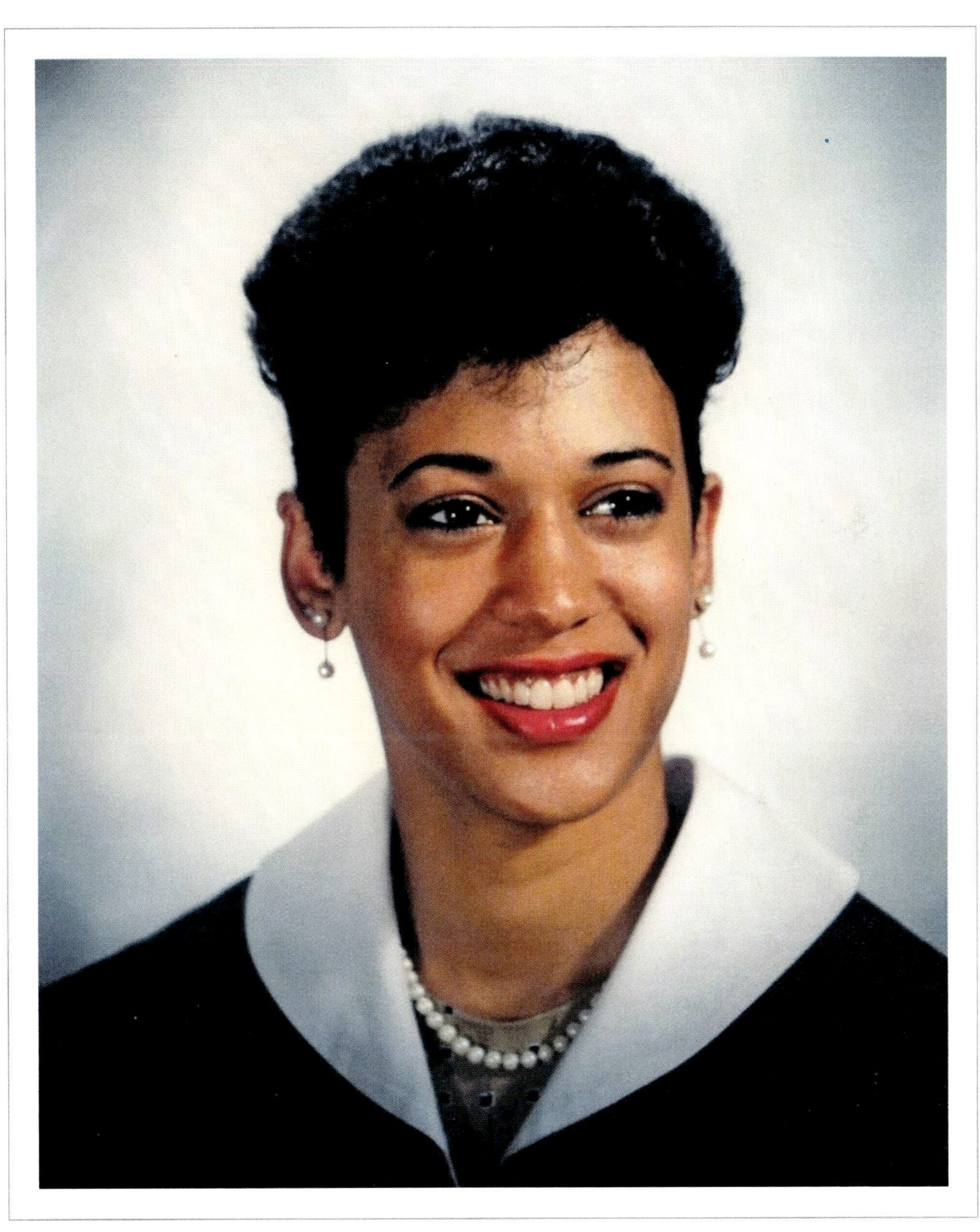

KAMALA HARRIS in her Howard University graduation photo, May 1986.

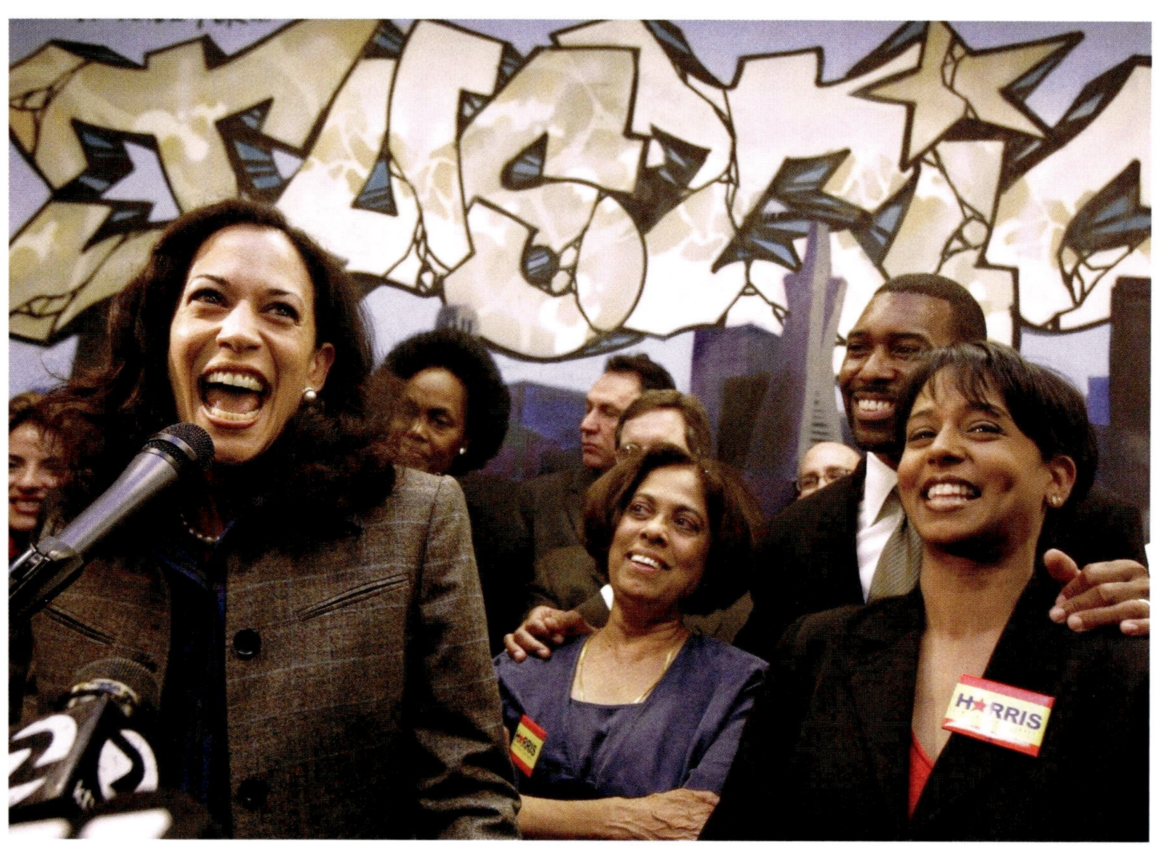

KAMALA HARRIS gives her victory speech after becoming the first woman and Afro/Indian American DA in California at her campaign headquarters in San Francisco, surrounded by friends and family members (*left to right*): Bayview–Hunters Point Point supervisor Sophie Maxwell; mother, Shyamala; brother-in-law, Tony West; and sister, Maya, on December 1, 2003.

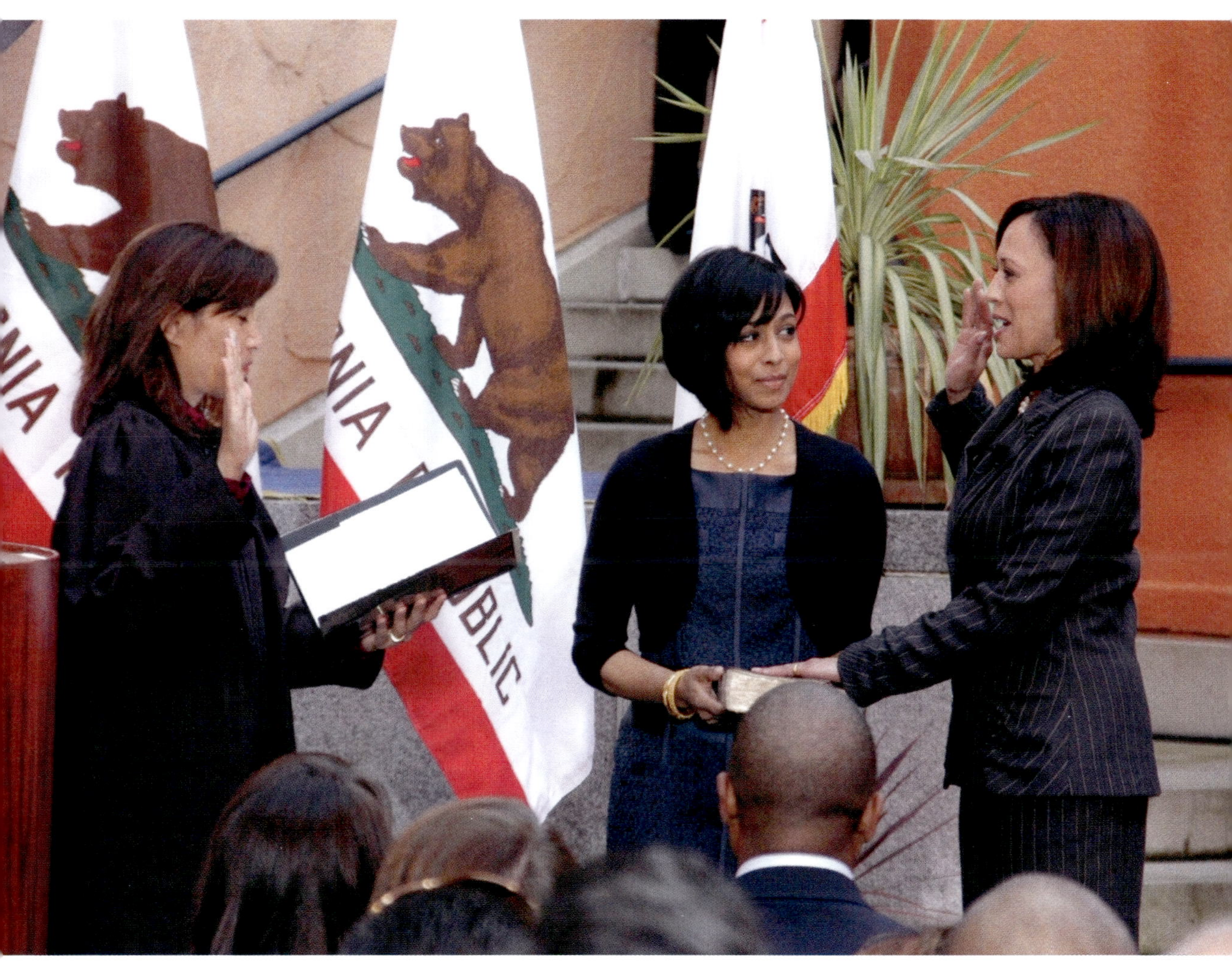

CALIFORNIA ATTORNEY GENERAL KAMALA HARRIS is sworn into her second term in office by California Supreme Court Chief Justice Tani Cantil-Sakauye on January 6, 2011, as her sister, Maya, looks on.

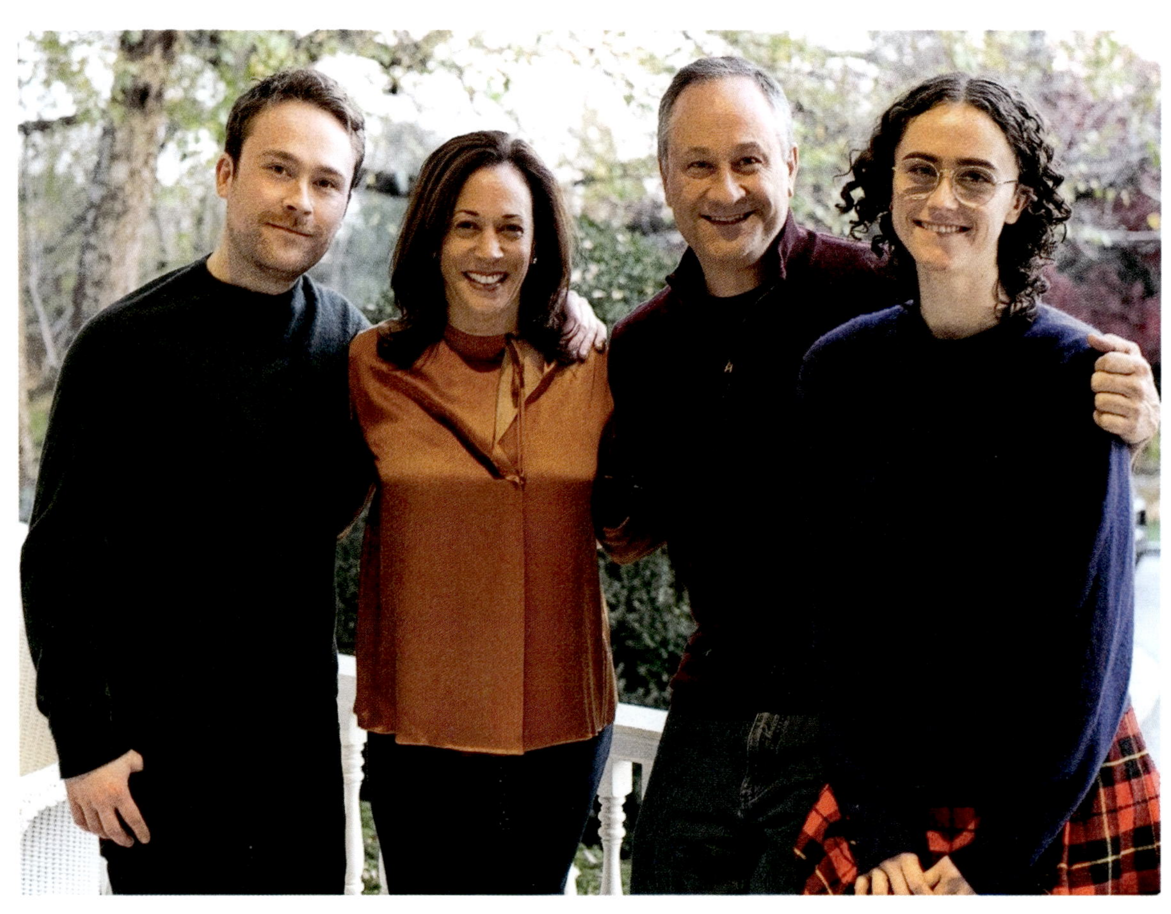

VICE PRESIDENT KAMALA HARRIS with her husband, Doug Emhoff, and their children, Cole and Ella, on Father's Day, June 2024. Ella and Cole, not wanting to call Harris "stepmom," gave her the name "Momala."

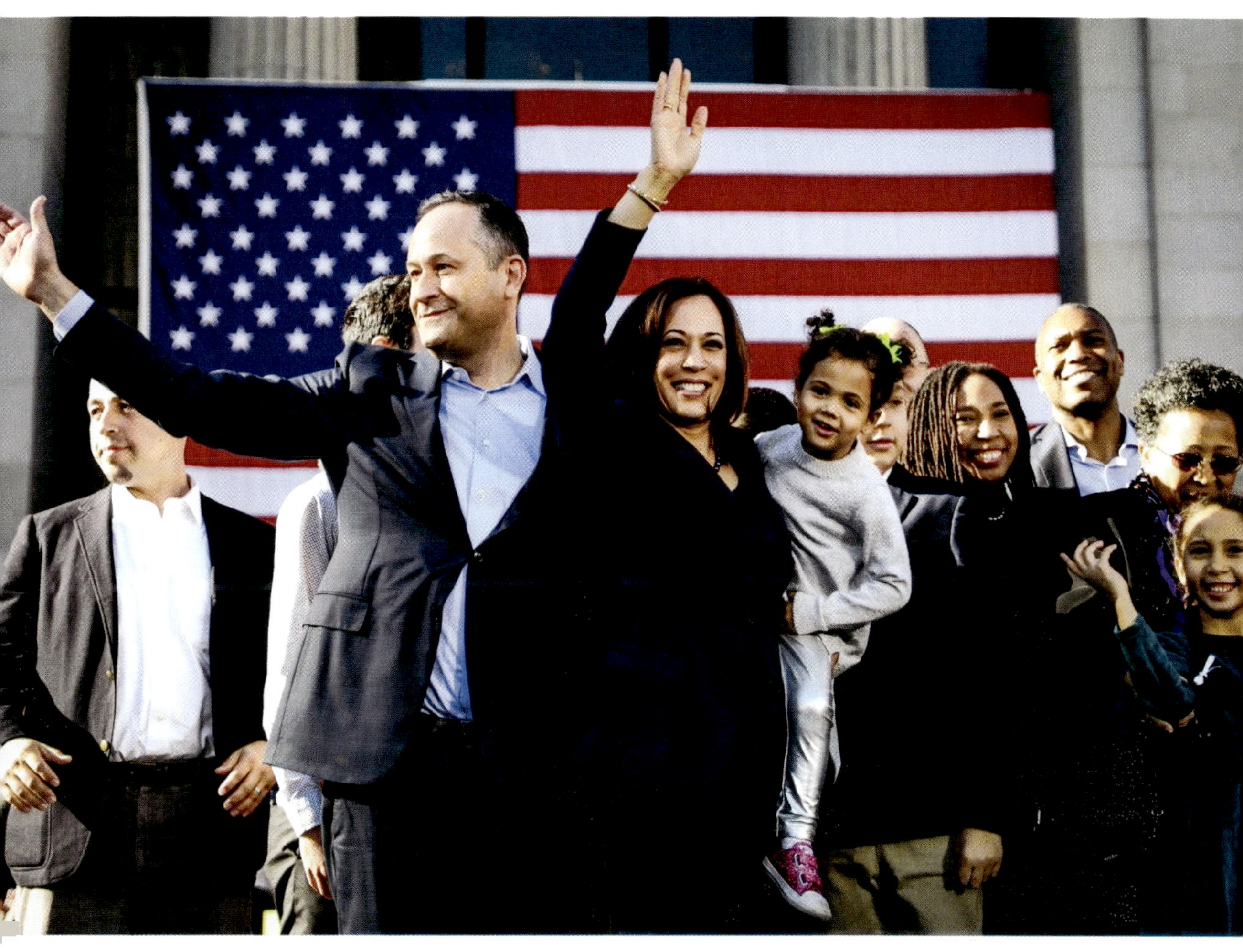

SENATOR KAMALA HARRIS holds her grandniece Amara as she and Doug wave to the crowd after her first presidential campaign rally in her hometown of Oakland on January 27, 2019.

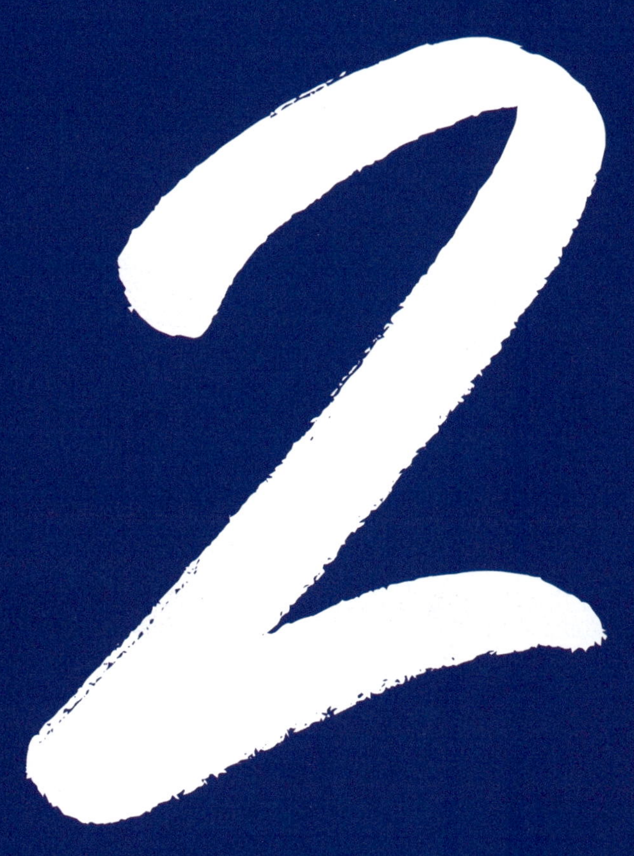

THE ASCENT

"I was a hard worker. A perfectionist. Someone who didn't take things for granted."

—KAMALA HARRIS

The official launch of Harris's elected political career came in 2003 when she decisively defeated incumbent San Francisco district attorney Terence Hallinan, whom she had once worked for. But the groundwork for success in politics was laid in the late 1990s with powerful relationships she made in San Francisco that kept expanding. As Dan Morain wrote in his biography, *Kamala's Way*, she did not have wealth or pedigree on her side, "but she was becoming a boldface name." She joined the board of trustees of the San Francisco Museum of Modern Art, which allowed her to grow her network but also become involved in community life. Willie Brown, the respected political powerbroker who also dated Harris in the 1990s, advised that it was particularly helpful for Black women who wanted to ascend in politics to become active on the boards of cultural and charitable institutions. In thirteen short years, Harris went from district attorney to California attorney general to United States senator. Her experience as prosecutor and attorney general, and her finely honed rhetorical skills, benefited her in the Senate. She created a viral moment in 2017 when her interrogation of Trump Attorney General Jeff Sessions about Russia's influence on the 2016 election got Sessions visibly rattled. She developed a reputation in the Senate as someone who could hold the Trump administration accountable, and she was more polished than most senators when they arrive.

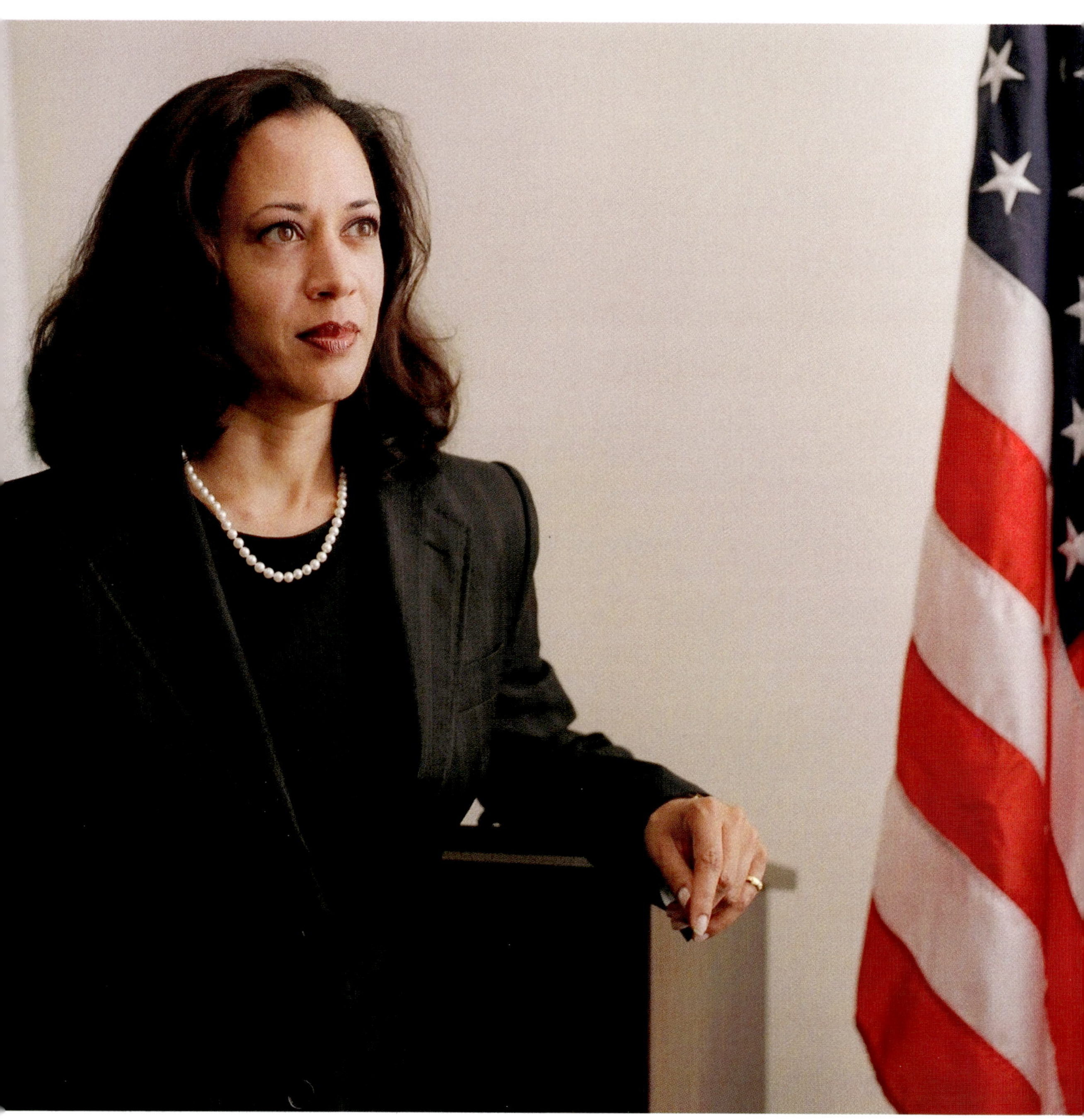

DISTRICT ATTORNEY KAMALA HARRIS in San Francisco.

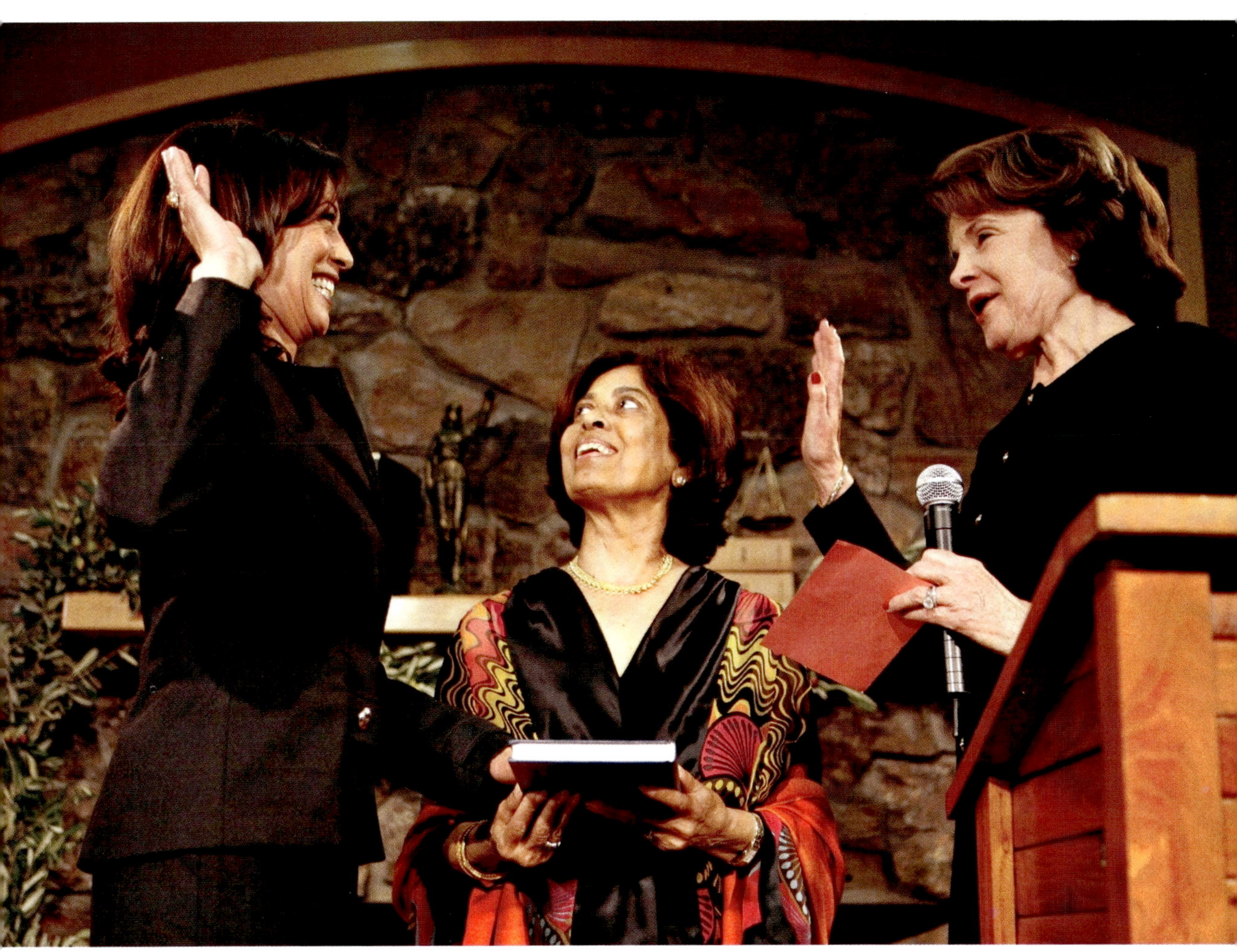

HARRIS BEING SWORN IN for her second term as district attorney of San Francisco in 2008 by Senator Dianne Feinstein.

CALIFORNIA ATTORNEY GENERAL KAMALA HARRIS speaks to the 2012 Democratic National Convention in Charlotte, North Carolina, her first major national appearance. She championed the reelection of President Barack Obama, introduced parts of her biography to the nation, and spoke of the American Dream that "belongs to all of us."

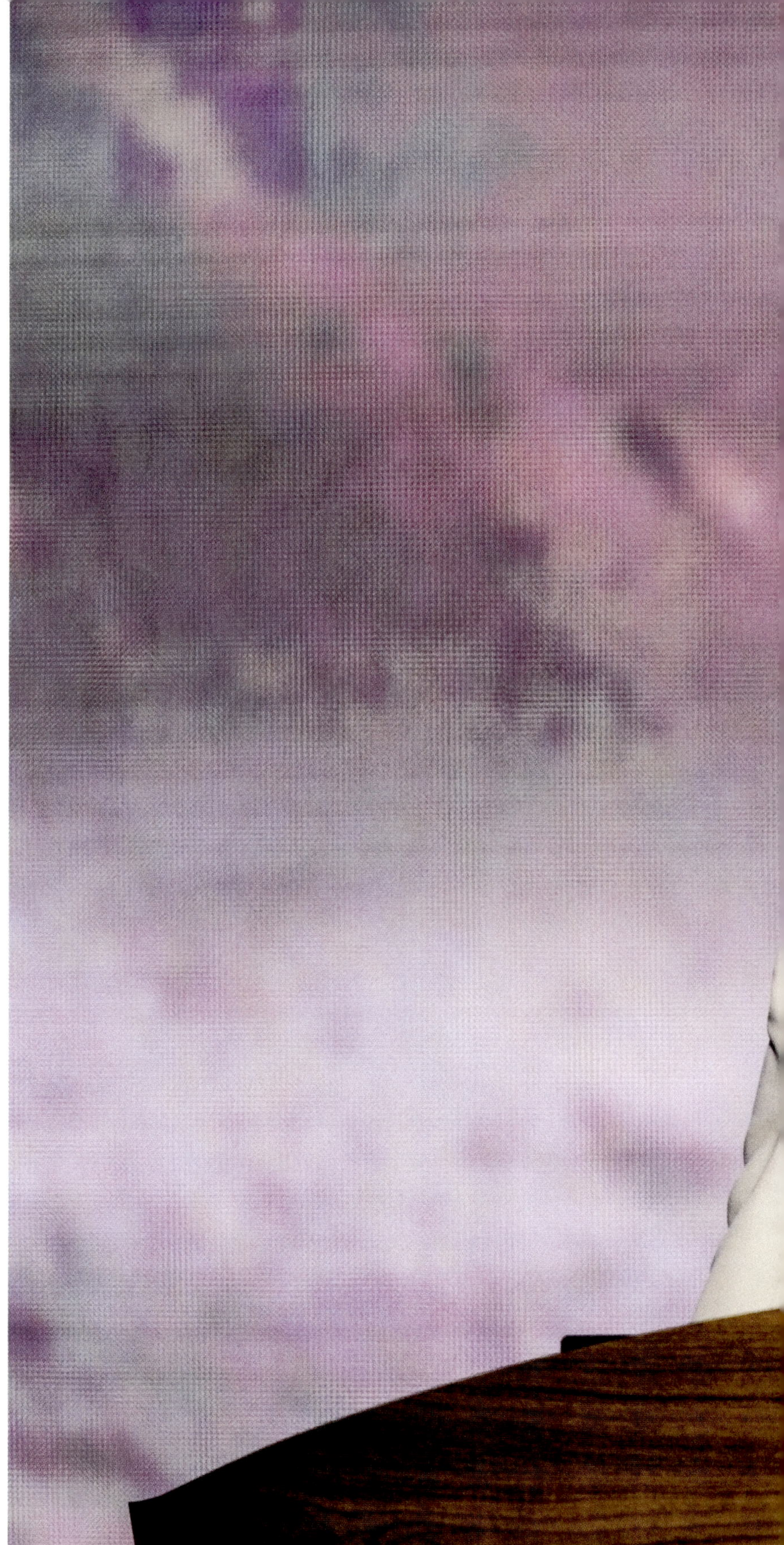

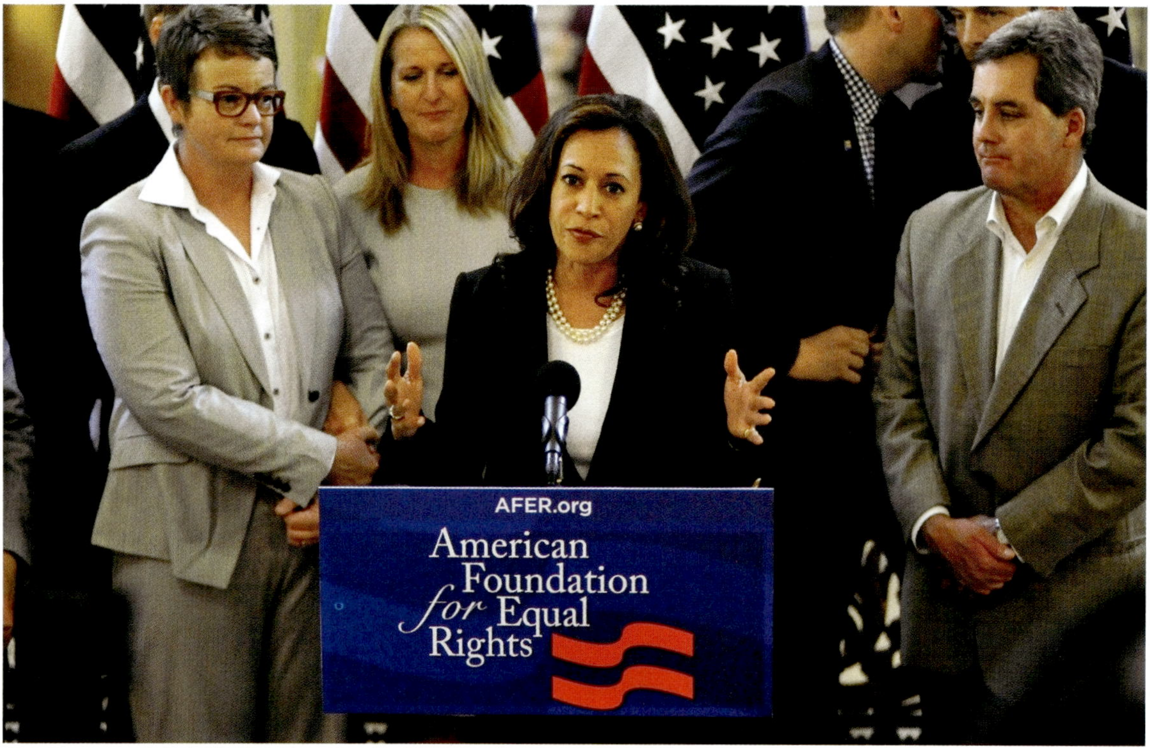

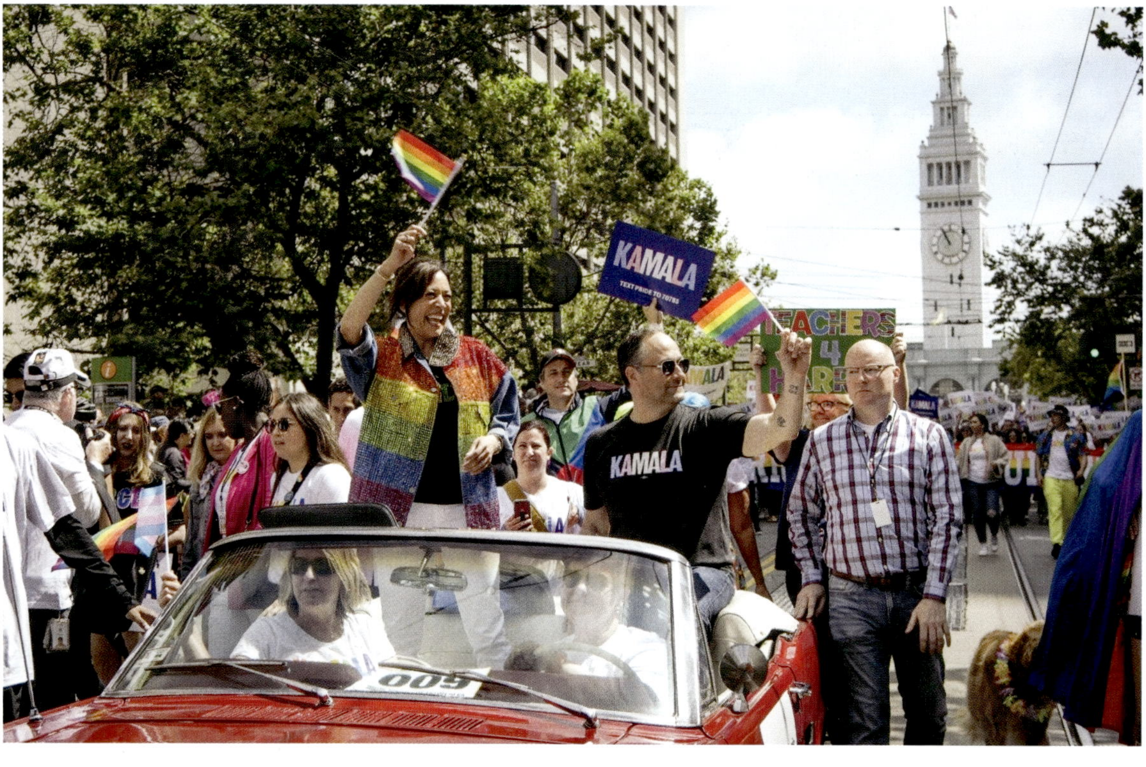

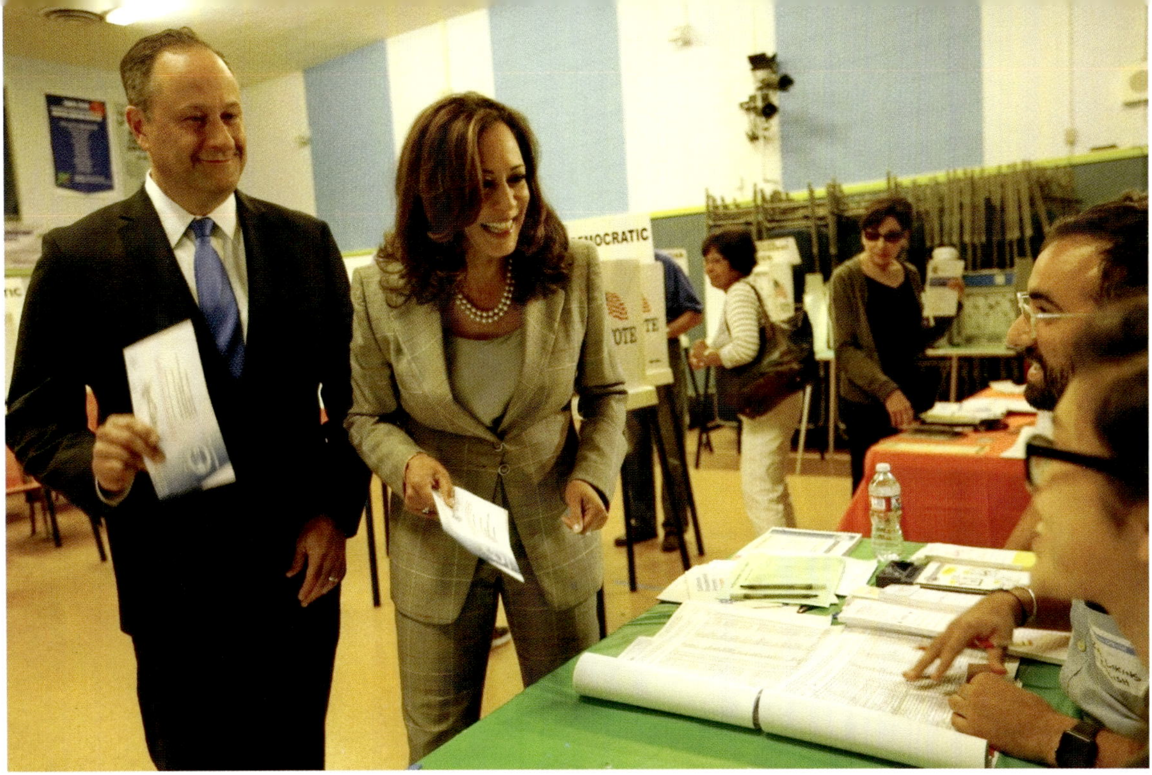

CALIFORNIA ATTORNEY GENERAL KAMALA HARRIS, running for the U.S. Senate seat of retiring senator Barbara Boxer, shows up to cast her vote with her husband at the Kenter Canyon Elementary Charter School auditorium in Los Angeles, California, on June 7, 2016.

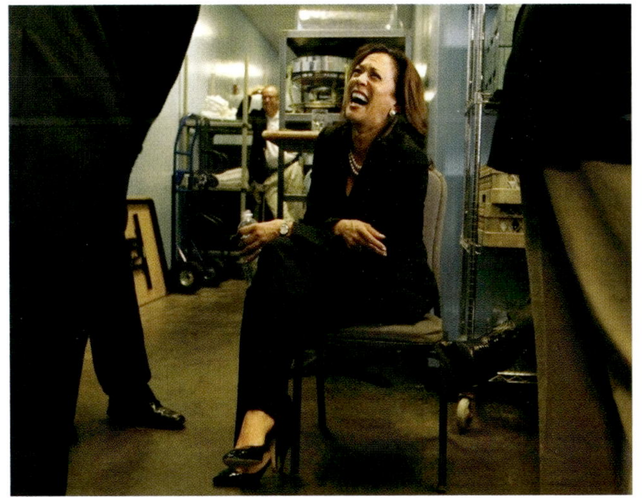

KAMALA HARRIS, running for California attorney general, shares a laugh backstage before a get-out-the-vote rally at the National Steinbeck Center in Salinas, California. She can be warm and lighthearted in more personal settings. Here she is one day before the election she won.

Facing page, top to bottom:

CALIFORNIA ATTORNEY GENERAL KAMALA HARRIS speaks to the media after marrying the same-sex couple Kris Perry (*left*) and Sandy Stier (*second from left*) at San Francisco City Hall on June 28, 2013. It was the first such marriage after the Ninth Circuit Court of Appeals lifted the stay on same-sex marriage in California.

SENATOR HARRIS at a Pride Parade in San Francisco. Harris has long been a champion of LGBTQ+ rights. She led the fight against hate crimes as San Francisco DA, pushed for expanding access to HIV-prevention medications in the Senate, and was outspoken against so-called Don't Say Gay laws in the states as vice president.

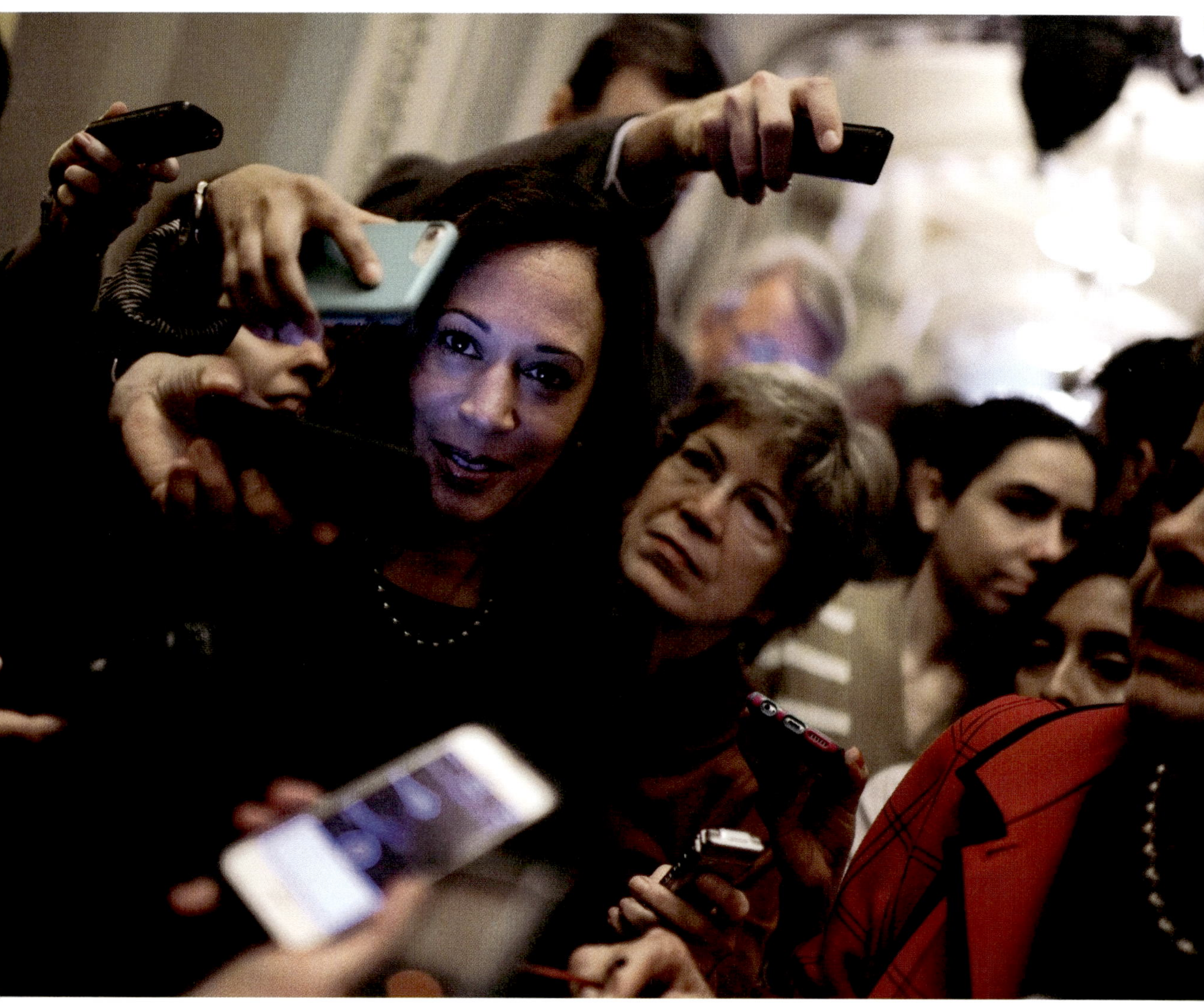

HARRIS, as a senator-elect, is surrounded by reporters in the Capitol on November 16, 2016, after the Senate Democratic Caucus leadership elections. Harris has had a mixed relationship with the media. At varying points in her career, she was hailed as a rising star and criticized for underachieving. During her 2024 campaign, she did some interviews uncommon for presidential nominees, such as appearing on the popular basketball podcast *All the Smoke*, cohosted by former NBA players Stephen Jackson and Matt Barnes.

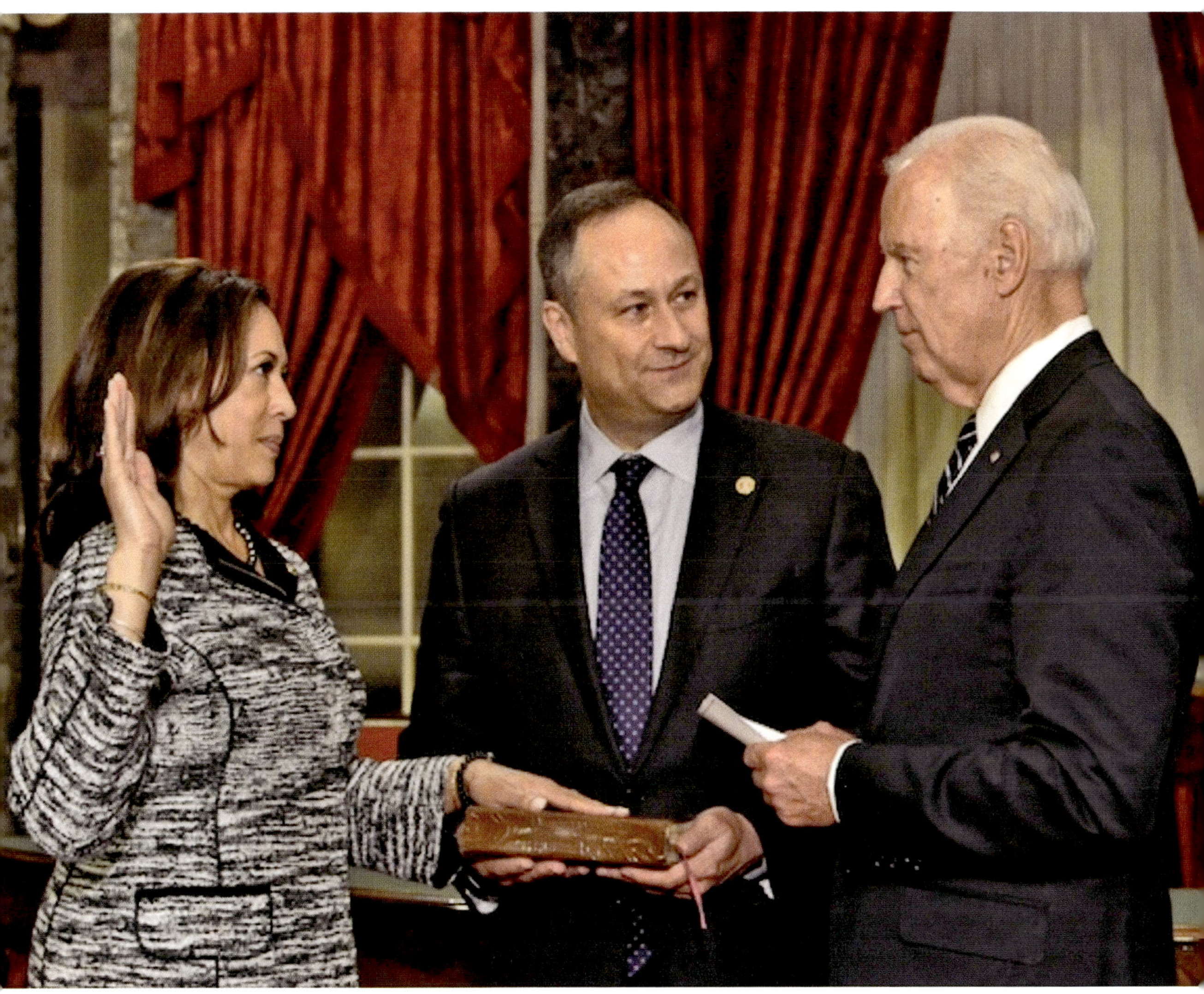

KAMALA HARRIS is sworn in to the Senate by Vice President Joe Biden on January 3, 2017, watched by her husband, Doug Emhoff.

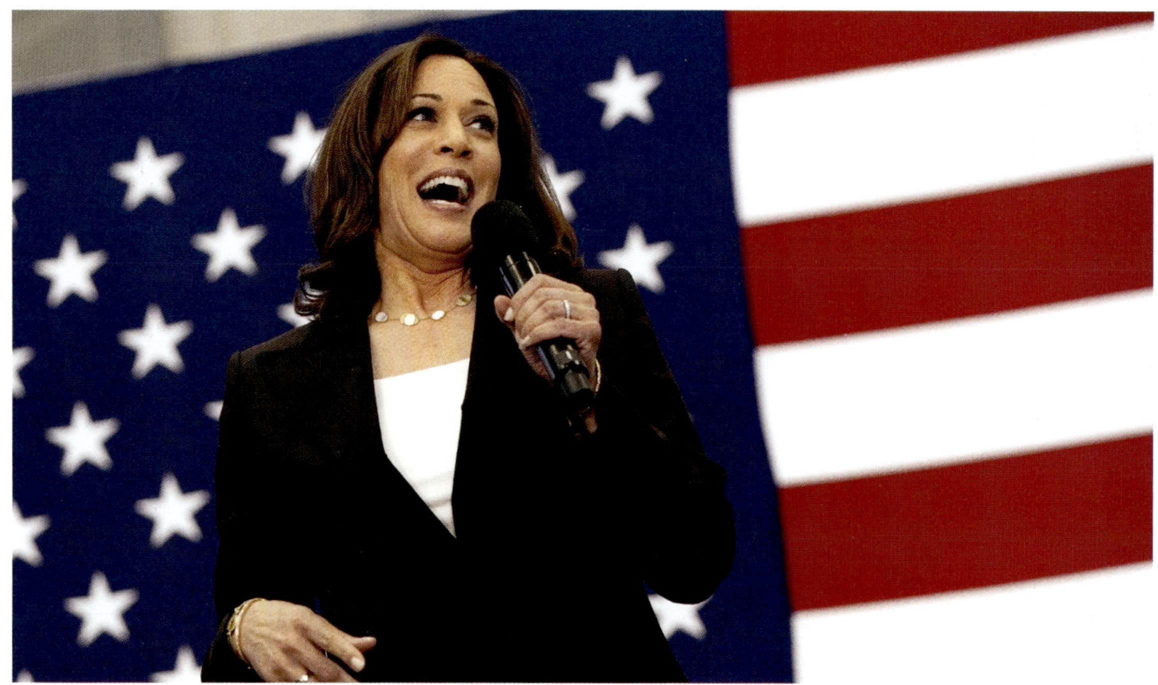

DEMOCRATIC PRESIDENTIAL CANDIDATE KAMALA HARRIS appears at her first Los Angeles rally since announcing her 2020 campaign. The candidate spoke about the need to combat gun violence, raise teacher pay, and provide middle-class tax relief.

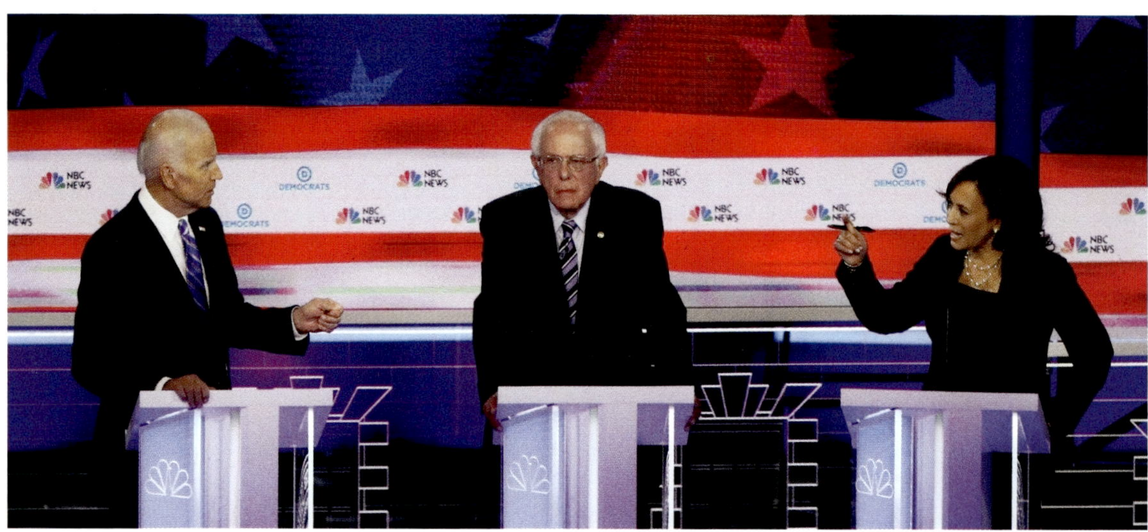

HARRIS and former vice president Joe Biden exchange sharp words during their first Democratic presidential primary debate, June 27, 2019, in Miami. The two candidates had a heated back-and-forth, initiated by Harris, about Biden's opposition to forced school busing. Harris said that as a child she was part of the second class of students who were bused to Thousand Oaks Elementary School in Berkeley to promote integration.

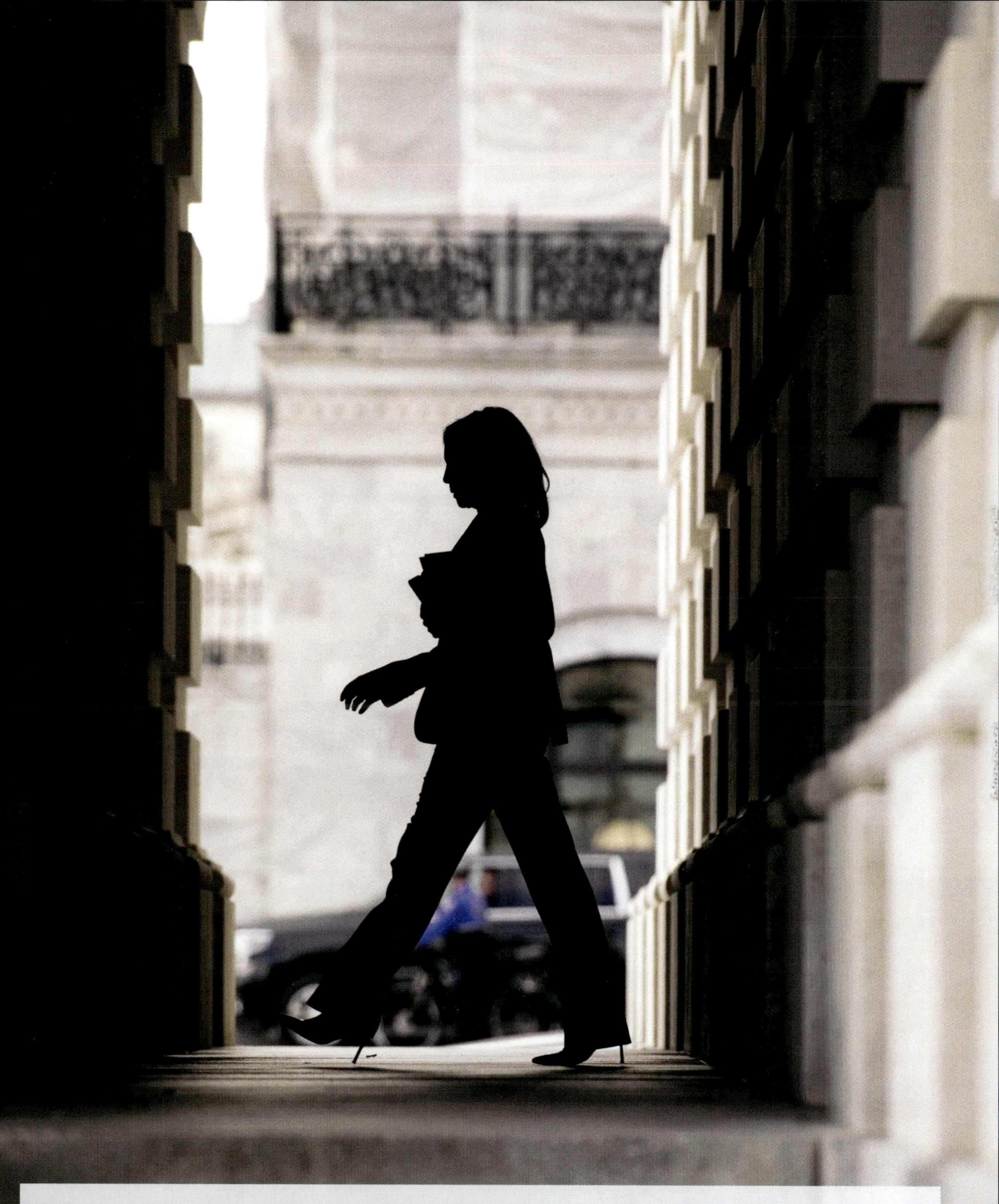

SENATOR HARRIS leaves the Capitol on February 3, 2020, after the conclusion of the first impeachment trial proceedings for President Donald Trump. He was acquitted of abuse of power and obstruction of Congress—articles of impeachment related to soliciting Ukrainian authorities to influence the 2020 elections.

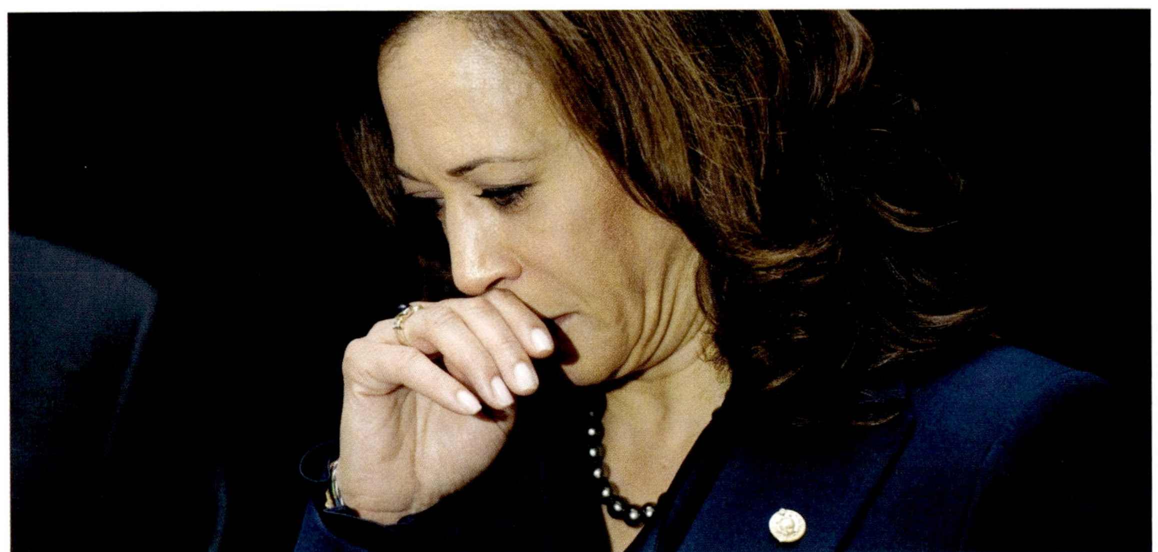

SENATOR KAMALA HARRIS, a member of the Judiciary Committee, pauses on September 28, 2018, while speaking with survivors of sexual assault and their supporters as they protest Judge Brett Kavanaugh's nomination to the Supreme Court. Harris was a forceful and effective questioner of Kavanaugh, who faced a contentious Senate hearing. He furiously fought back against sexual assault allegations recounted in harrowing detail by his accuser and ended up being confirmed to the high court.

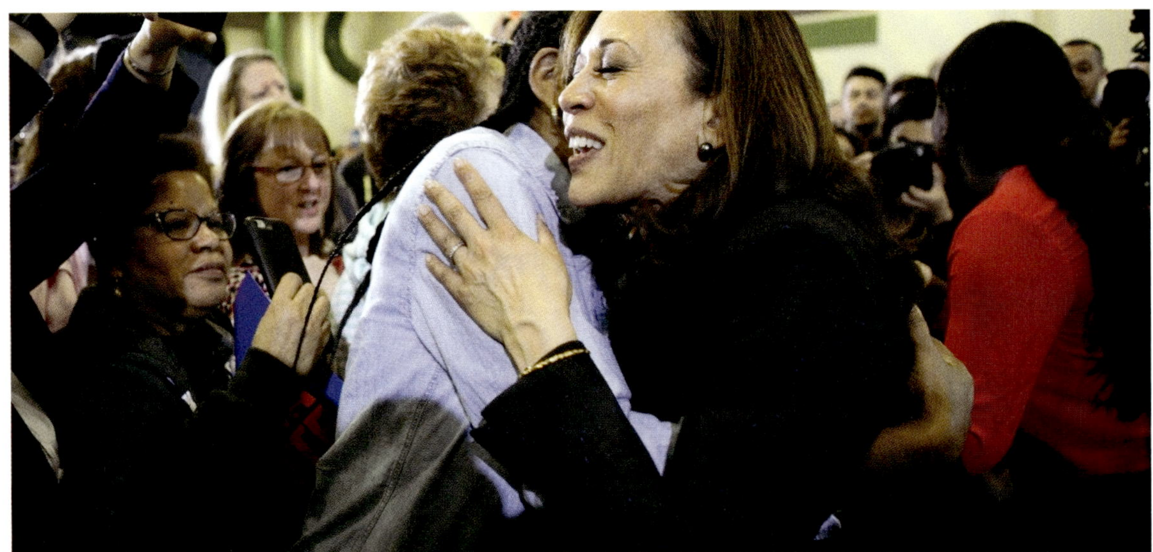

DEMOCRATIC PRESIDENTIAL CANDIDATE SENATOR KAMALA HARRIS greets members of the audience before taking the stage during the Women's Caucus at the California Democratic Convention, held at the Moscone Center in San Francisco, on June 1, 2019. Her 2020 campaign started with big, enthusiastic crowds and much promise, but it never caught fire, and she officially dropped out of the race in December 2019.

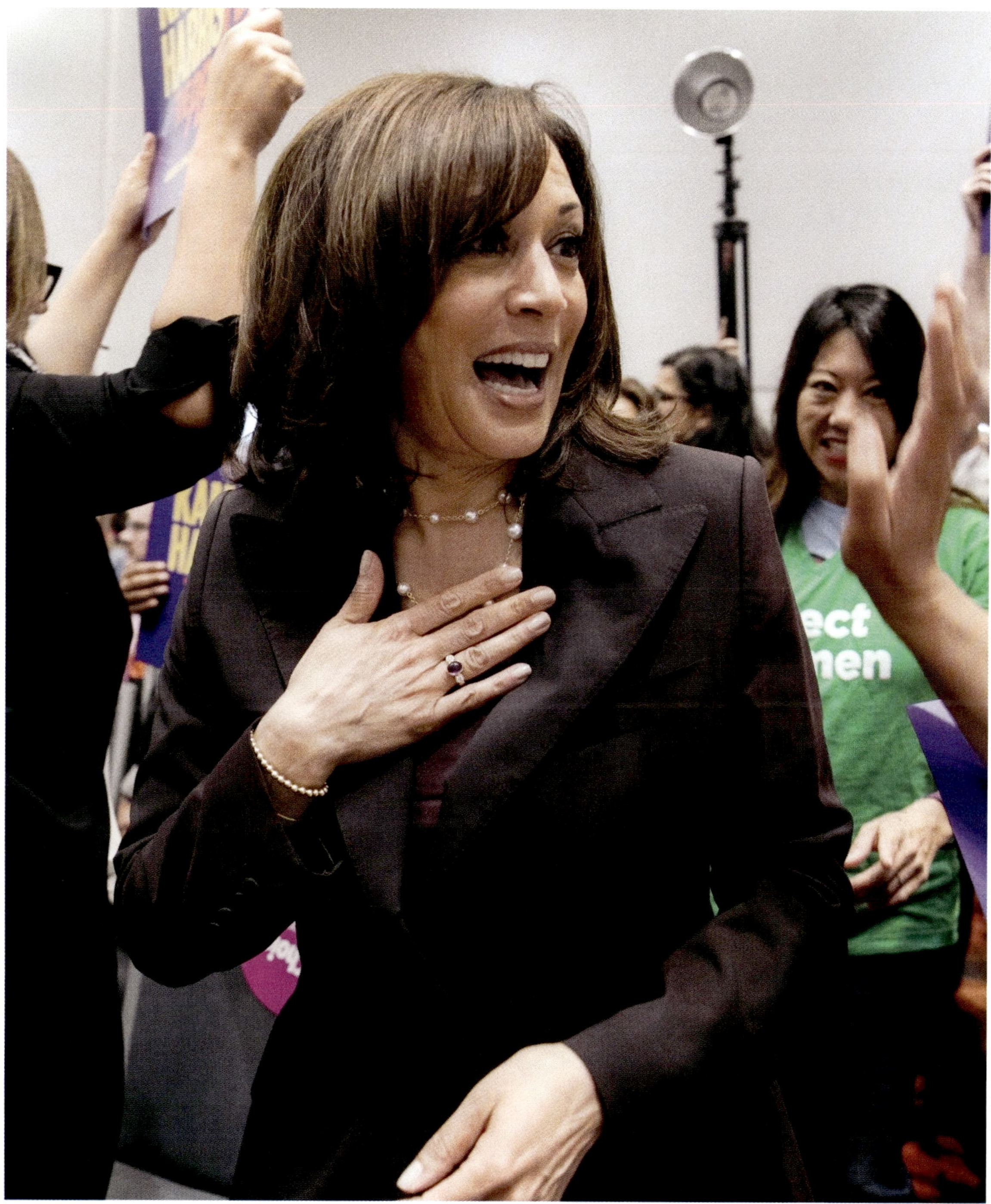

DEMOCRATIC PRESIDENTIAL CANDIDATE SENATOR KAMALA HARRIS greets people following a town hall meeting at Canyon Springs High School on March 1, 2019, in North Las Vegas. Her ability to convey a common touch with hugs and hand placement is a notable feature of her campaign style.

3

POWERFUL ROOMS

"What I want young women and girls to know is: You are powerful and your voice matters. You're going to walk into many rooms in your life and career where you may be the only one who looks like you or who has had the experiences you've had. But you remember that when you are in those rooms, you are not alone."

—KAMALA HARRIS

Being elected to high office gets you into rooms of consequence, where power is observed and wielded. This series of photos shows Harris in Senate hearing rooms; in private, whispered consultation with a colleague; and surrounded by reporters who swarm notable members of Congress whenever the opportunity presents. In these rooms, Harris can be intense when the issue and questioning call for her steely vigor. She can also be playful, as when elbow-bumping Nancy Pelosi, who will go down as one of the most powerful House Speakers in American history.

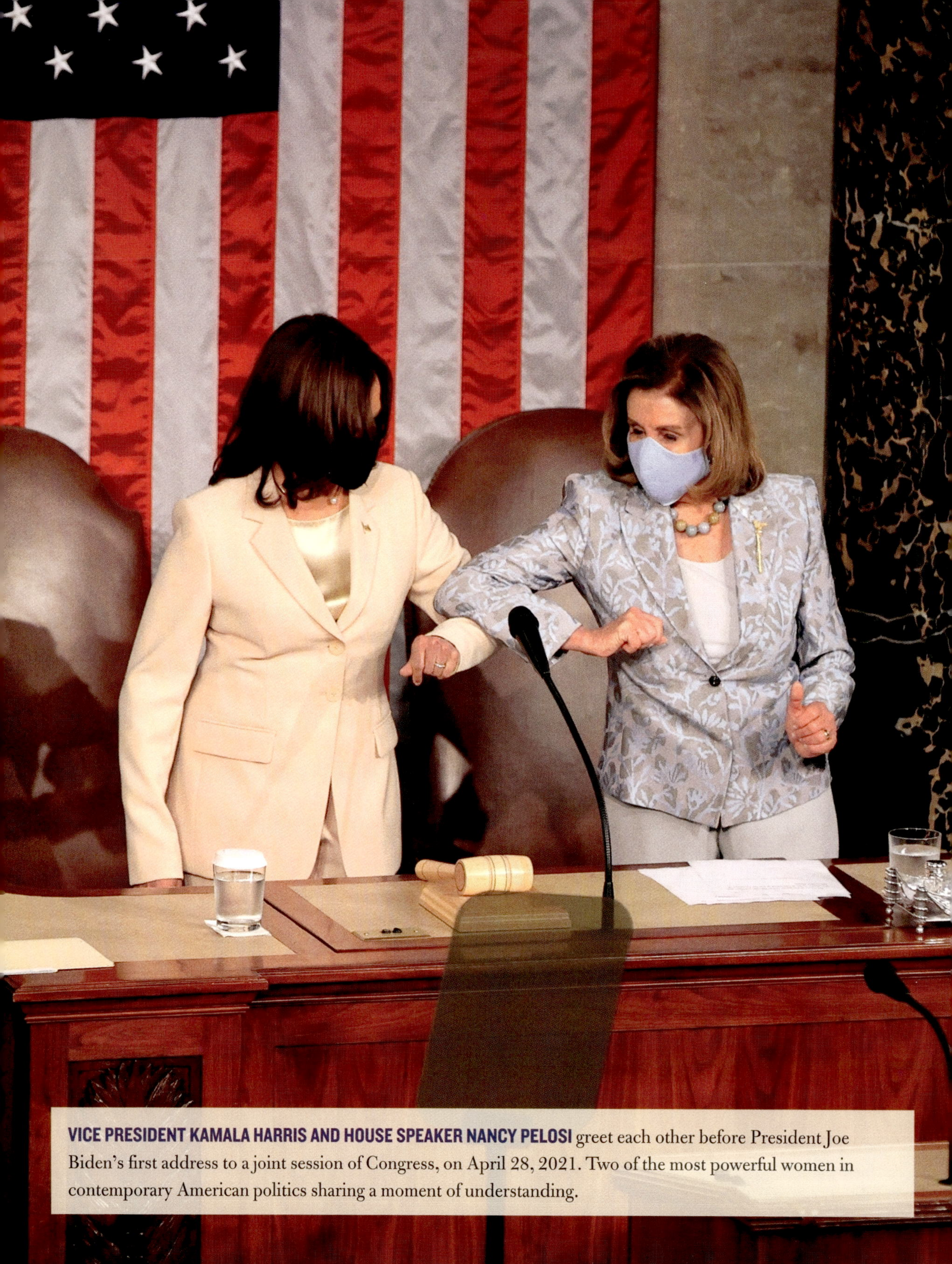

VICE PRESIDENT KAMALA HARRIS AND HOUSE SPEAKER NANCY PELOSI greet each other before President Joe Biden's first address to a joint session of Congress, on April 28, 2021. Two of the most powerful women in contemporary American politics sharing a moment of understanding.

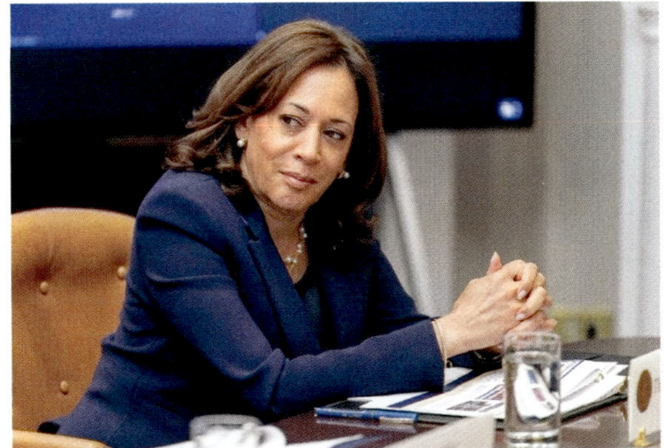

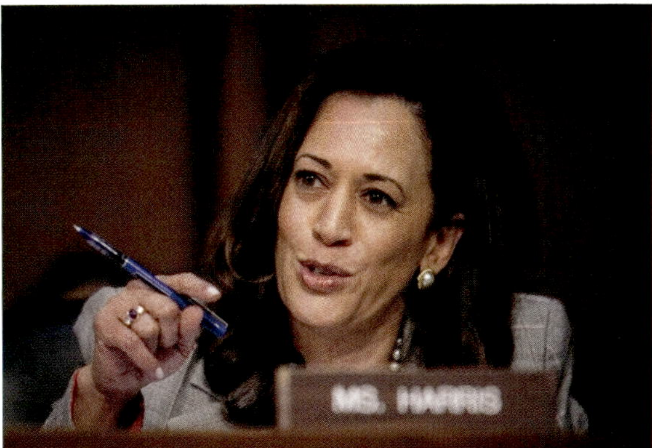

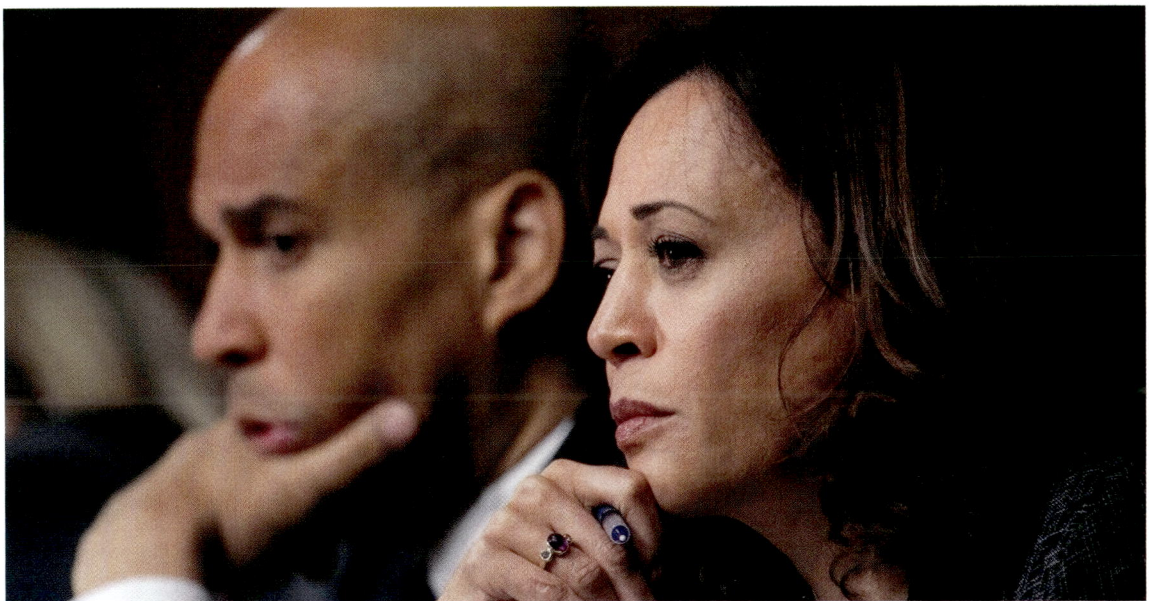

Above, clockwise:

VICE PRESIDENT KAMALA HARRIS reflecting on her job as senator, which often involved battles behind the scenes that the public never saw.

SENATOR KAMALA HARRIS and Attorney General Jeff Sessions having a contentious back-and-forth at a Senate Intelligence Committee hearing about if he had communications with Russian nationals he hadn't disclosed. The committee was investigating Russian interference in the 2016 election. Senator Richard Burr, the committee chairman, at one point had to weigh in. Harris's incisiveness as a former prosecutor was often on display in Senate meeting rooms.

SENATOR CORY BOOKER OF NEW JERSEY AND SENATOR KAMALA HARRIS listen as Dr. Christine Blasey Ford testifies during the Senate Judiciary Committee hearing on the Supreme Court nomination of Brett Kavanaugh. You can see the pained expressions as Blasey details her allegations of being sexually assaulted by Kavanaugh in the early 1980s. Though they ran against each other as presidential contenders in the 2020 campaign, Harris and Booker shared a close relationship in the Senate.

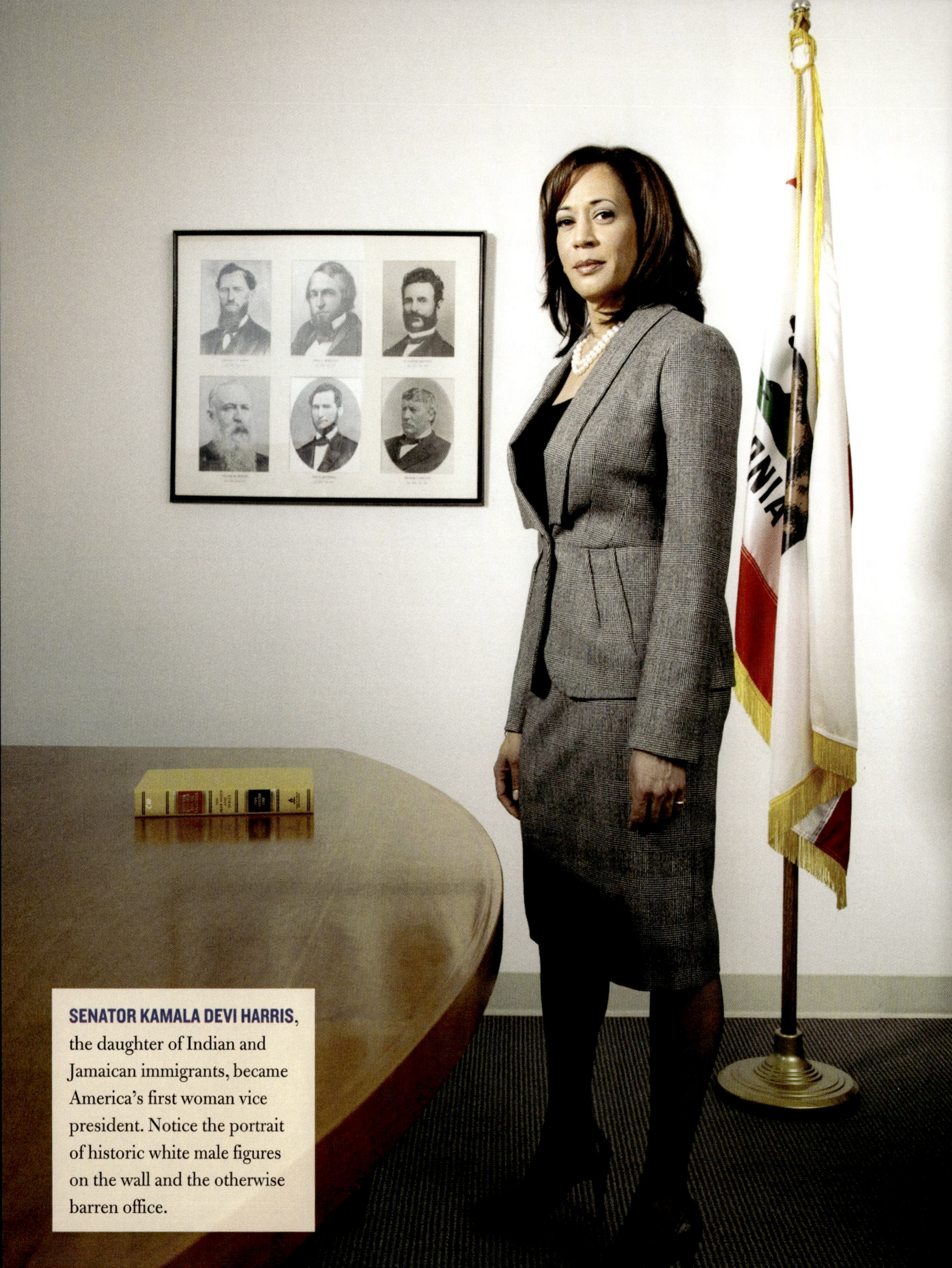

SENATOR KAMALA DEVI HARRIS, the daughter of Indian and Jamaican immigrants, became America's first woman vice president. Notice the portrait of historic white male figures on the wall and the otherwise barren office.

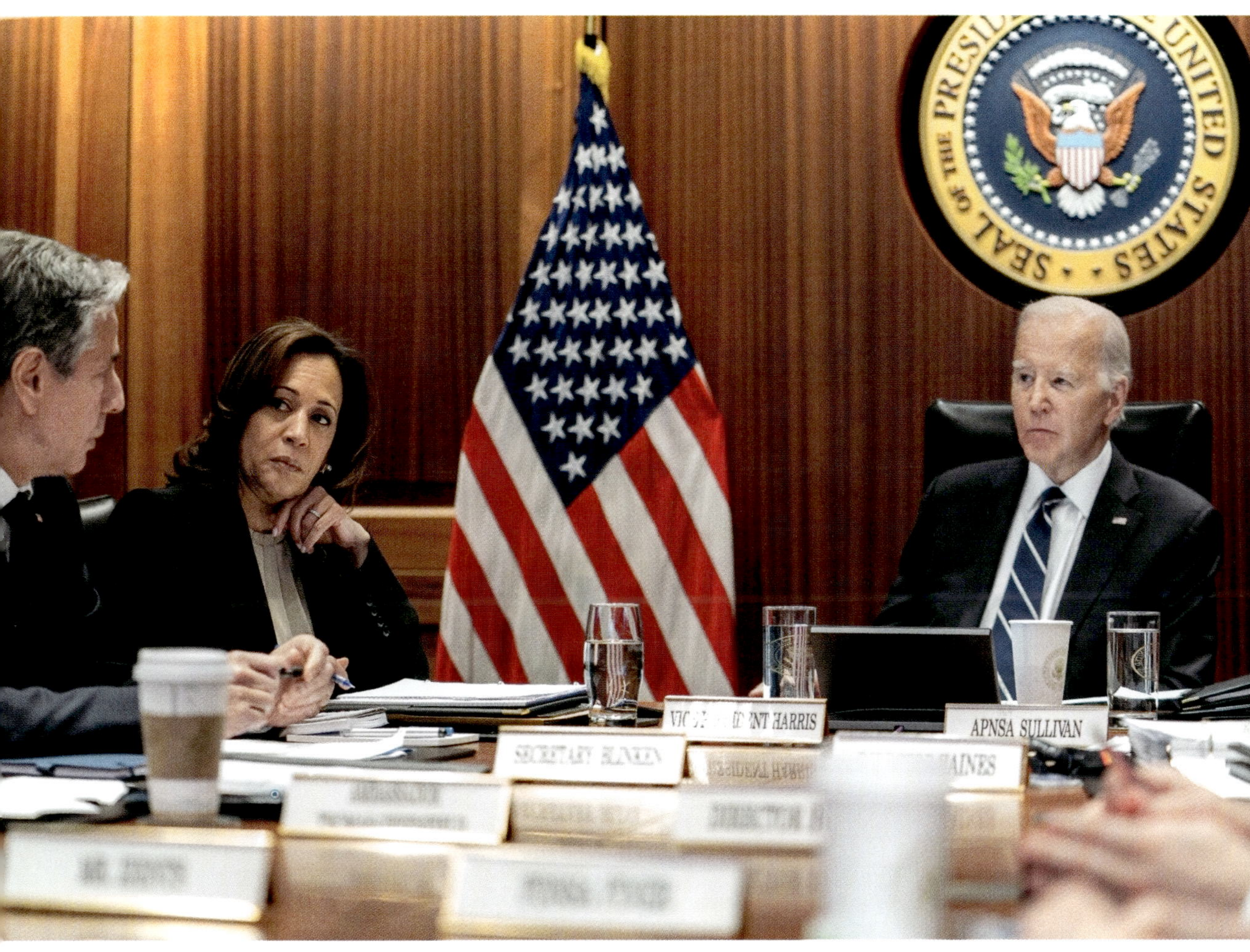

PRESIDENT JOE BIDEN AND VICE PRESIDENT KAMALA HARRIS listen to Secretary of State Antony Blinken during a meeting with national security advisors on October 10, 2023, in the White House Situation Room.

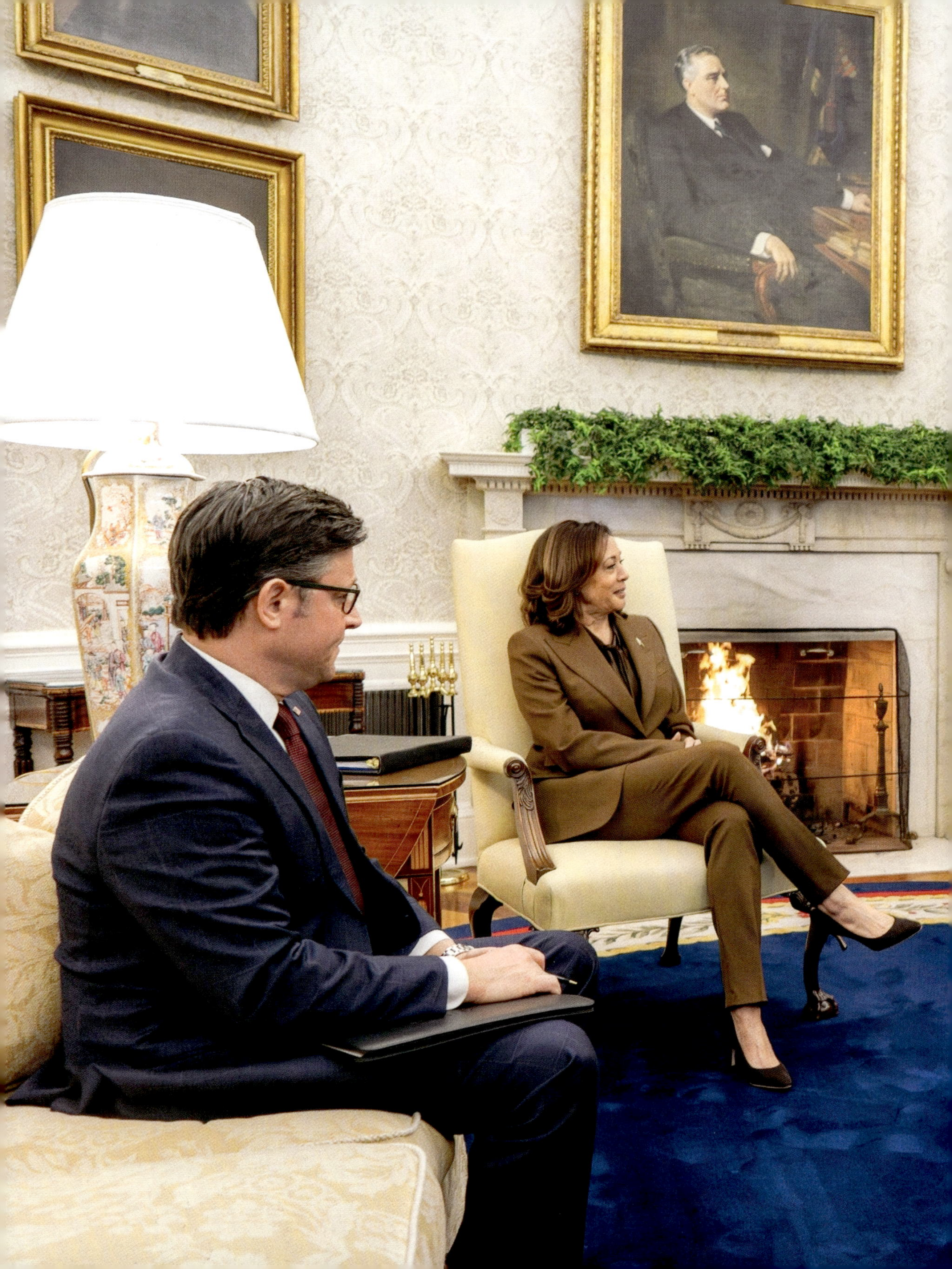

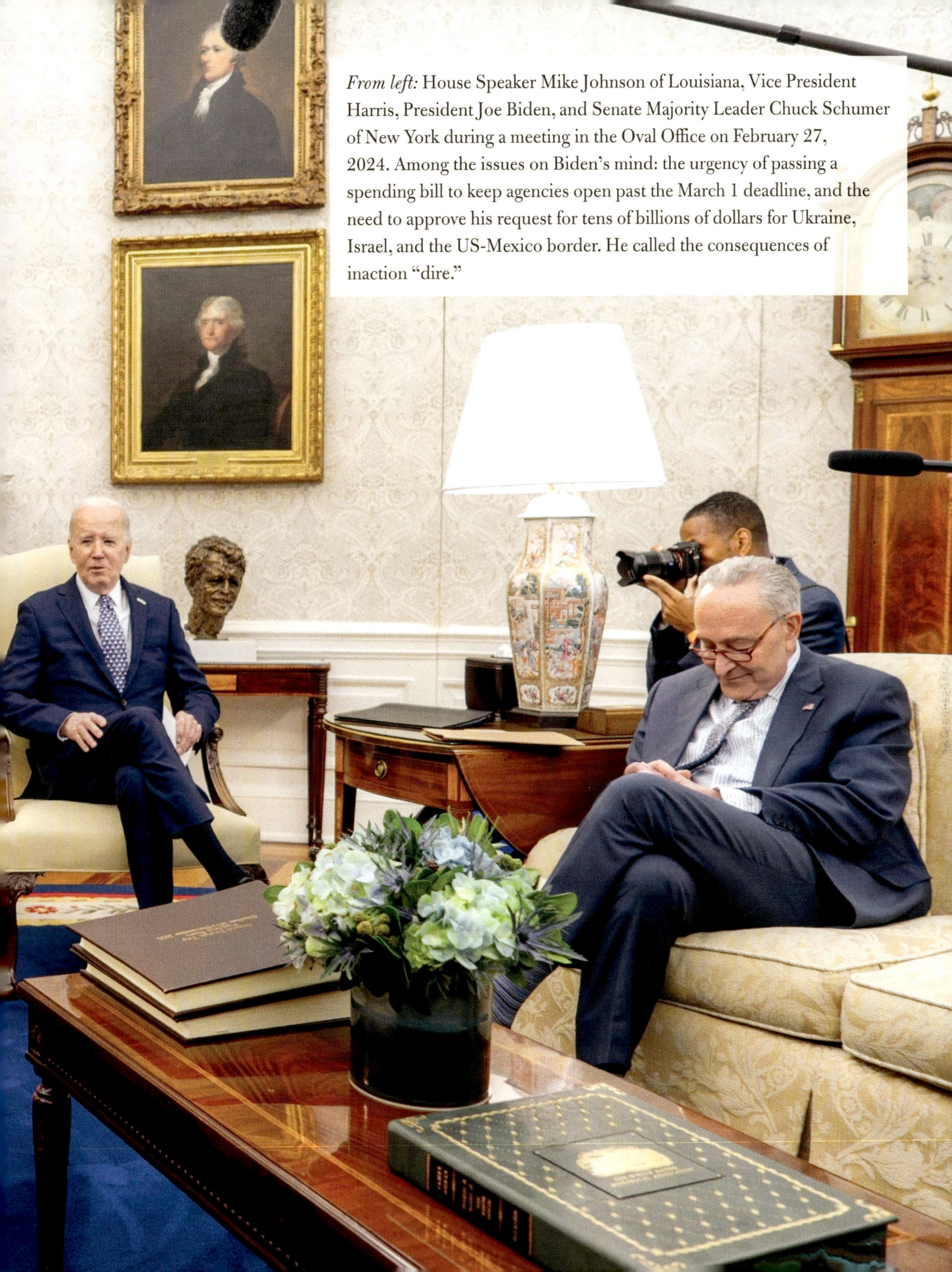

From left: House Speaker Mike Johnson of Louisiana, Vice President Harris, President Joe Biden, and Senate Majority Leader Chuck Schumer of New York during a meeting in the Oval Office on February 27, 2024. Among the issues on Biden's mind: the urgency of passing a spending bill to keep agencies open past the March 1 deadline, and the need to approve his request for tens of billions of dollars for Ukraine, Israel, and the US-Mexico border. He called the consequences of inaction "dire."

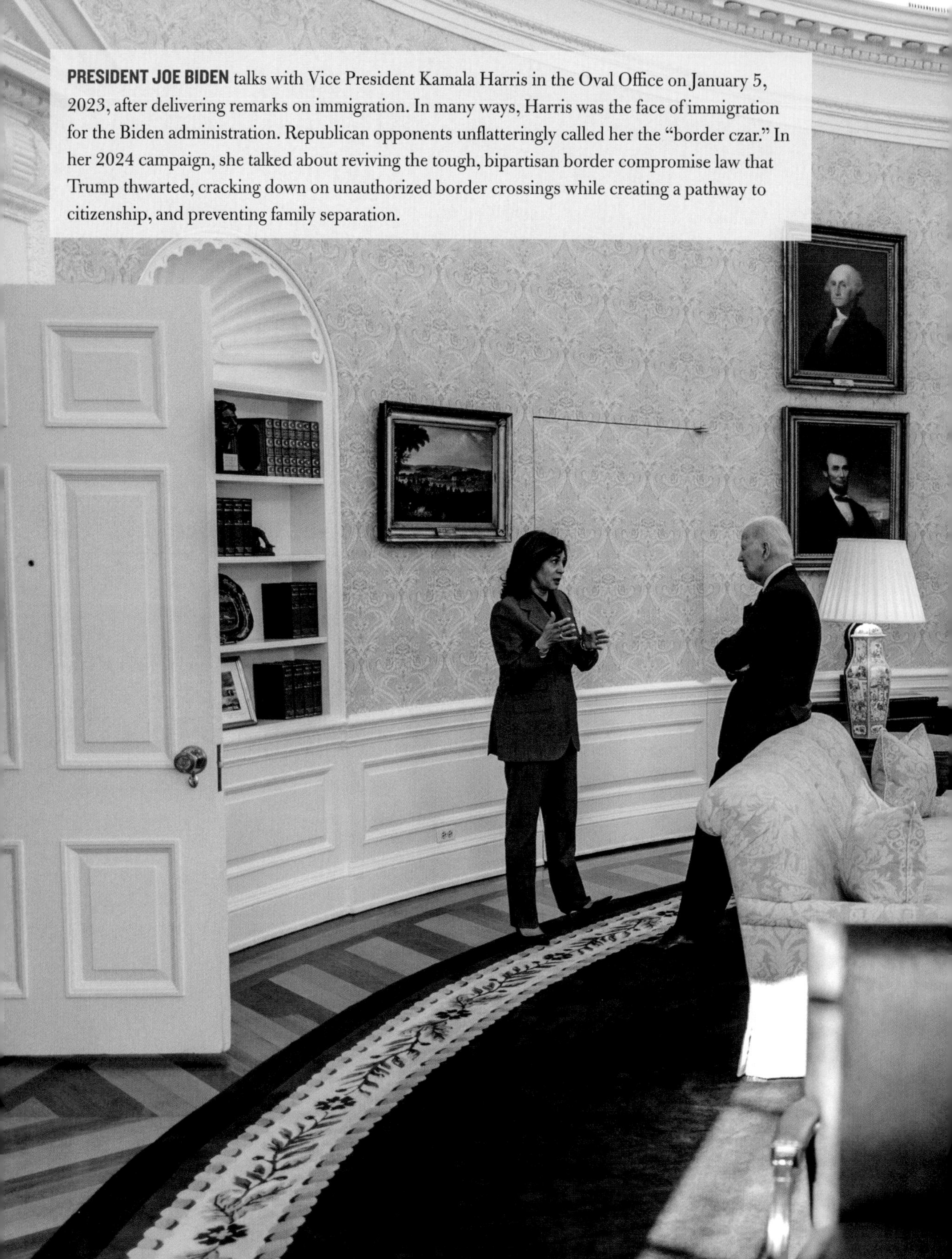

PRESIDENT JOE BIDEN talks with Vice President Kamala Harris in the Oval Office on January 5, 2023, after delivering remarks on immigration. In many ways, Harris was the face of immigration for the Biden administration. Republican opponents unflatteringly called her the "border czar." In her 2024 campaign, she talked about reviving the tough, bipartisan border compromise law that Trump thwarted, cracking down on unauthorized border crossings while creating a pathway to citizenship, and preventing family separation.

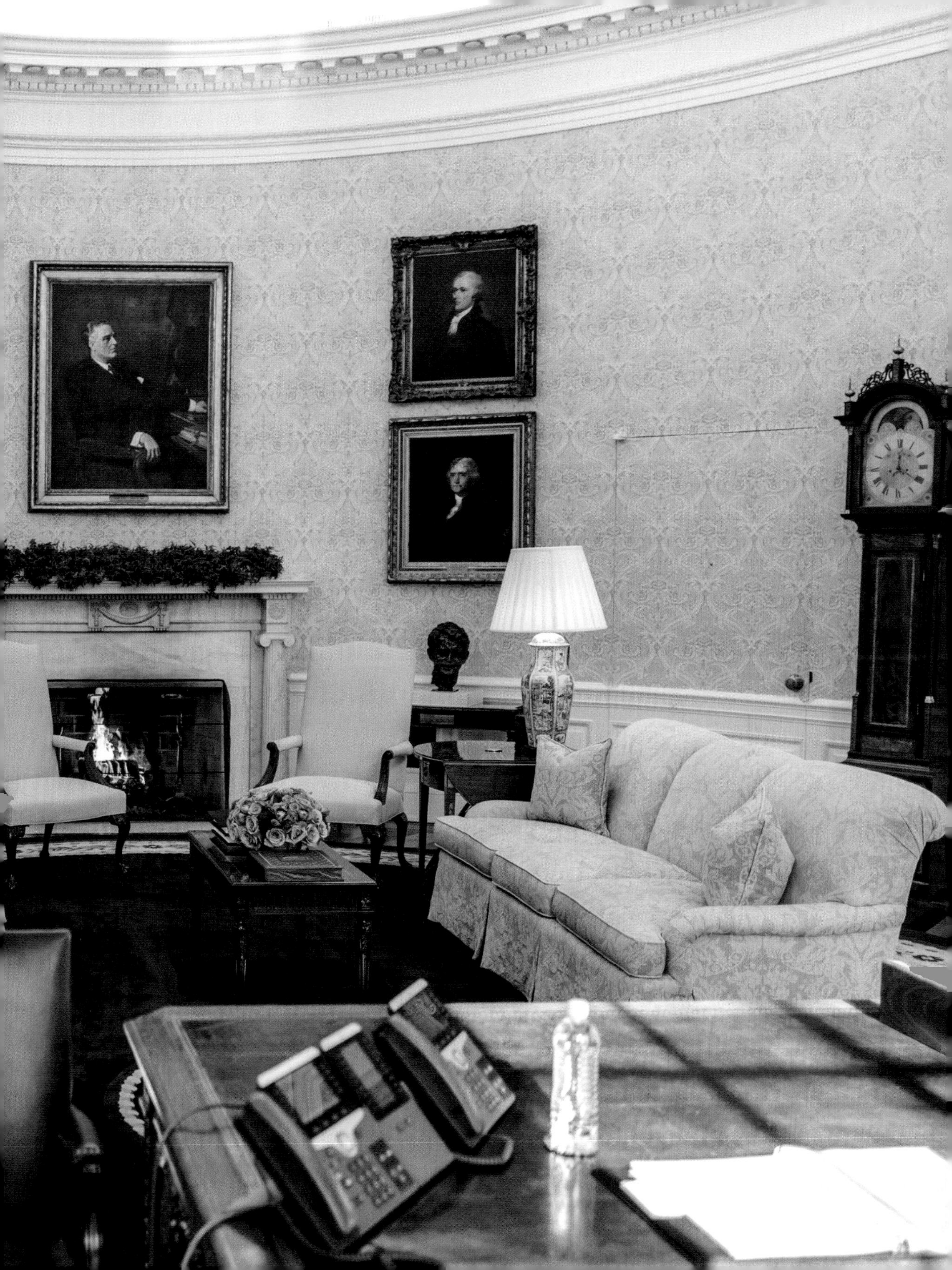

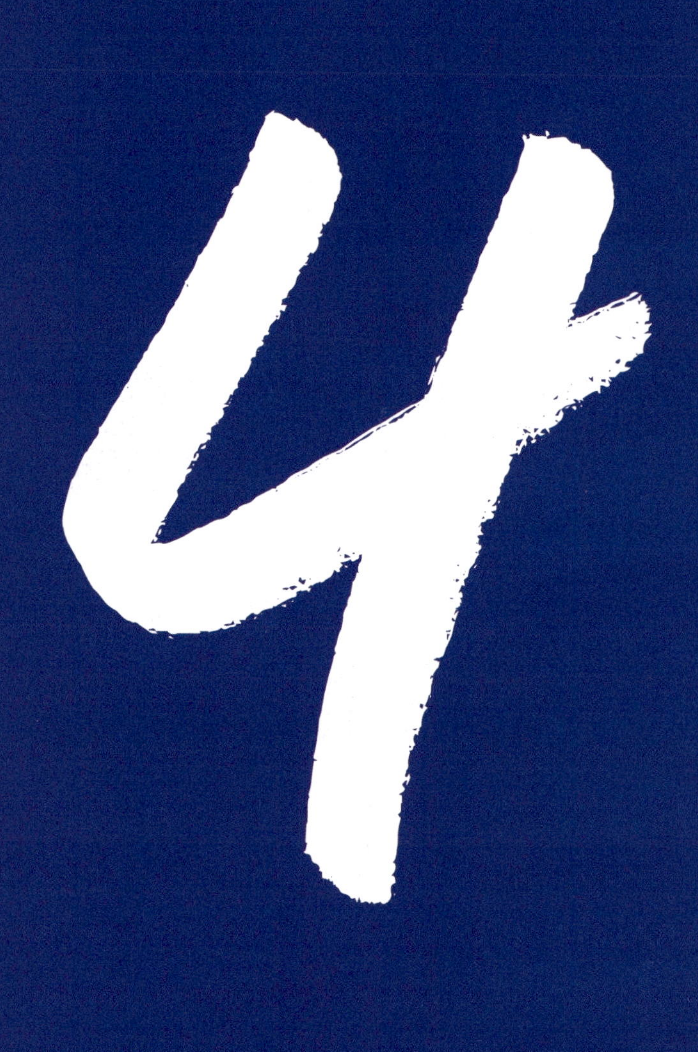

2020

"While I may be the first woman in this office, I will not be the last, because every little girl watching tonight sees that this is a country of possibilities."

—KAMALA HARRIS

The 2020 campaign season was a roller-coaster ride of promise, disappointment, and ultimately validation for Harris. Running for president can be exhilarating—those who come to your events cheer you on, chant slogans, and make you believe You're the One, as these photos show. And your face reflects that you feel the love. But then your polling tells you otherwise, your financial coffers tell you otherwise, and you begin to wonder if you're connecting. You have a great debate moment challenging the front-runner, Joe Biden, on school desegregation, and you start to believe again. But it's not enough. Senator Harris left the race, despondent at being unable to break through. Biden ended up winning the Democratic nomination, and with some thoughtful consideration as well as some backdoor politicking by Representative James Clyburn, Harris was selected to run as Biden's vice president. That was redemption. That was historic.

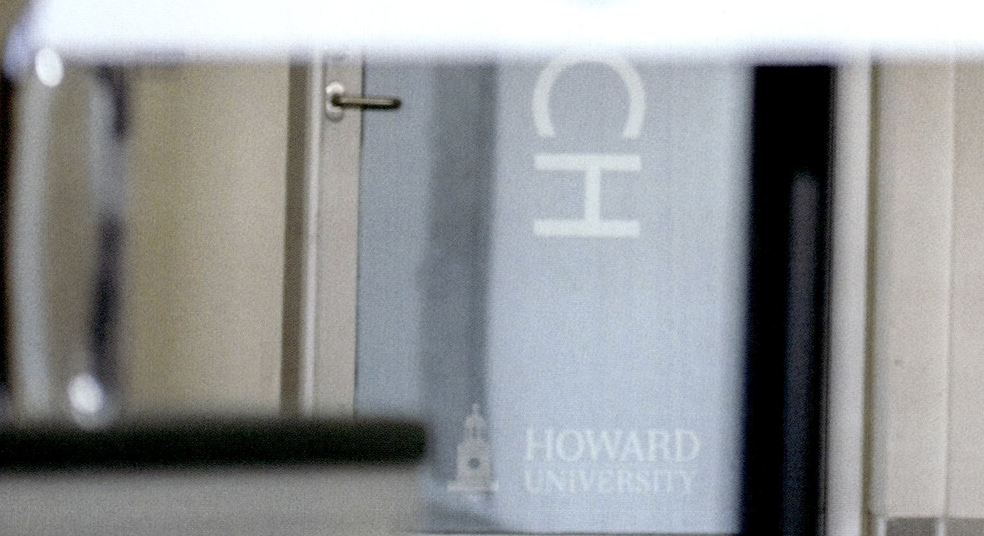
KAMALA HARRIS FOR THE PEOPLE
HOWARD UNIVERSITY

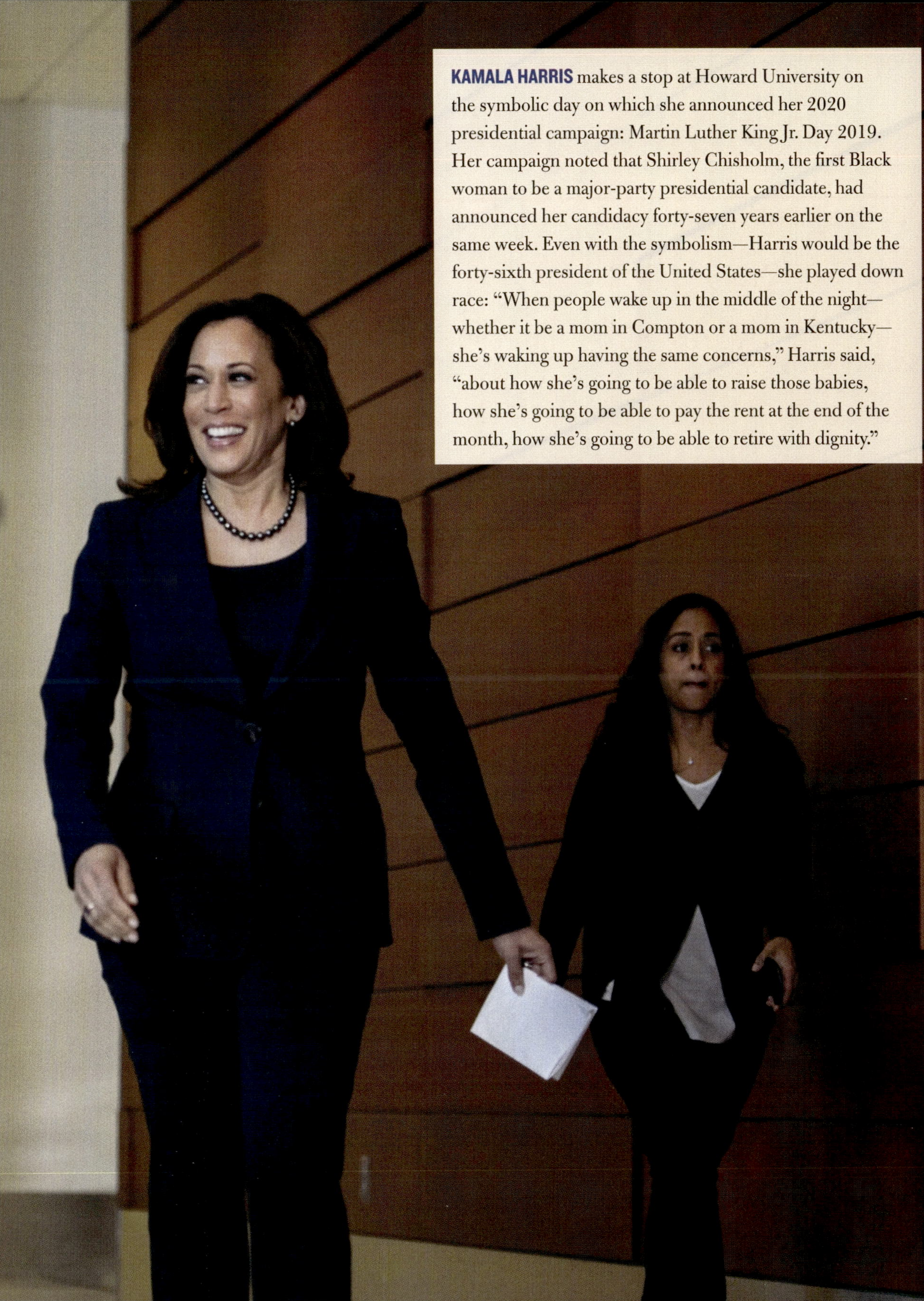

KAMALA HARRIS makes a stop at Howard University on the symbolic day on which she announced her 2020 presidential campaign: Martin Luther King Jr. Day 2019. Her campaign noted that Shirley Chisholm, the first Black woman to be a major-party presidential candidate, had announced her candidacy forty-seven years earlier on the same week. Even with the symbolism—Harris would be the forty-sixth president of the United States—she played down race: "When people wake up in the middle of the night—whether it be a mom in Compton or a mom in Kentucky—she's waking up having the same concerns," Harris said, "about how she's going to be able to raise those babies, how she's going to be able to pay the rent at the end of the month, how she's going to be able to retire with dignity."

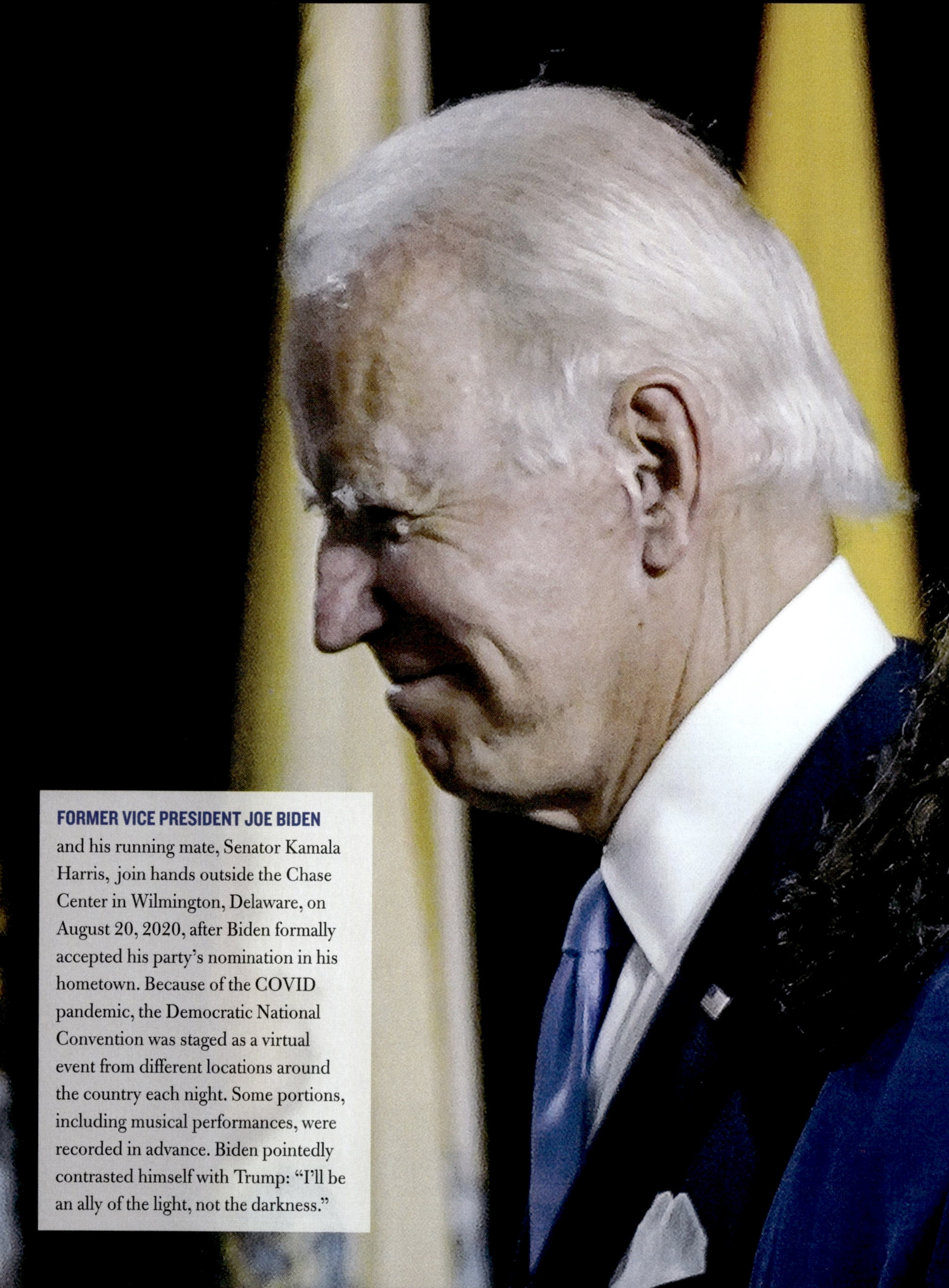

FORMER VICE PRESIDENT JOE BIDEN and his running mate, Senator Kamala Harris, join hands outside the Chase Center in Wilmington, Delaware, on August 20, 2020, after Biden formally accepted his party's nomination in his hometown. Because of the COVID pandemic, the Democratic National Convention was staged as a virtual event from different locations around the country each night. Some portions, including musical performances, were recorded in advance. Biden pointedly contrasted himself with Trump: "I'll be an ally of the light, not the darkness."

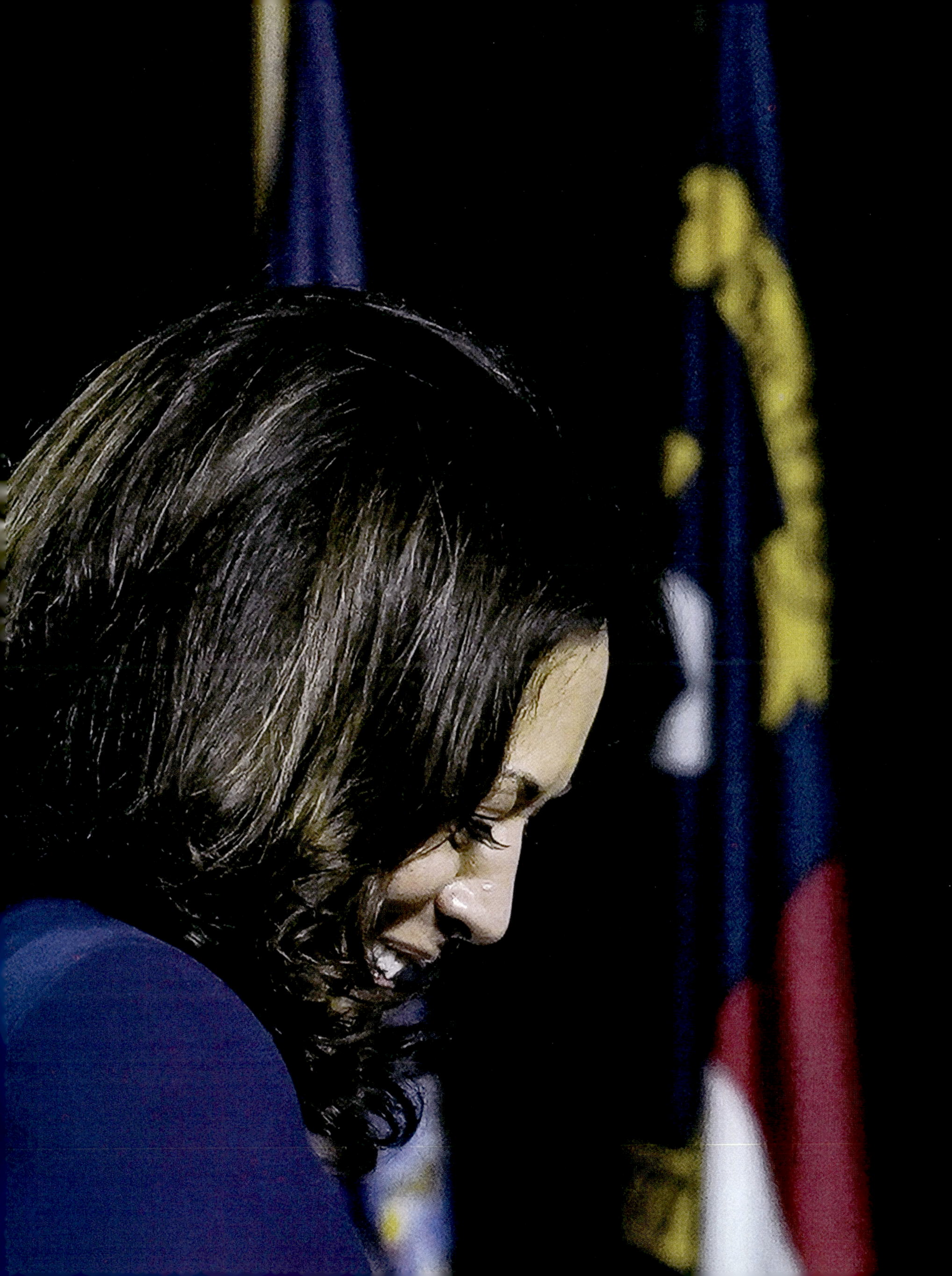

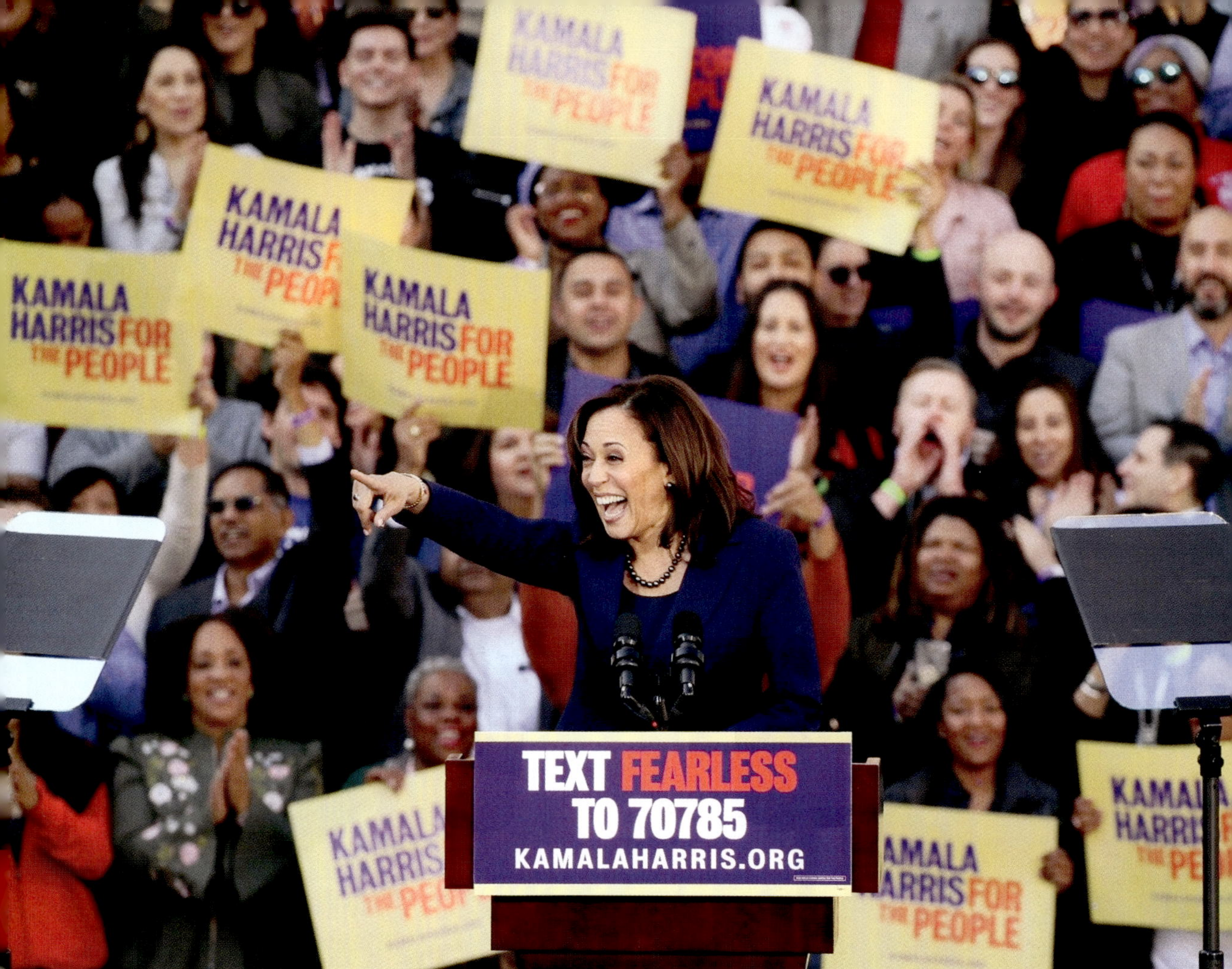

SENATOR KAMALA HARRIS formally kicks off her 2020 campaign for president of the United States on January 27, 2019, at a rally at Frank H. Ogawa Plaza in her hometown of Oakland, California.

Facing page:

A SOMBER OCCASION for Senator Harris as she participates in a moment of silence to honor George Floyd and the Black Lives Matter movement in Emancipation Hall at the U.S. Capitol on June 4, 2020. The stark murder of Floyd by a Minneapolis police officer set off protests around the world and ignited a new debate about criminal justice and policing. In the weeks following Floyd's killing, Harris voiced support for the "defund the police" movement, saying it rightly questioned the size of police budgets versus money that went to education, housing, and other social and community services. She also explicitly called for demilitarizing police departments. But after she joined Biden as his running mate, Biden and the campaign made clear that a Biden-Harris administration would oppose defunding police departments.

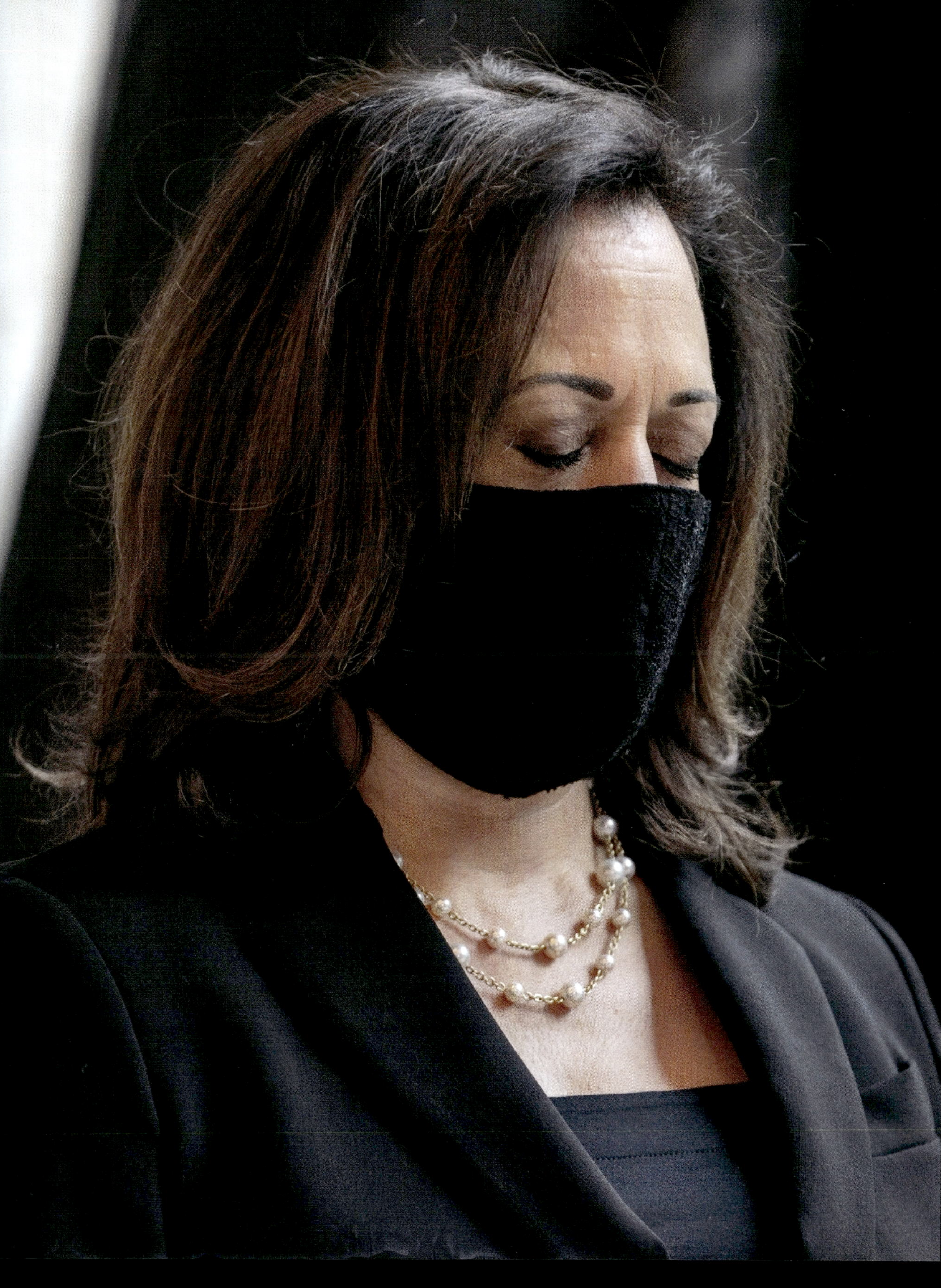

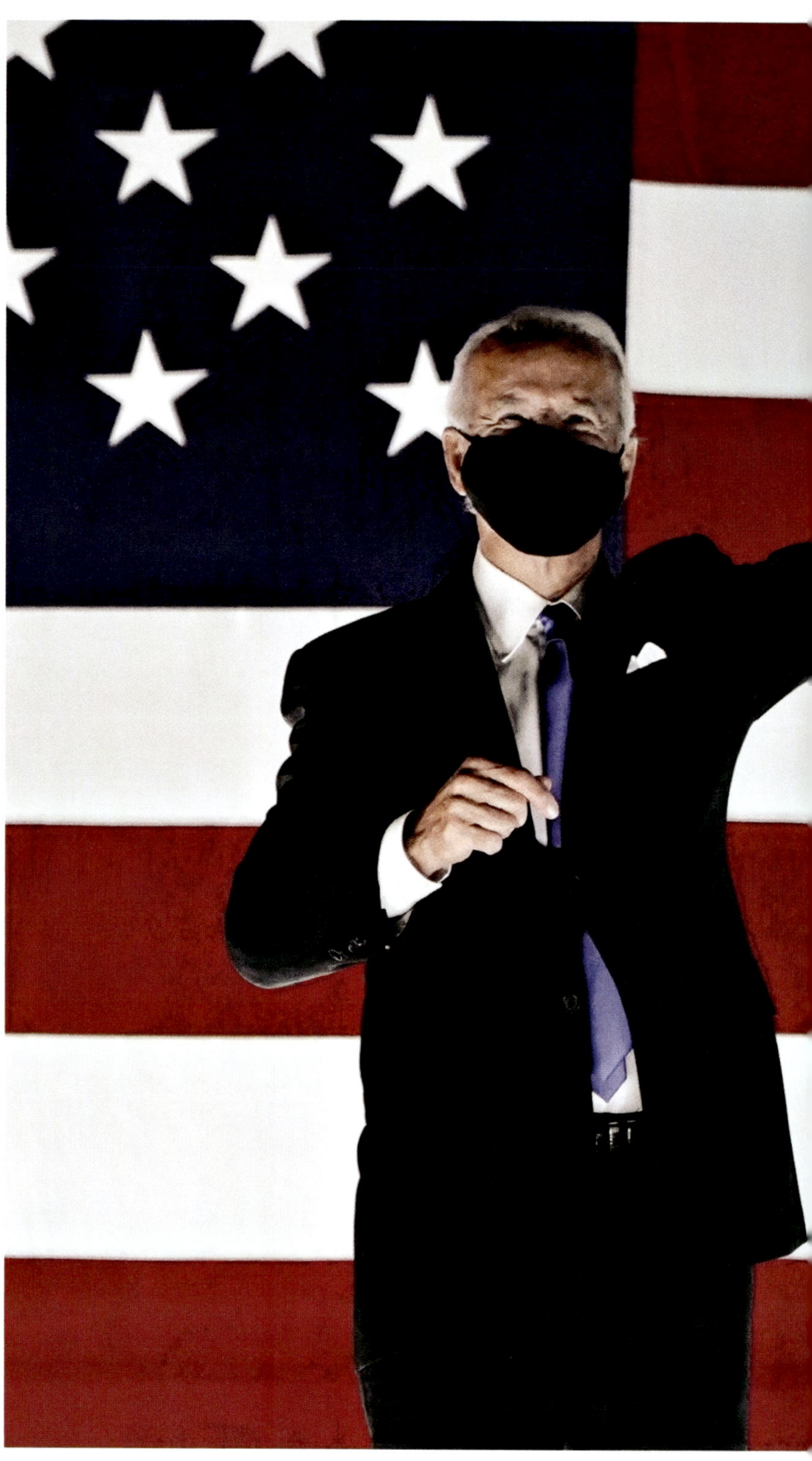

JOE BIDEN AND SENATOR KAMALA HARRIS at a rally at the University of North Florida, Jacksonville.

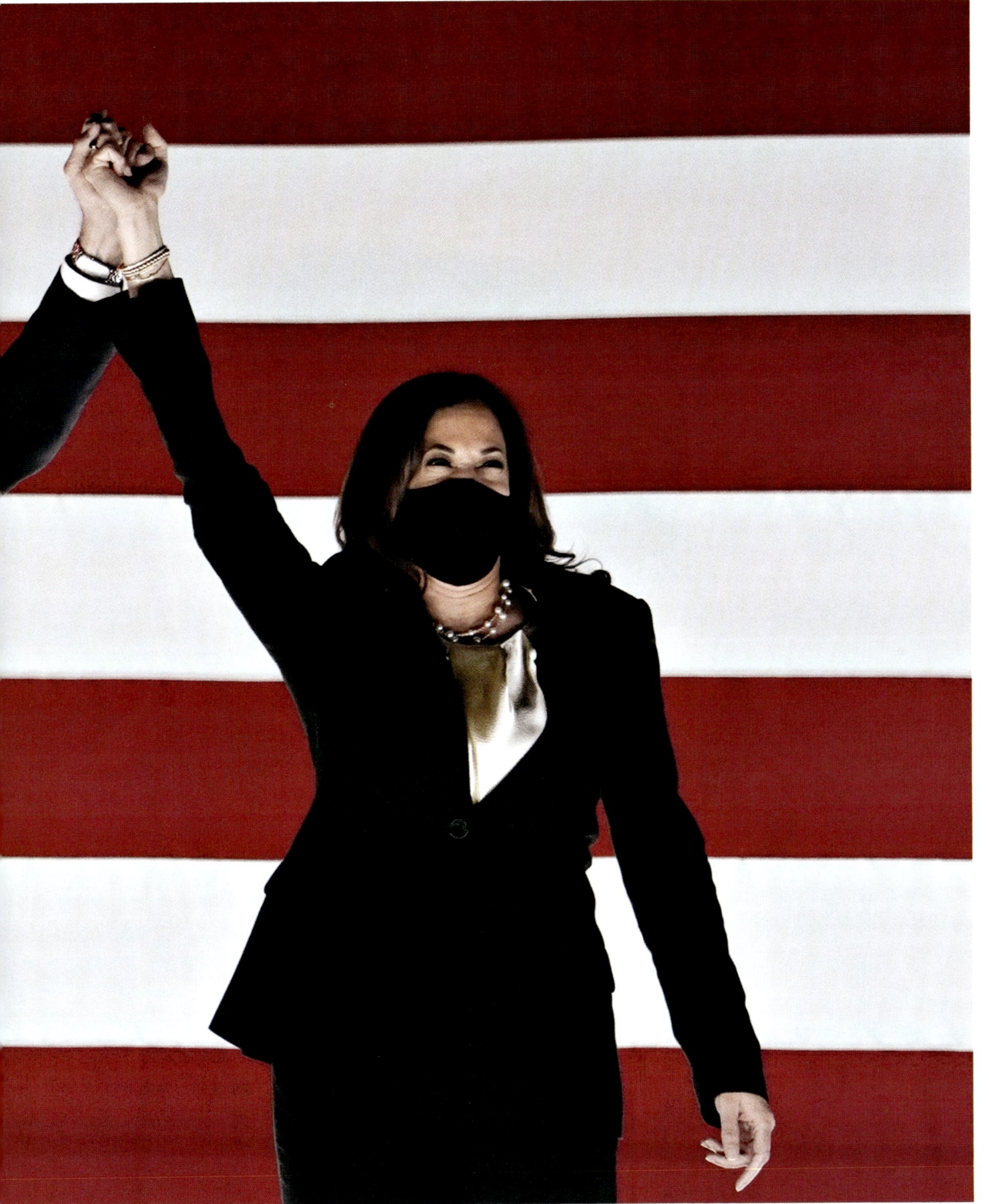

5

VICE PRESIDENT

"From the courthouse to the White House,

that has been my life's work."

—KAMALA HARRIS

Kamala Harris was sworn in as vice president on January 20, 2021, at the height of COVID. There are many photos of her wearing a mask, though only a few in this collection. Despite being a historic vice president, her public presence was somewhat limited early on because of the pandemic. Black and South Asian communities felt a special kind of pride, and many women beamed that they were now just one notch away from the presidency. These photos show Harris performing a series of official duties—greeting military servicemembers and arriving at the scene of hurricane relief efforts in Houston, for instance. Vice presidents are often dispatched in times of crisis to convey the administration's concern. But they have considerable latitude in where to speak, what projects to take on, and how best to represent themselves and the president. A new dimension to Harris's vice presidency is the Second Gentleman, a role for Doug Emhoff. Photos of him accompanying the vice president are role-reversal shots we had never seen before.

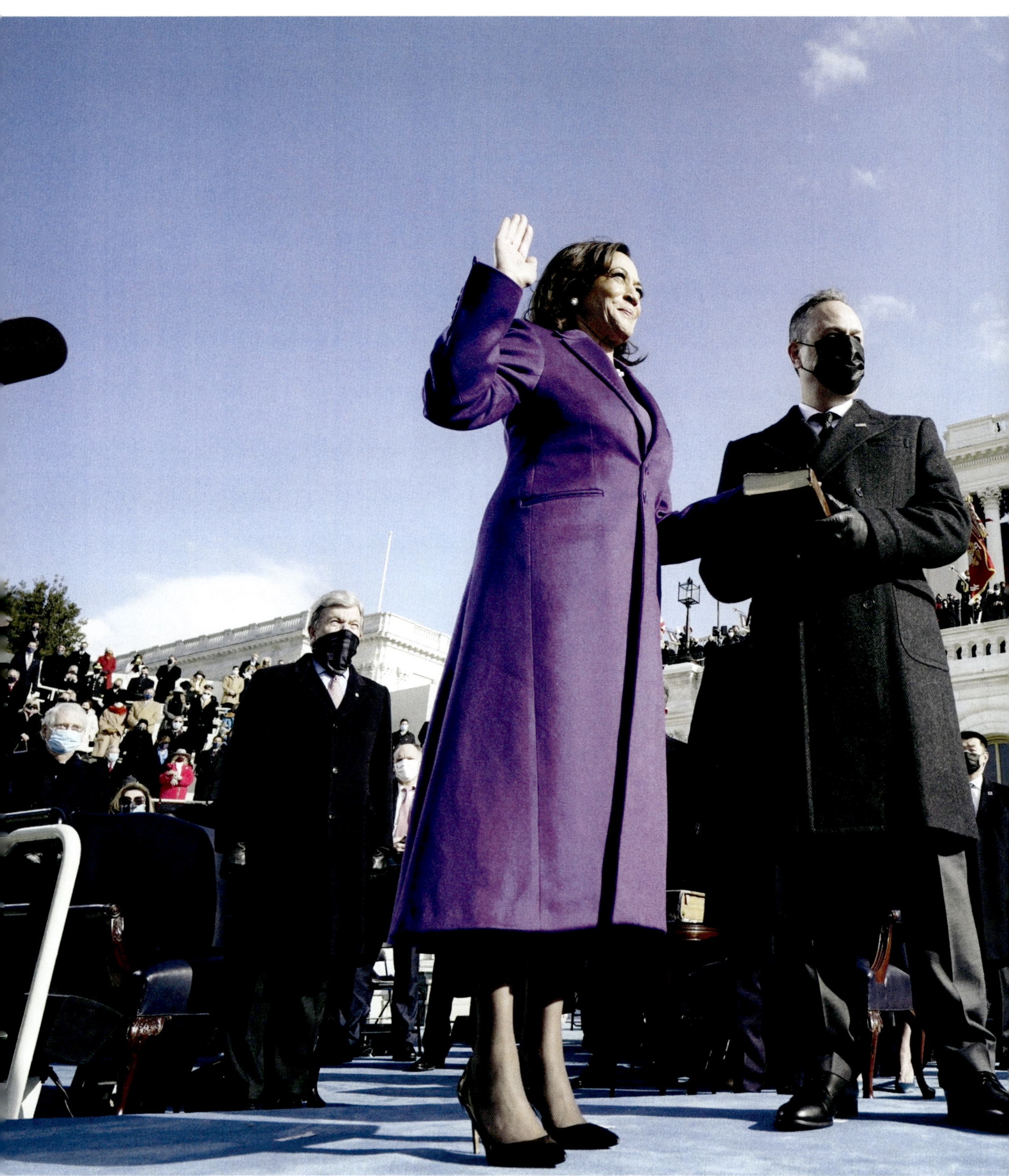

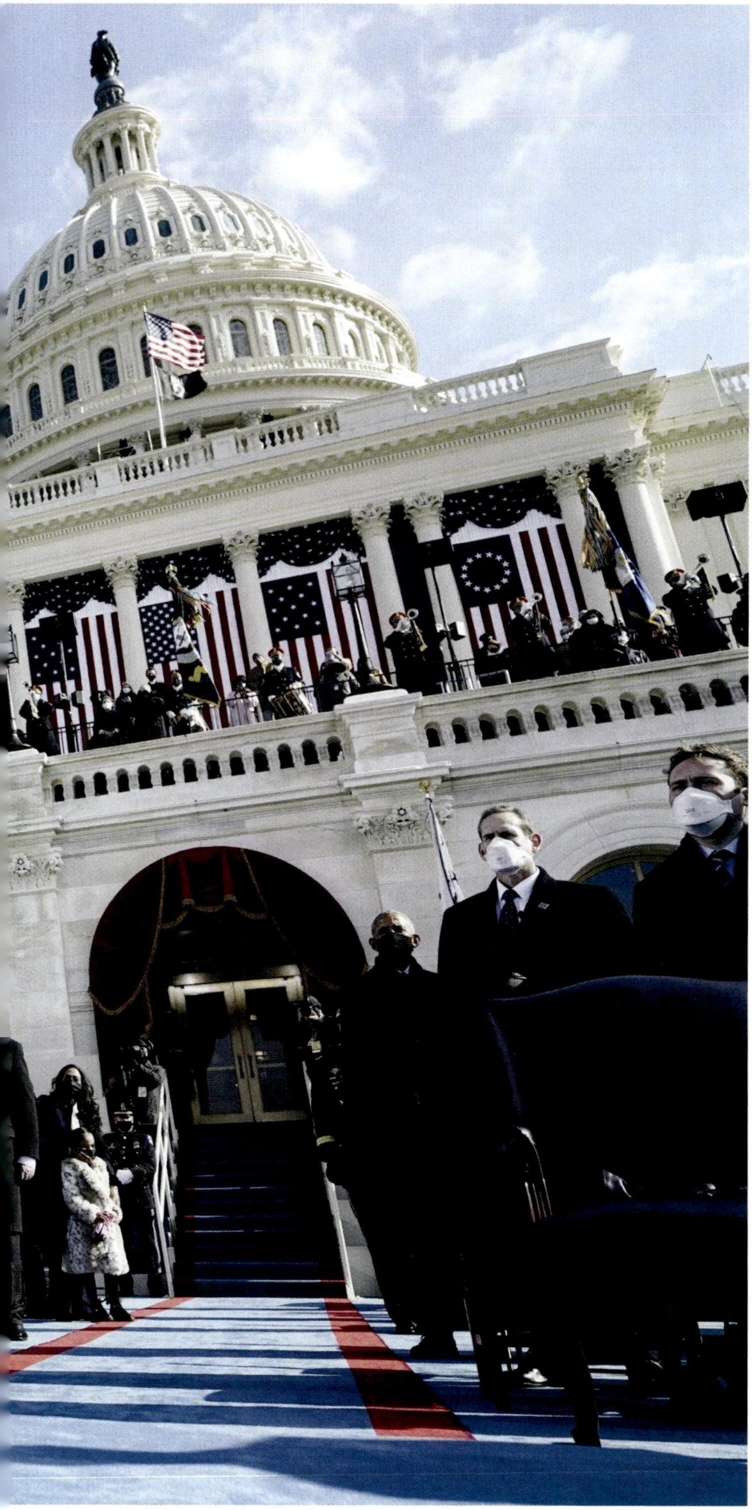

OFFICIAL White House portrait.

KAMALA HARRIS is sworn in as vice president as her husband, Doug Emhoff, holds a Bible during the fifty-ninth presidential inauguration on the west front of the Capitol on January 20, 2021.

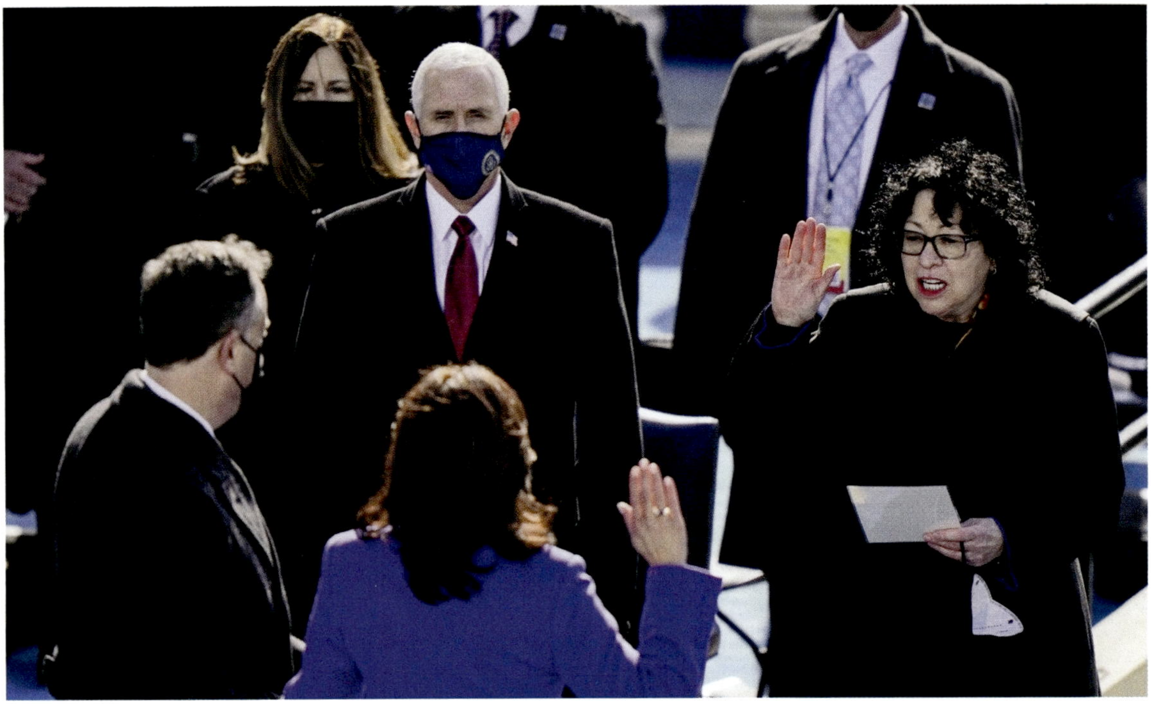

SUPREME COURT JUSTICE SONIA SOTOMAYOR (*right*) administers the oath of office to incoming vice president Kamala Harris as outgoing vice president Mike Pence (*wearing blue mask*) watches.

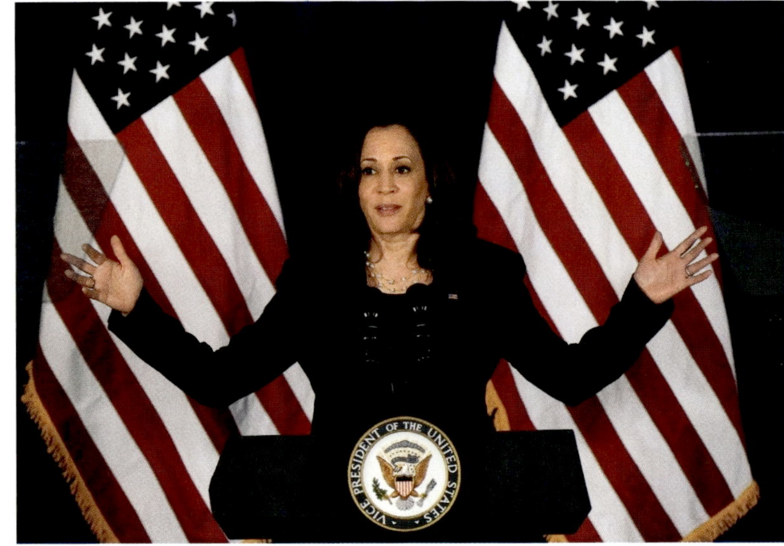

VICE PRESIDENT HARRIS delivers remarks at the Louis Stokes Library on the campus of her alma mater, Howard University, on July 8, 2021, in Washington, DC. Organized by the Democratic National Committee, the event focused on voting rights.

Facing page:

VICE PRESIDENT HARRIS walks through an honor cordon of side boys as she arrives to visit the Arleigh Burke–class guided-missile destroyer USS *Howard* at Fleet Activities Yokosuka, September 28, 2022, in Yokosuka, Japan.

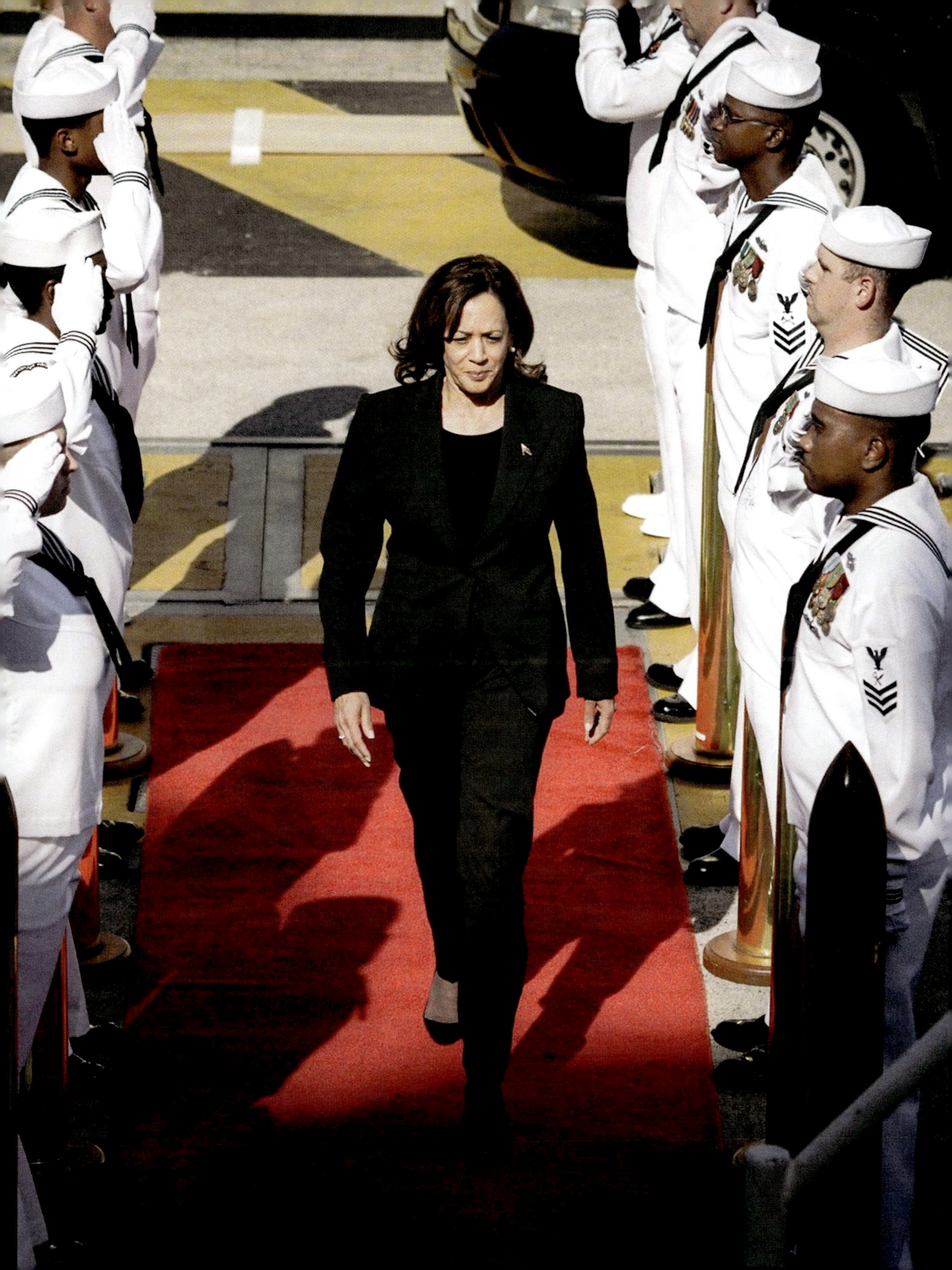

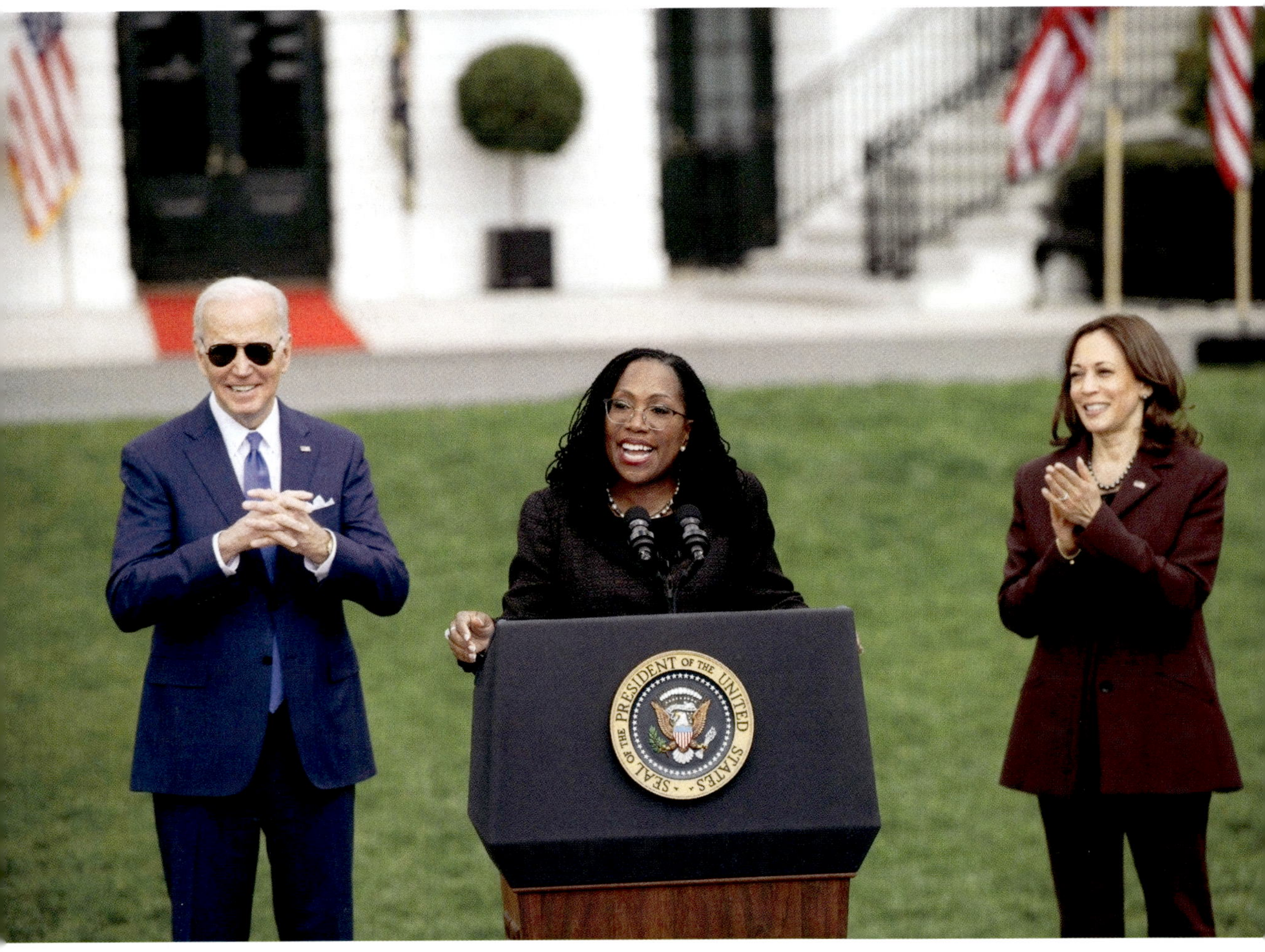

JUDGE KETANJI BROWN JACKSON gives remarks at a White House celebration on April 8, 2022, a day after becoming the first African American woman to be confirmed to the U.S. Supreme Court. Said President Joe Biden, who nominated her, "Whoa! It's about time!" Vice President Kamala Harris, who presided over the Senate confirmation vote, said she had taken time to draft a note to her goddaughter. "I told her that I felt such a deep sense of pride and joy," Harris reflected, "and about what this moment means for our nation and for her future."

Facing page:

VICE PRESIDENT HARRIS arrives at the Houston Emergency Center to speak to local officials and be briefed on the region's recovery efforts from Hurricane Beryl on July 24, 2024. She arrived in Houston the day before to speak to the American Federation of Teachers' annual convention

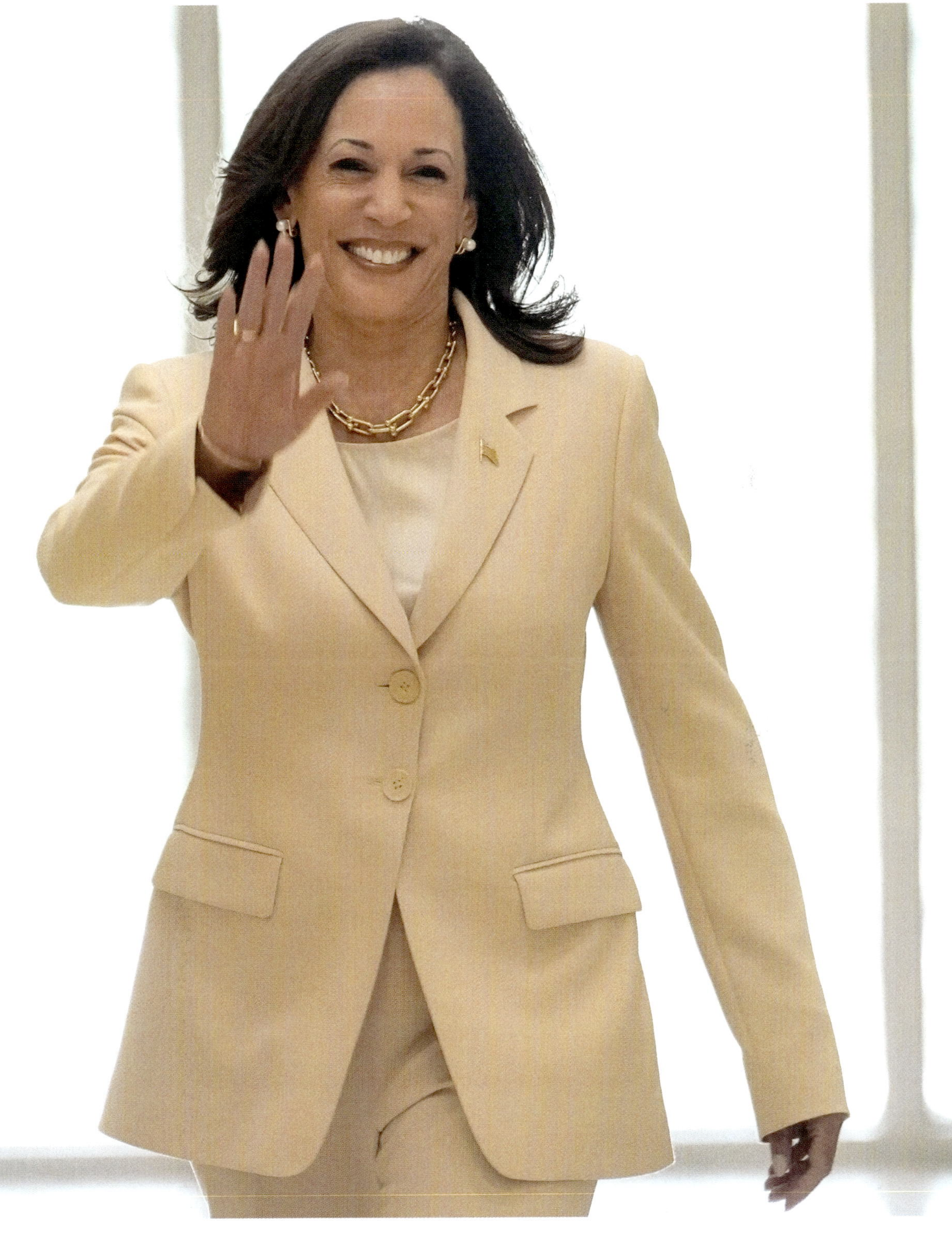

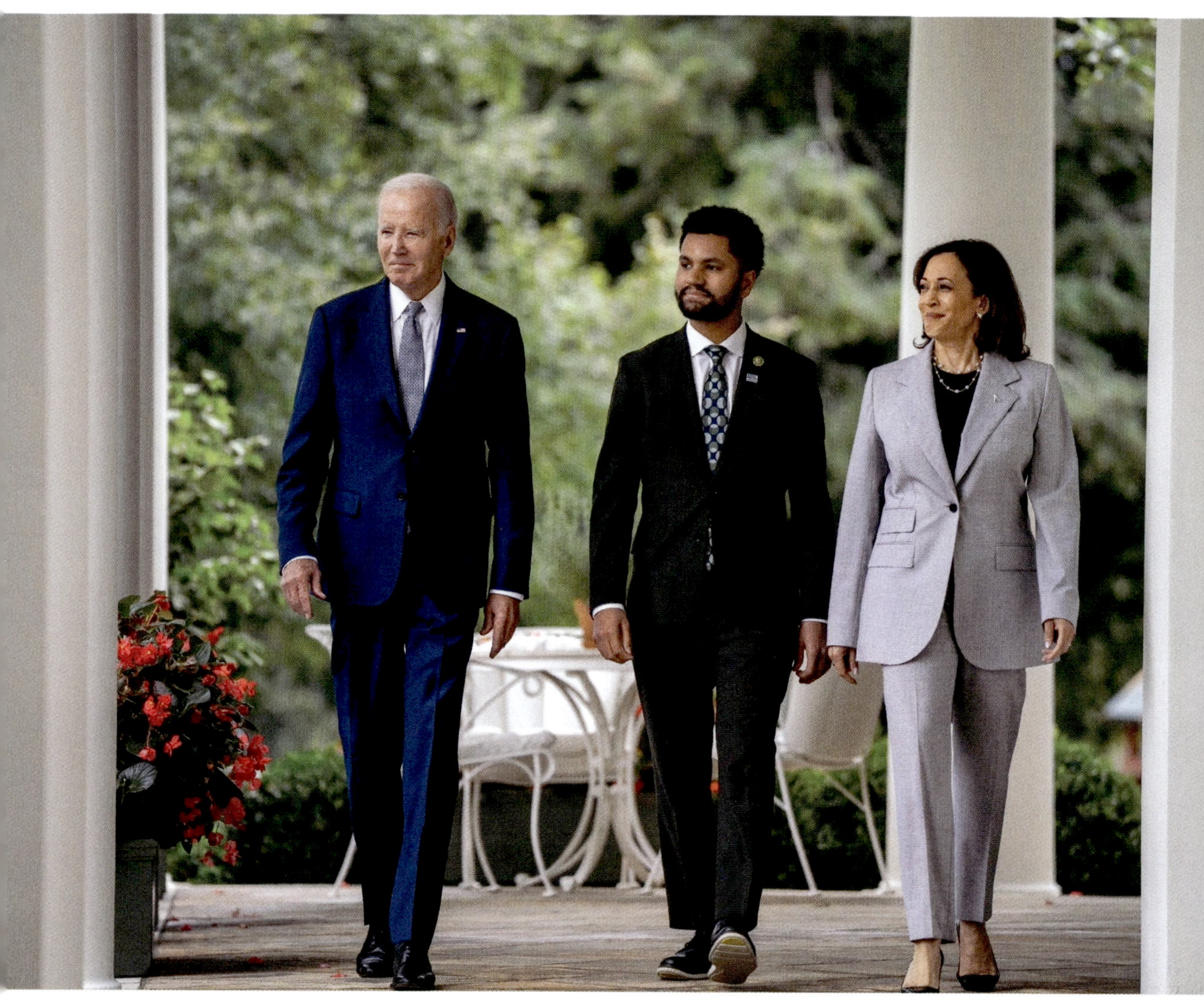

PRESIDENT JOE BIDEN, Vice President Harris, and Democratic Representative Maxwell Frost of Florida arrive at the Rose Garden for an announcement on the first-ever White House Office of Gun Violence Prevention on September 22, 2023.

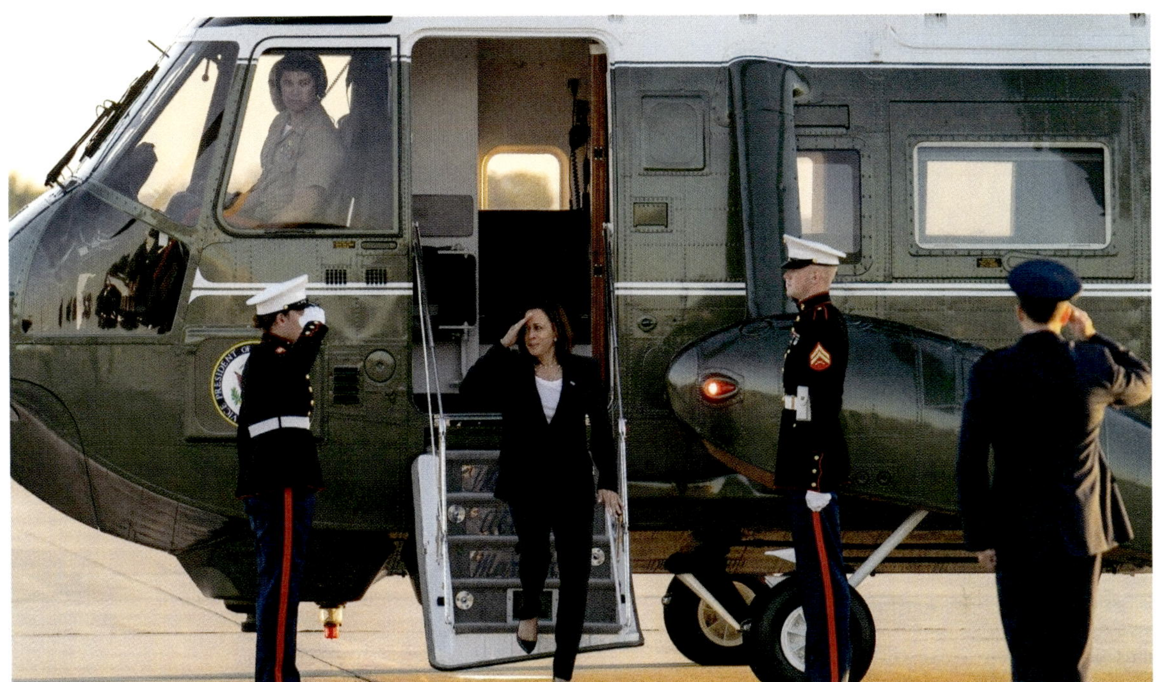

VICE PRESIDENT KAMALA HARRIS salutes U.S. Marines as she disembarks Marine Two at Joint Base Andrews in Maryland, on June 25, 2021, to begin her trip to El Paso, Texas.

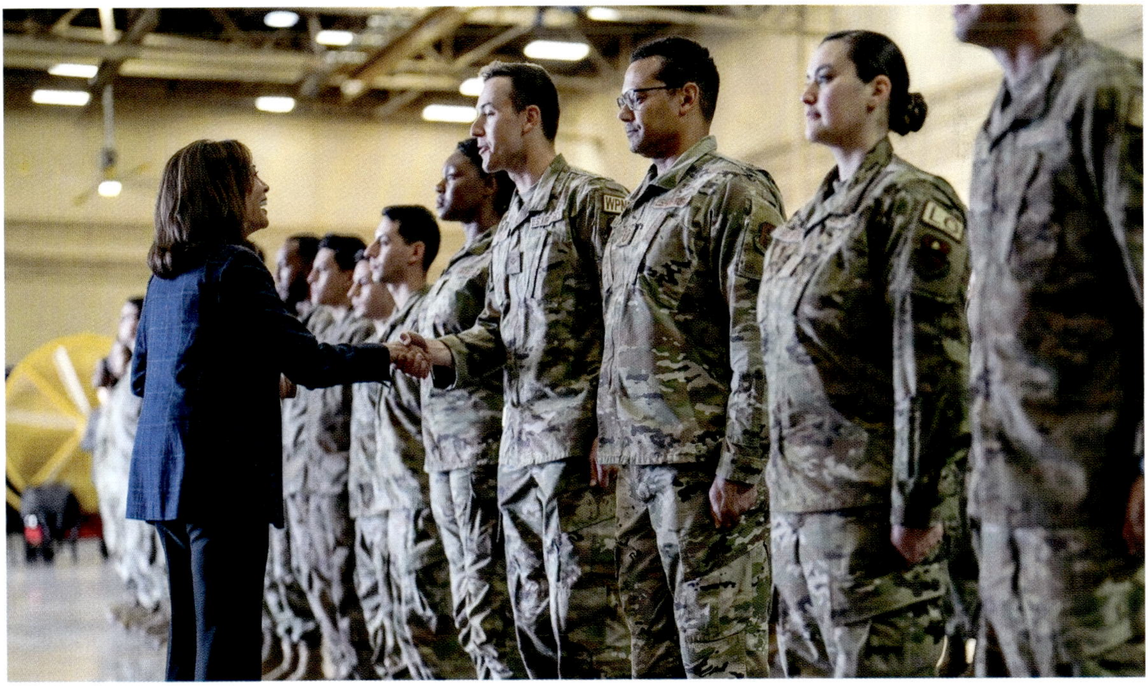

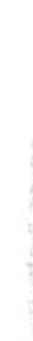

VICE PRESIDENT HARRIS greets aviators at Luke Air Force Base on January 19, 2023, in Maricopa County, Arizona.

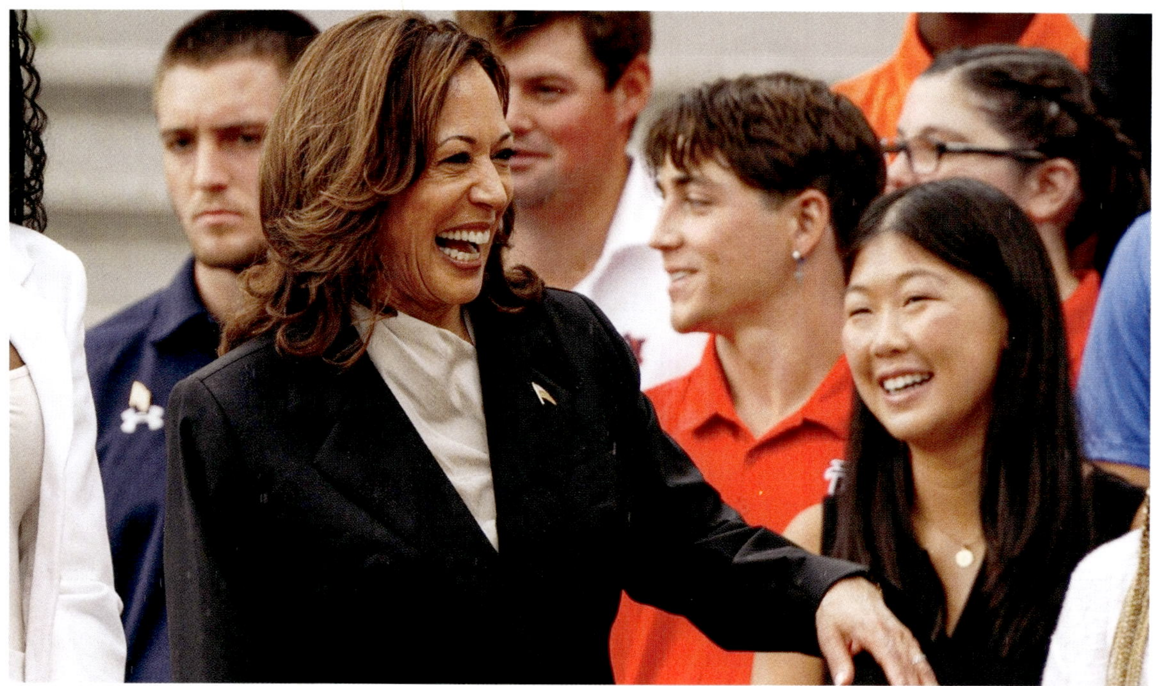

VICE PRESIDENT HARRIS hosting NCAA championship teams in Washington, DC, on the South Lawn of the White House. It was Harris's first public appearance since Joe Biden exited the 2024 presidential election and she became the presumptive front-runner for the Democratic nomination.

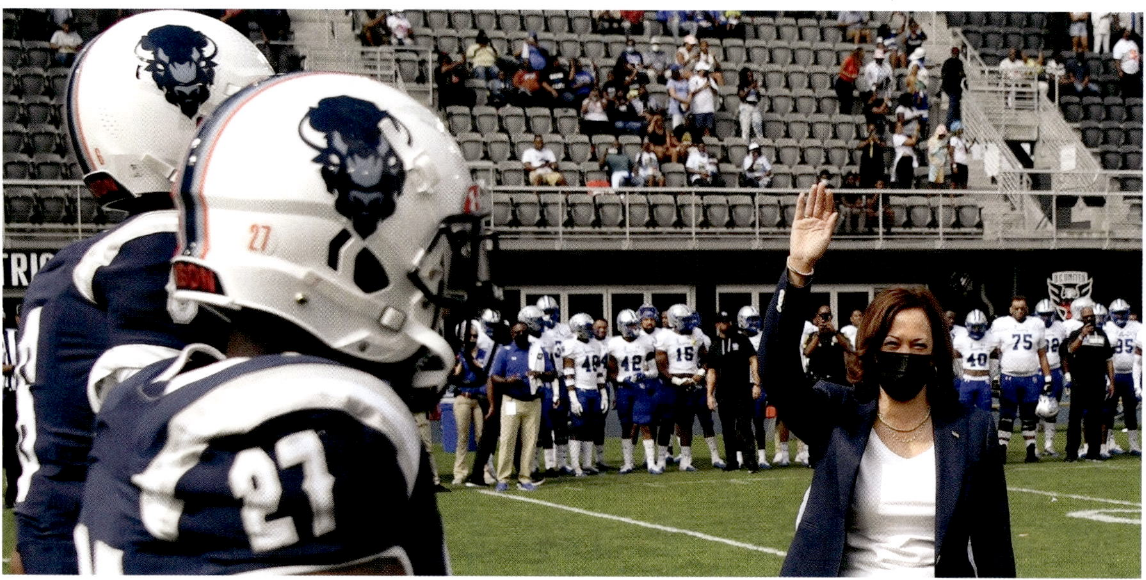

VICE PRESIDENT HARRIS participates in the coin toss at the opening of the football game between Howard University and Hampton University, an intense rivalry among Historically Black Colleges and Universities, at Audi Field in Washington, DC, on September 18, 2021.

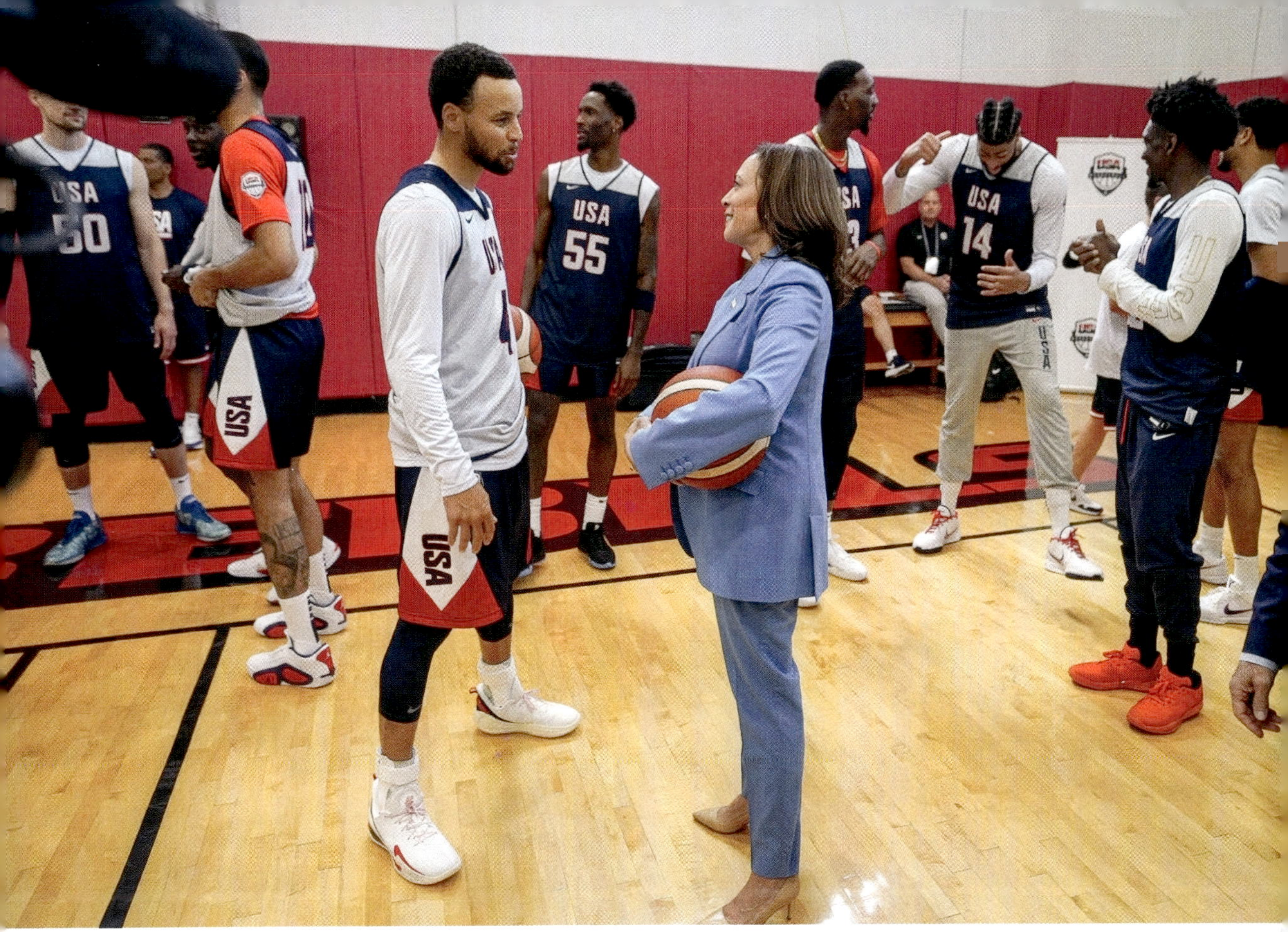

KAMALA HARRIS has long been a Golden State Warriors fan. Here, she meets with Warrior Steph Curry and the rest of the U.S. men's national basketball team practicing in Las Vegas. Assistant coach Erik Spoelstra called her visit a "pretty special moment for the entire group."

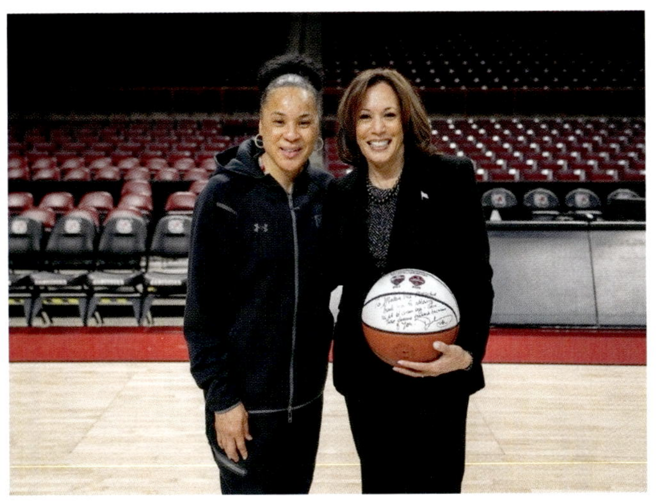

VICE PRESIDENT HARRIS poses for a photo with South Carolina Gamecocks women's basketball coach Dawn Staley during a surprise stop at Colonial Life Arena in Columbia, South Carolina, on January 15, 2024.

VICE PRESIDENT HARRIS arrives to speak during her visit to a Planned Parenthood clinic in Saint Paul, Minnesota, on March 14, 2024. Harris made reproductive rights a pillar of her presidential campaign.

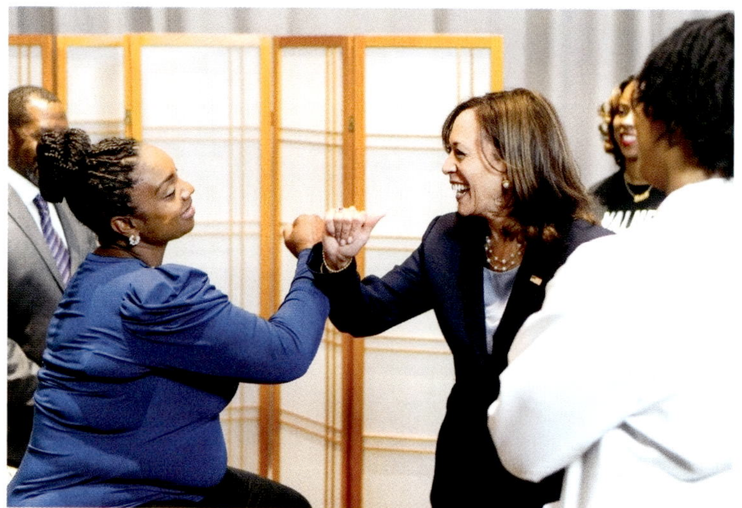

VICE PRESIDENT HARRIS shows she is comfortable in every setting. Here, she meets with patient Hope Williams, who was expecting her fourth child.

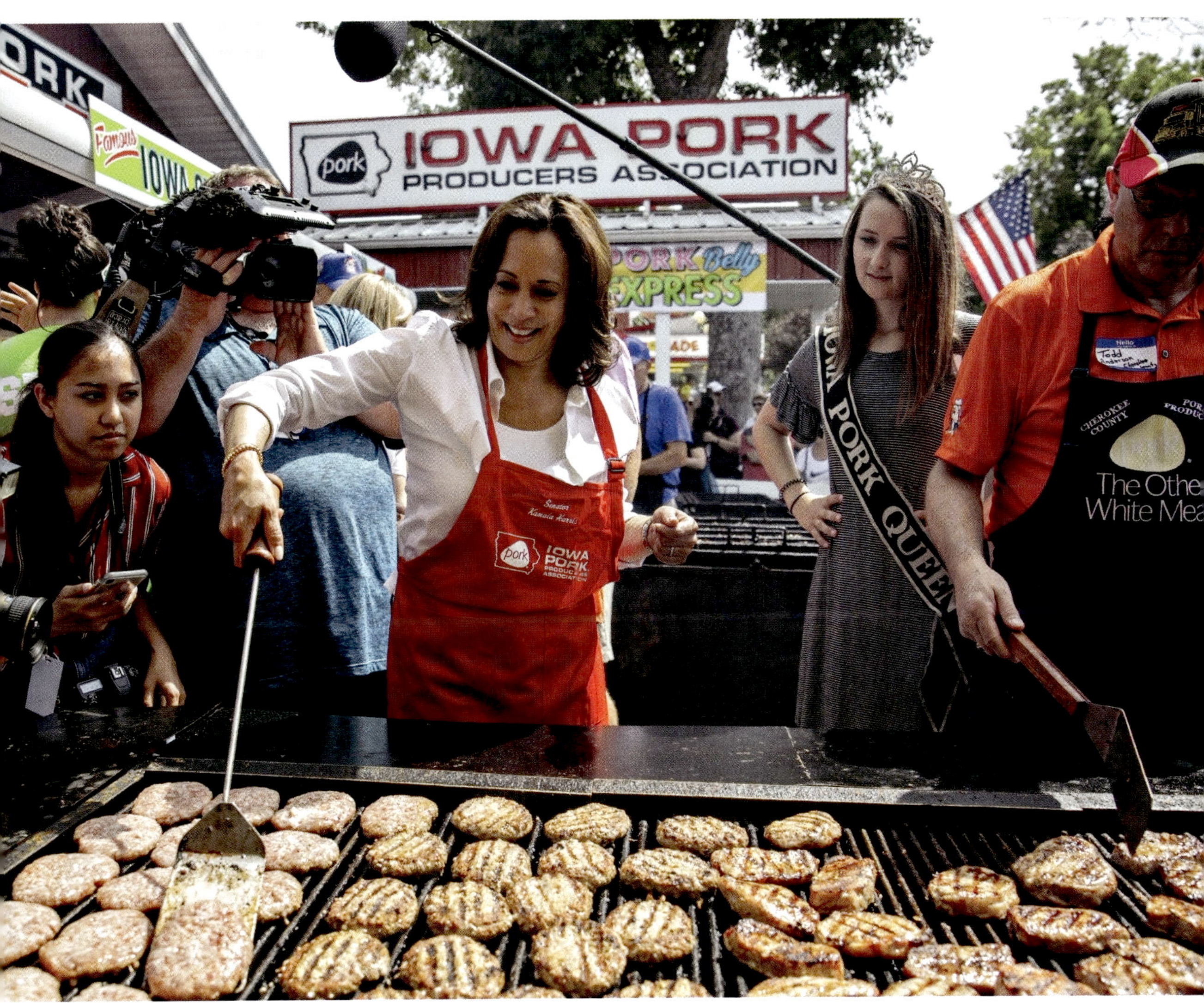

UNLIKE MANY public figures, Kamala's political food photo ops make her seem no different from her constituents.

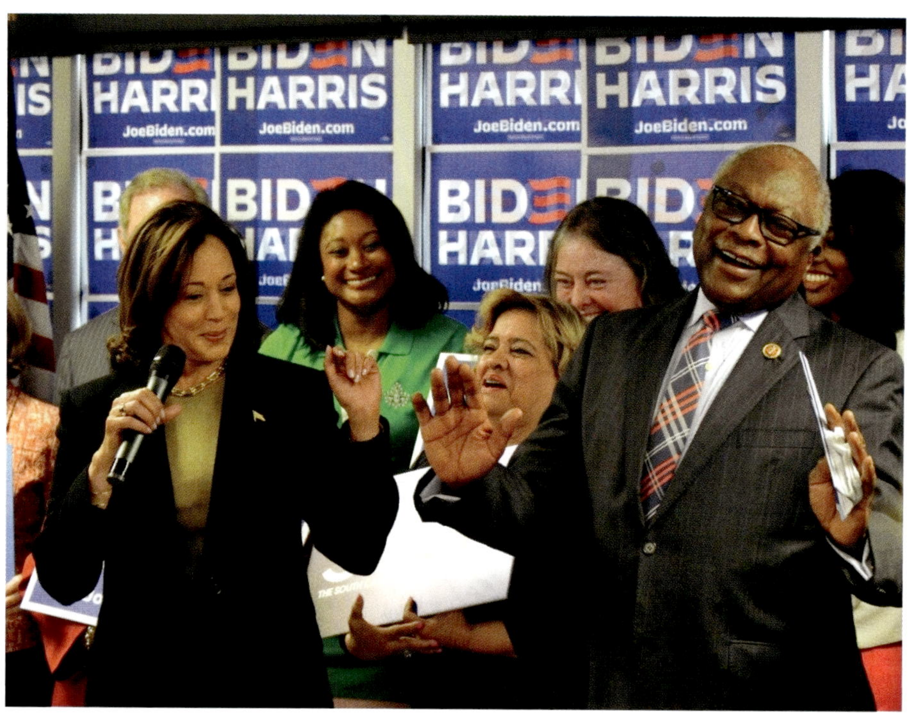

VICE PRESIDENT HARRIS jokes with Representative Jim Clyburn at an event in the South Carolina Democratic Party headquarters in Columbia on November 10, 2023.

VICE PRESIDENT HARRIS walks onstage to speak at the kickoff for the Fight for Reproductive Freedoms Tour on January 22, 2024, at the International Union of Painters and Allied Trades District Council 7 in Big Bend, Wisconsin.

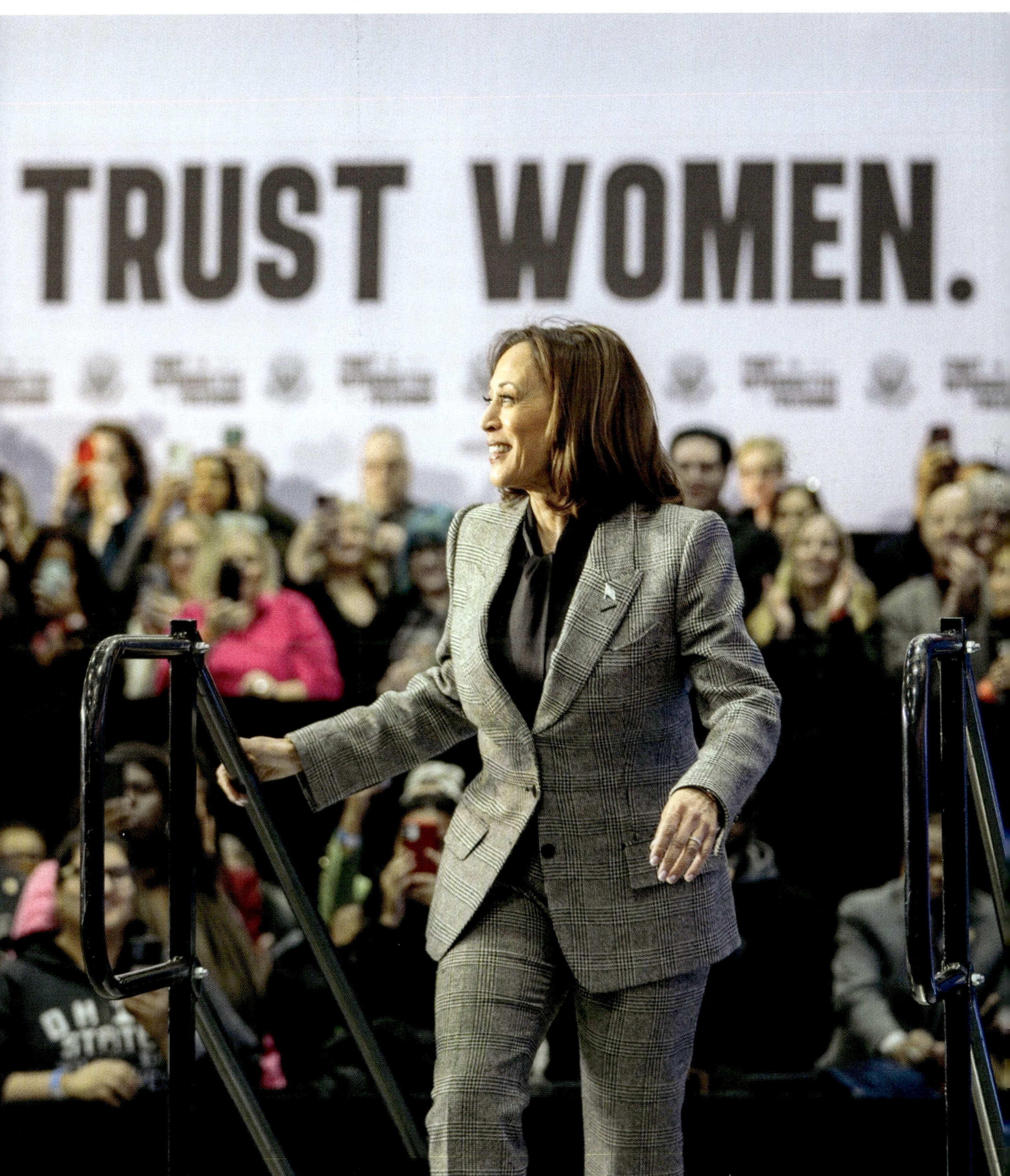
TRUST WOMEN.

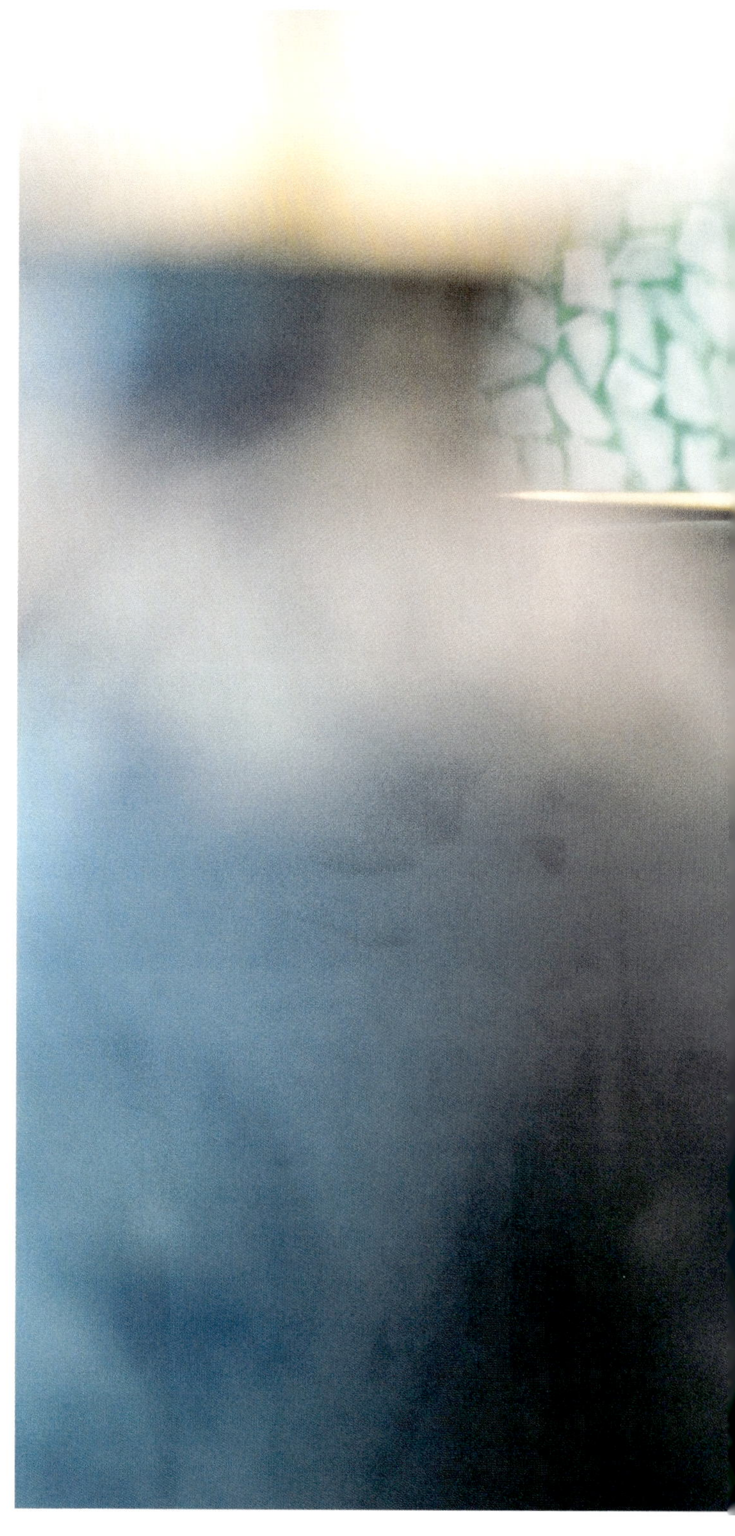

VICE PRESIDENT HARRIS holds an on-phone and in-person meeting in her West Wing office on August 4, 2021, in preparation for her trip to Singapore. Hanging behind her is the painting *White Daisies Rhapsody* (1973) by Alma Thomas. The painting is on loan from the Smithsonian American Art Museum.

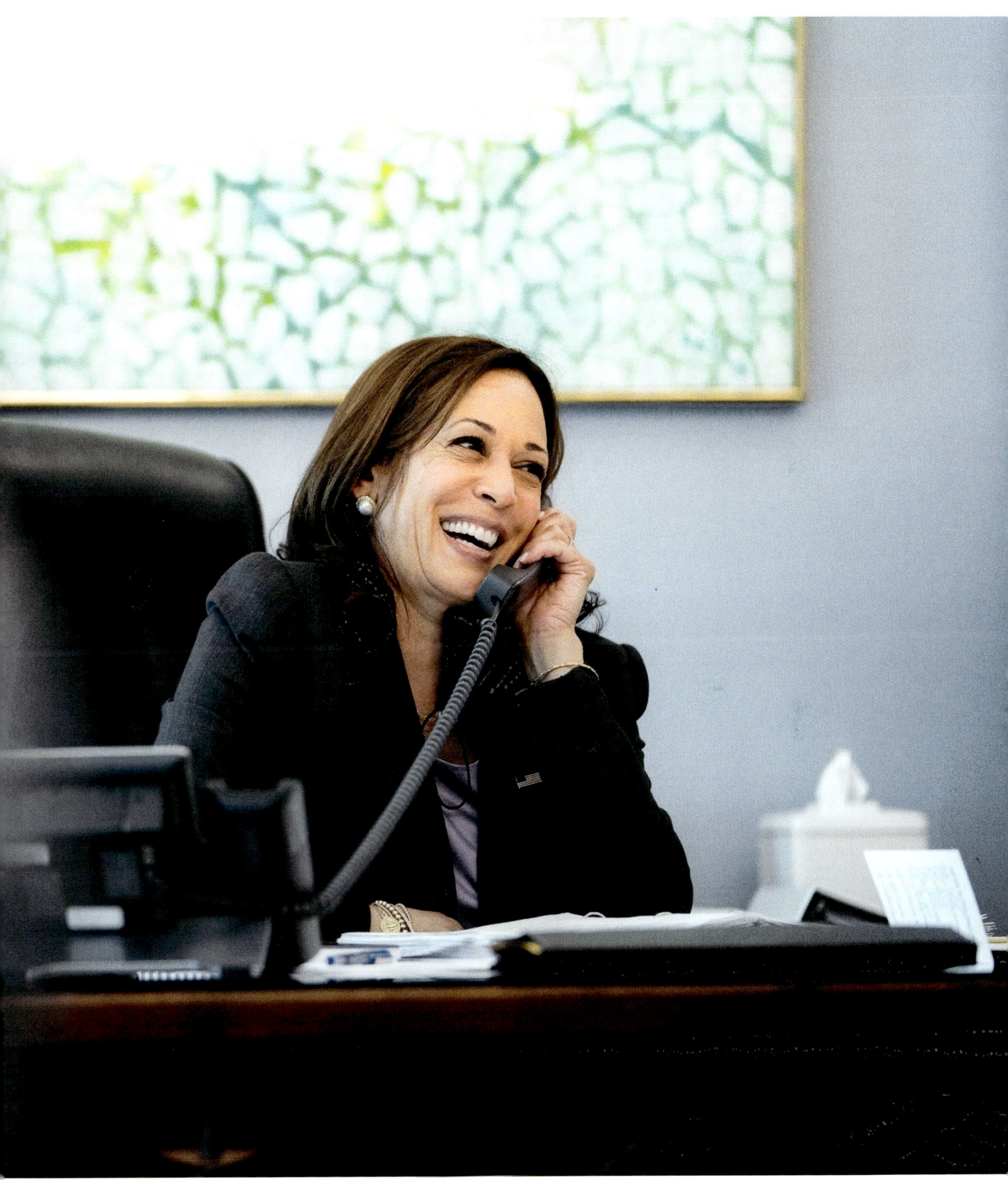

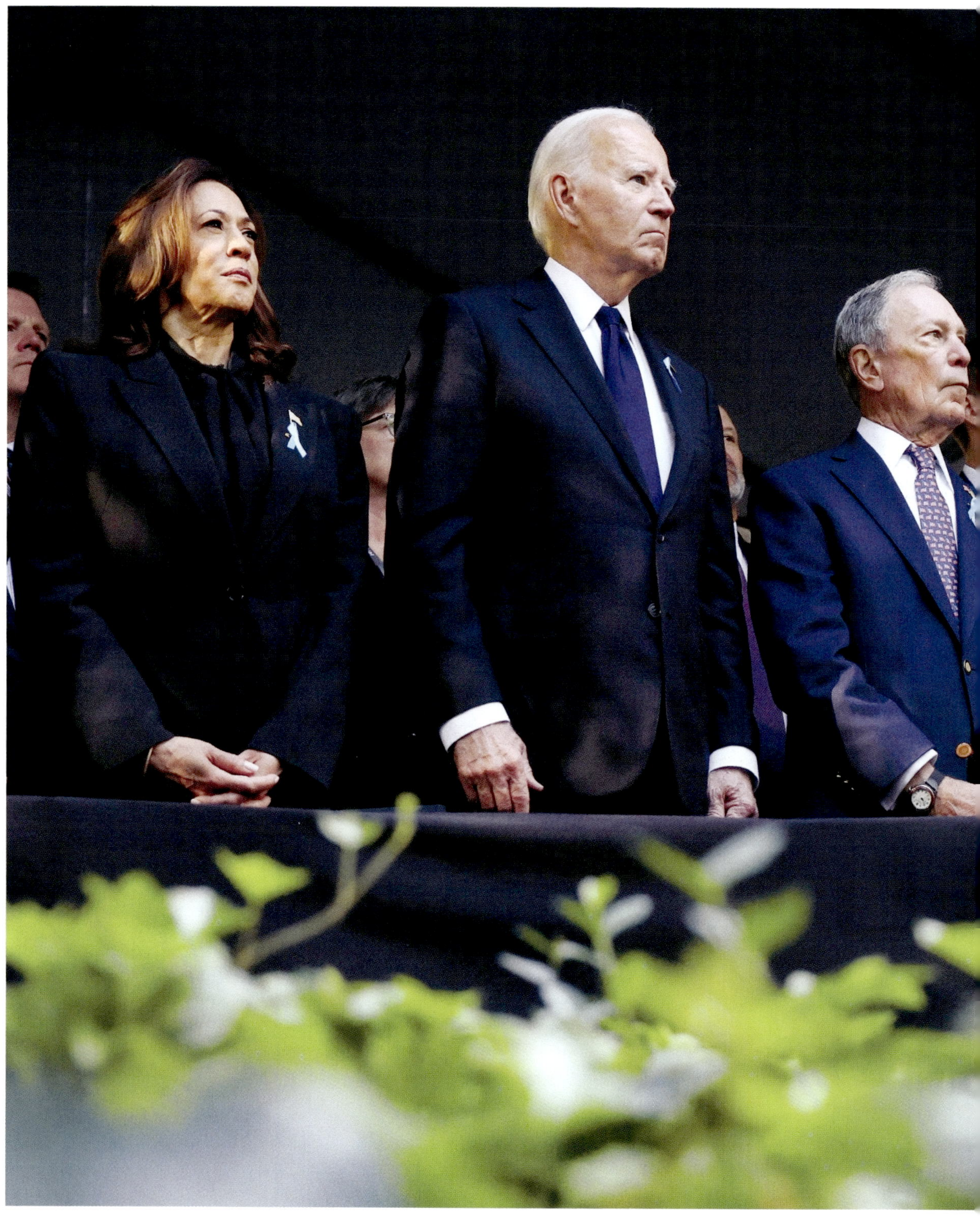

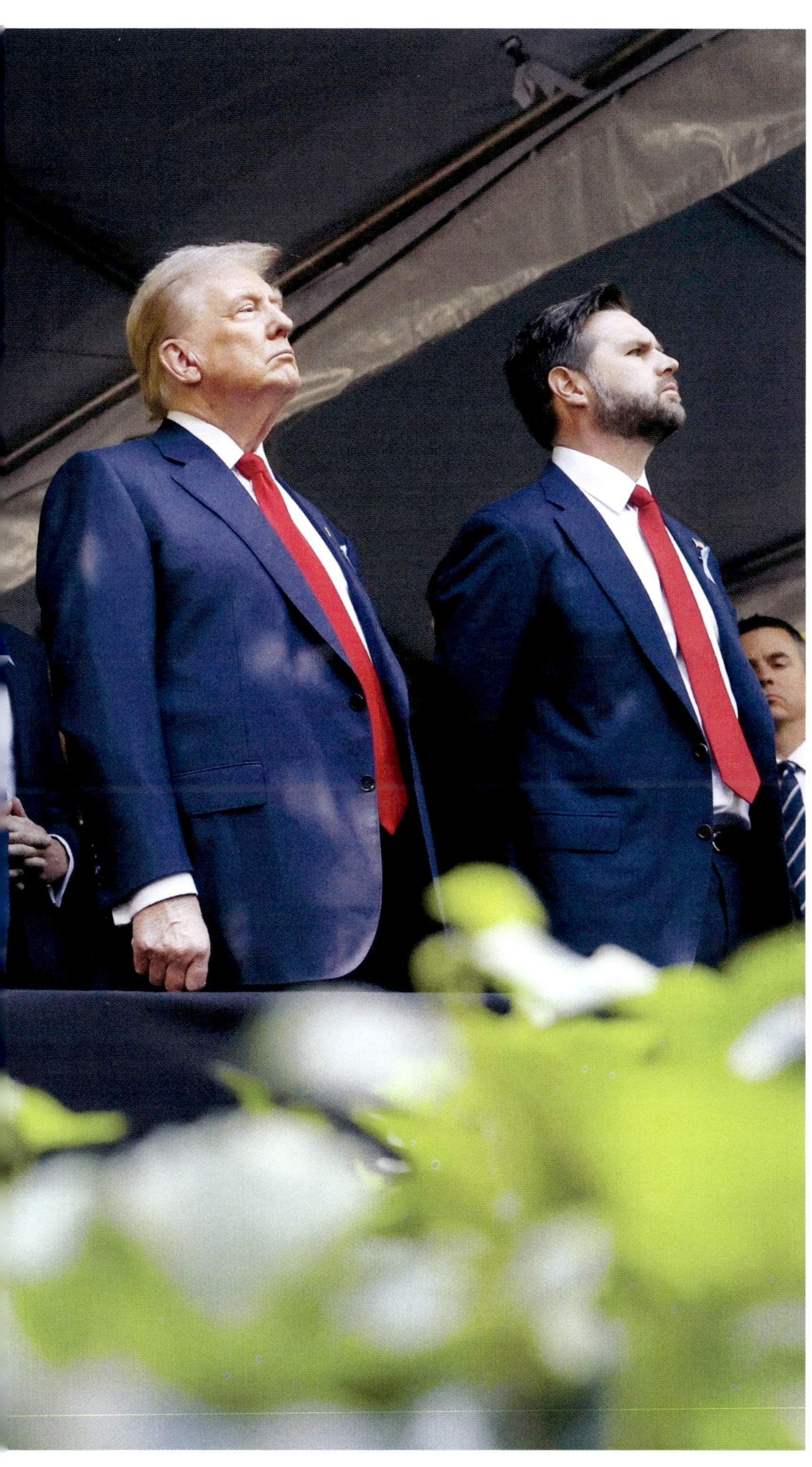

ONE OF the few days of bipartisan comity in America: the anniversary of the 9/11 terrorist attacks on the United States. Here, Democratic presidential nominee Kamala Harris, President Joe Biden, former New York City mayor Michael Bloomberg, former president Donald Trump, and Republican vice-presidential nominee JD Vance attend the annual 9/11 commemoration ceremony at the National September 11 Memorial & Museum in New York City.

BIDEN AND HARRIS in the Rose Garden at the White House. A pivotal moment in 2024, as the president confides in his vice president after making the difficult decision to not seek reelection.

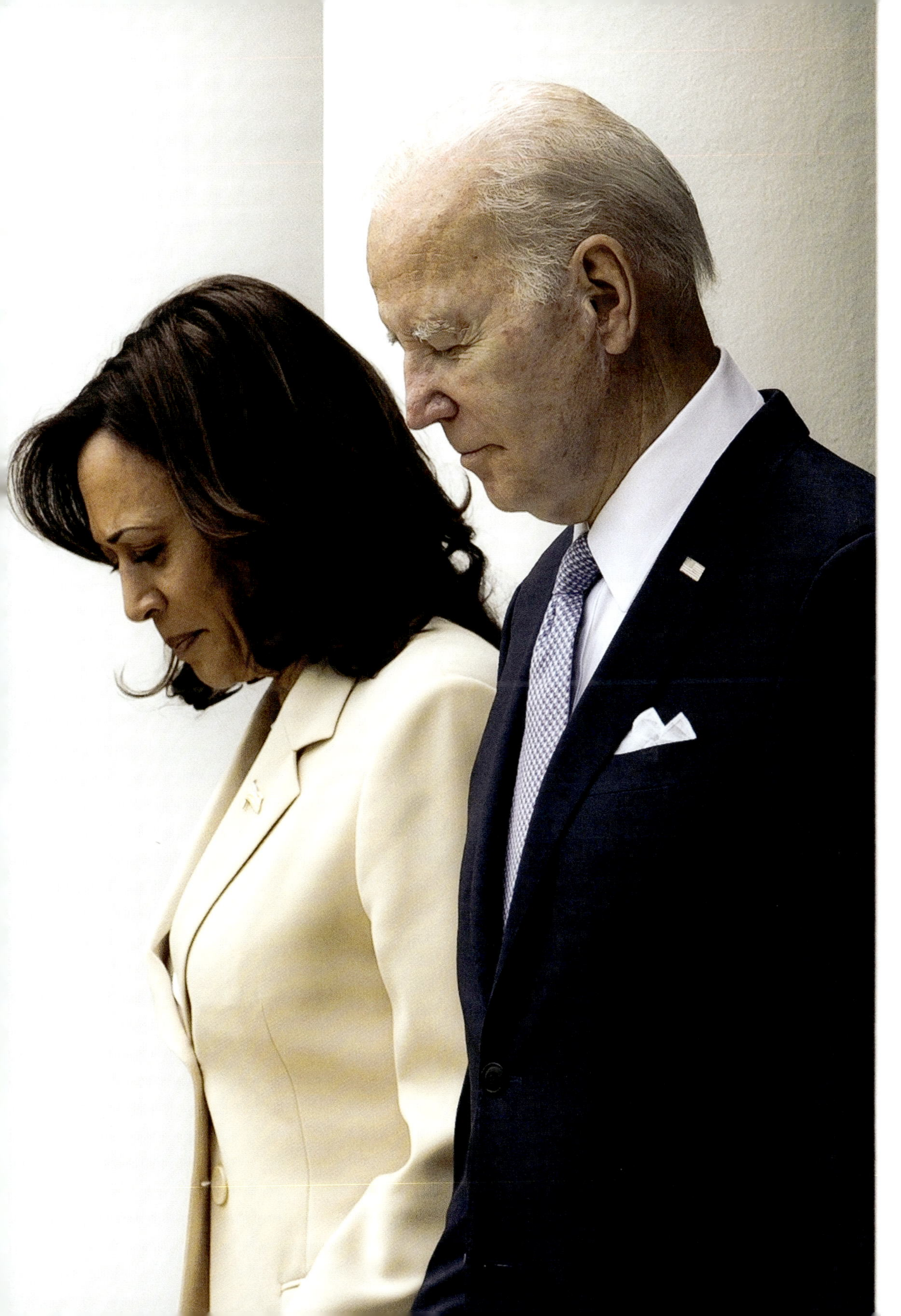

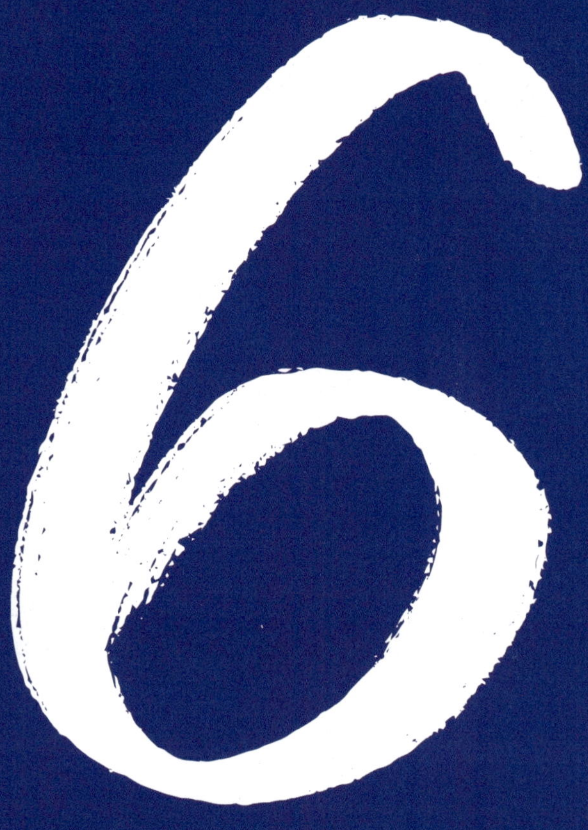

2024

"It's important to remind the former president, you're not running against Joe Biden, you are running against me."

—KAMALA HARRIS

The 2024 campaign season began with Harris in a supporting role and ended with her as the lead, picking a Minnesota-high-school-football-coach-turned-governor as her running mate. The photos here take you through the journey—the sober moment when Biden confides in her after his decision to abandon reelection, and the swagger of Megan Thee Stallion performing in Atlanta on Harris's behalf. The photos show her exuberance at being given a chance to beat Trump, and the confidence of others in her—the Obamas, governors Wes Moore of Maryland and Josh Shapiro of Pennsylvania, the sign-holders ready for a reproductive rights champion who will fight for them. The photos also show a revealing montage of facial expressions from the first Harris-Trump debate, one of the signature events of the campaign.

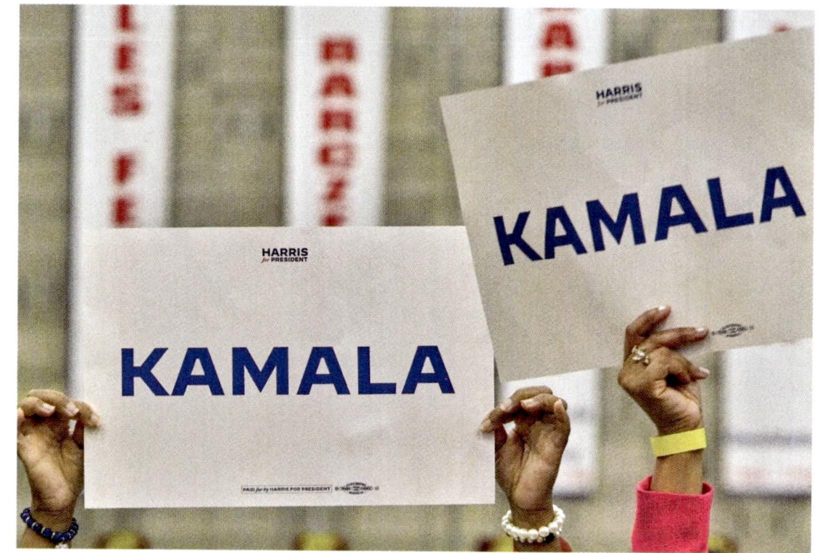

VICE PRESIDENT KAMALA HARRIS, the presumptive Democratic nominee, holds a campaign event in West Allis, Wisconsin, on July 23, 2024. Clean and crisp, the signs say just KAMALA.

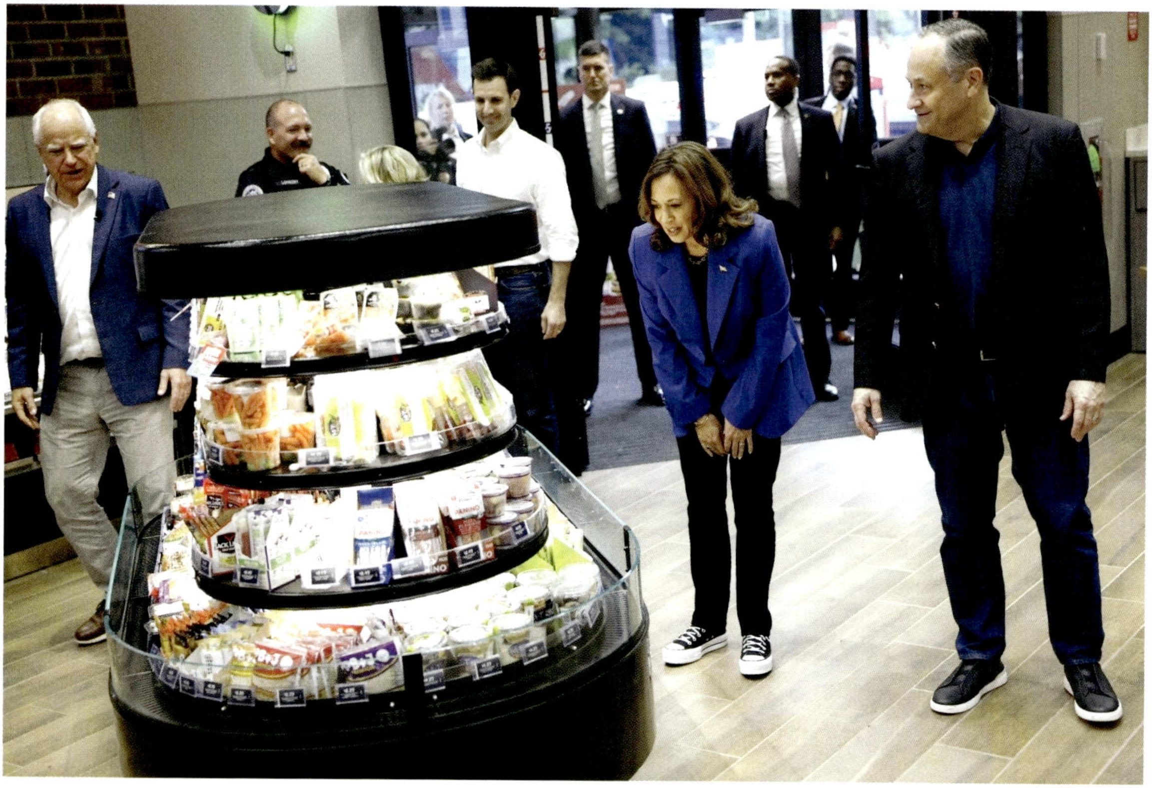

DEMOCRATIC PRESIDENTIAL NOMINEE KAMALA HARRIS and Second Gentleman Doug Emhoff visit a Sheetz gas station on August 18, 2024, in Coraopolis, Pennsylvania. Harris and Emhoff, along with Democratic vice-presidential nominee Tim Walz and his wife, Gwen, were participating in a campaign bus tour throughout cities around western Pennsylvania.

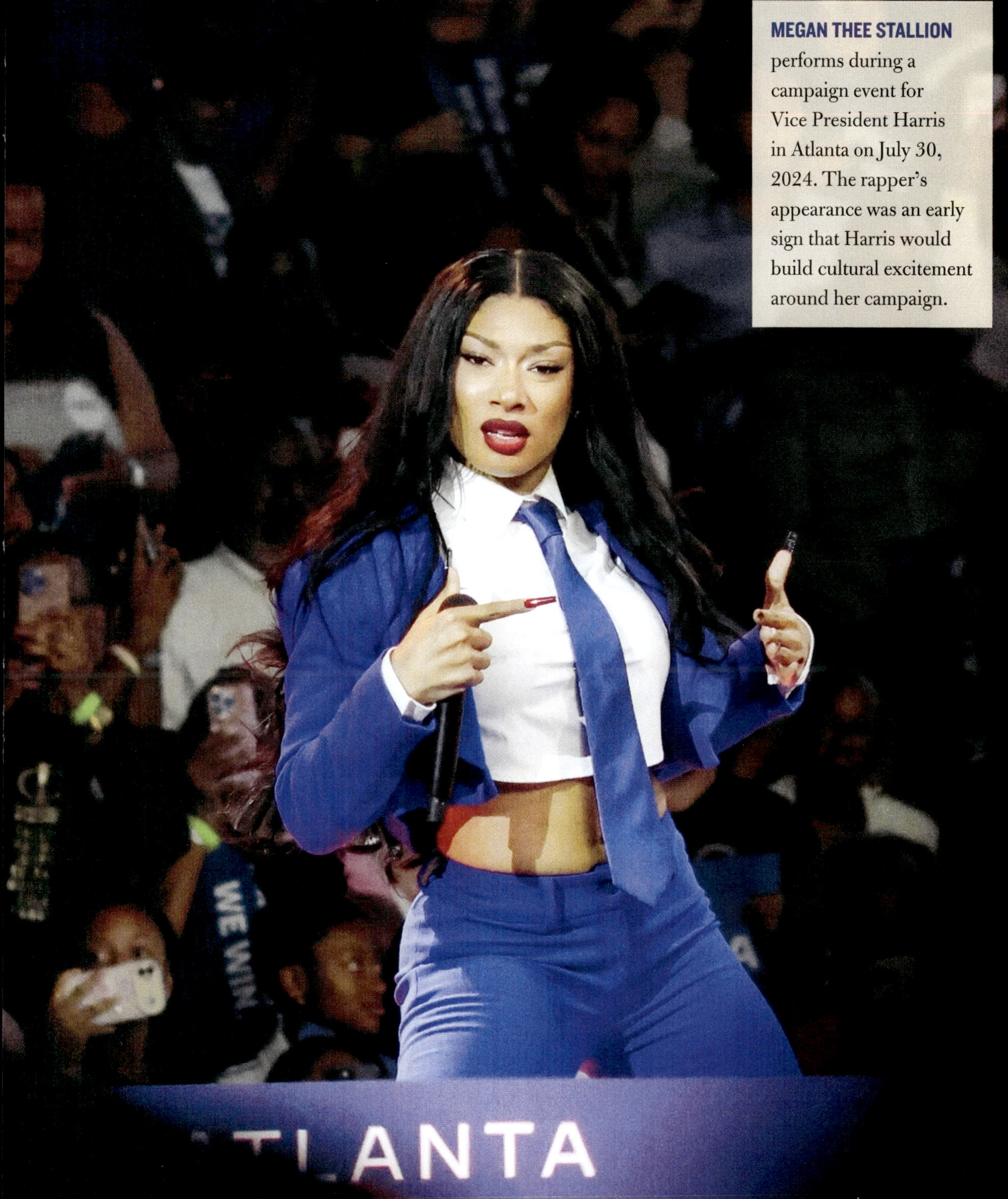

MEGAN THEE STALLION performs during a campaign event for Vice President Harris in Atlanta on July 30, 2024. The rapper's appearance was an early sign that Harris would build cultural excitement around her campaign.

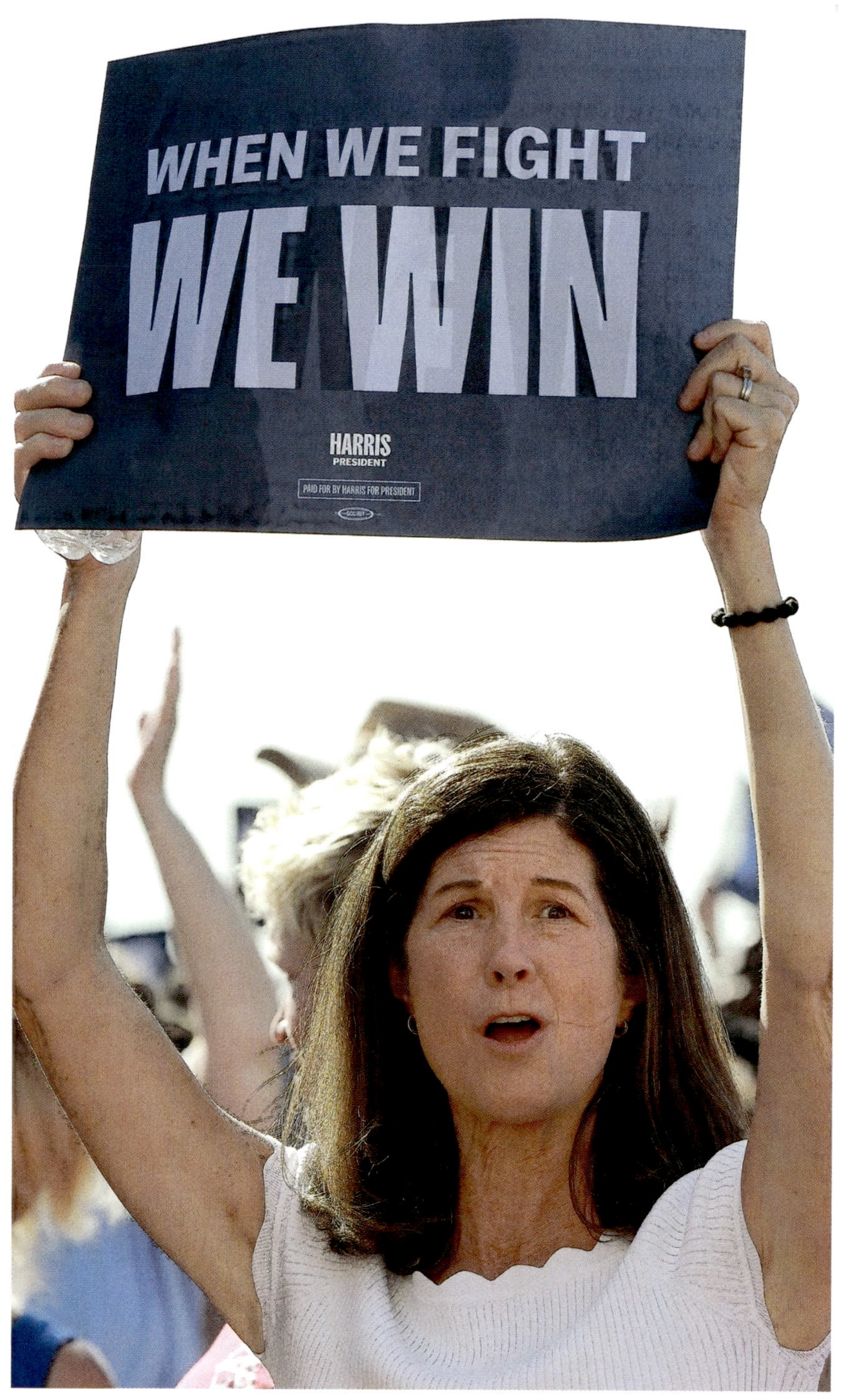

A SUPPORTER holds up a WHEN WE FIGHT WE WIN sign while attending a campaign rally for the Harris-Walz ticket at the Detroit Metropolitan Wayne County Airport in Romulus, Michigan, on August 7, 2024.

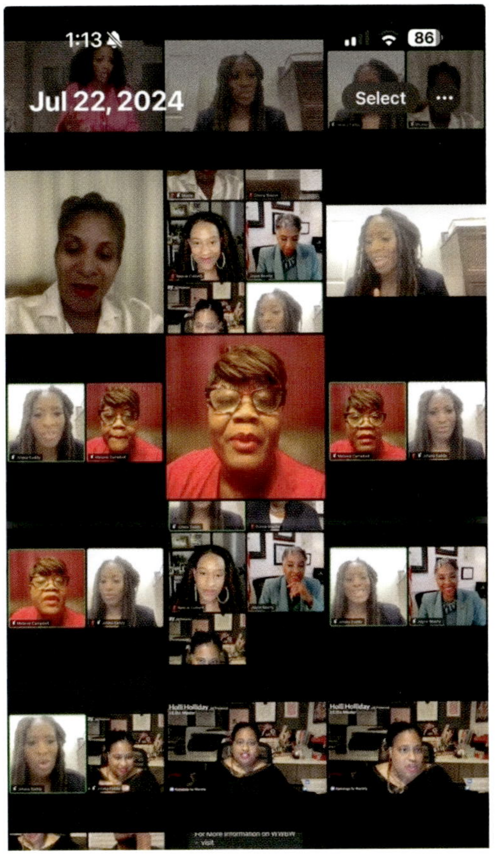

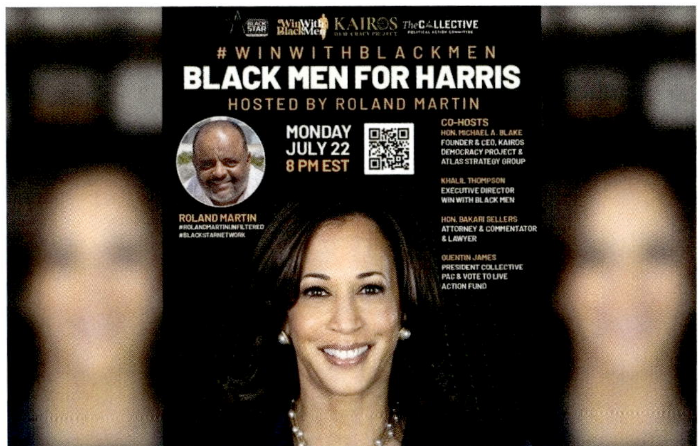

Left to right:

MORE THAN 44,000 Black women, organized by the grassroots group Win With Black Women, joined a Zoom call to mobilize support for Harris early on and raised $1.5 millionon July 21. The effort was replicated by other grassroots coalitions of Black men, white women, white men, and more.

MEDIA ENTREPRENEUR ROLAND MARTIN led a virtual event on StreamYard and YouTube to build support for Harris among Black men, whose loyalty to the Democratic ticket had been questioned. The event drew 54,000 Black men and raised more than $1.3 million.

VICE PRESIDENT HARRIS AND TIM WALZ, Democratic vice-presidential nominee and governor of Minnesota, developed a quick rapport. Here, they share a laugh during a campaign event in Philadelphia on August 6, 2024. Harris tapped Walz as her running mate, enlisting him to build an electoral coalition of coastal progressives and Midwest moderates to block Donald Trump from the White House.

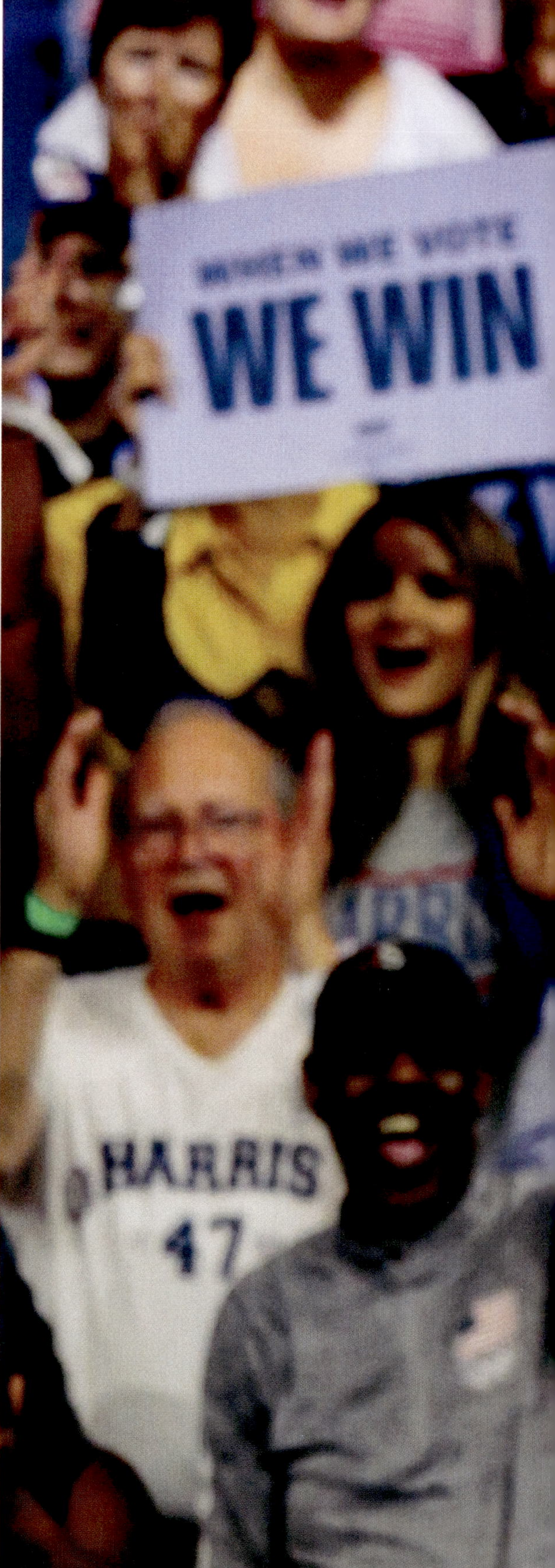

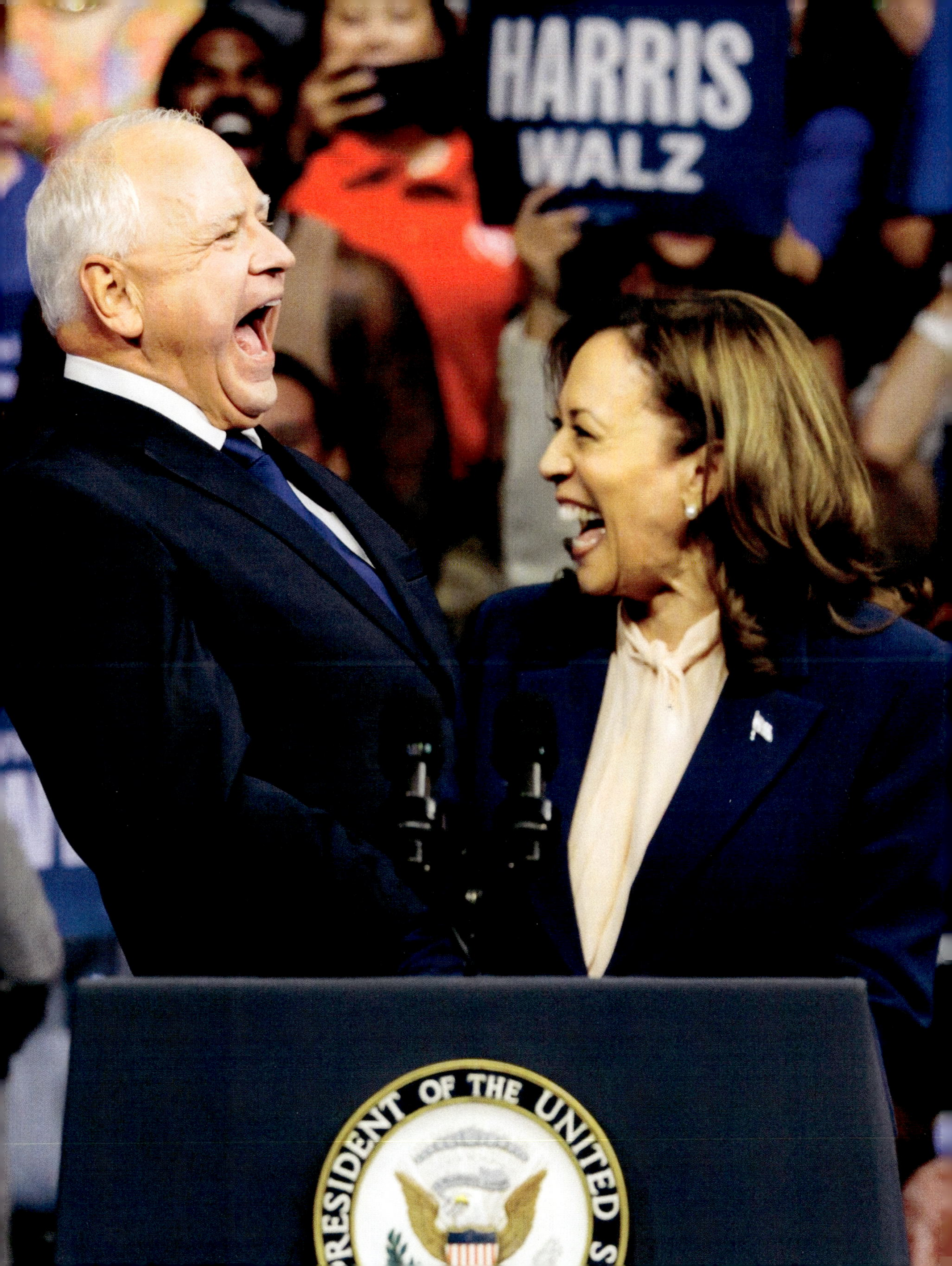
HARRIS
WALZ

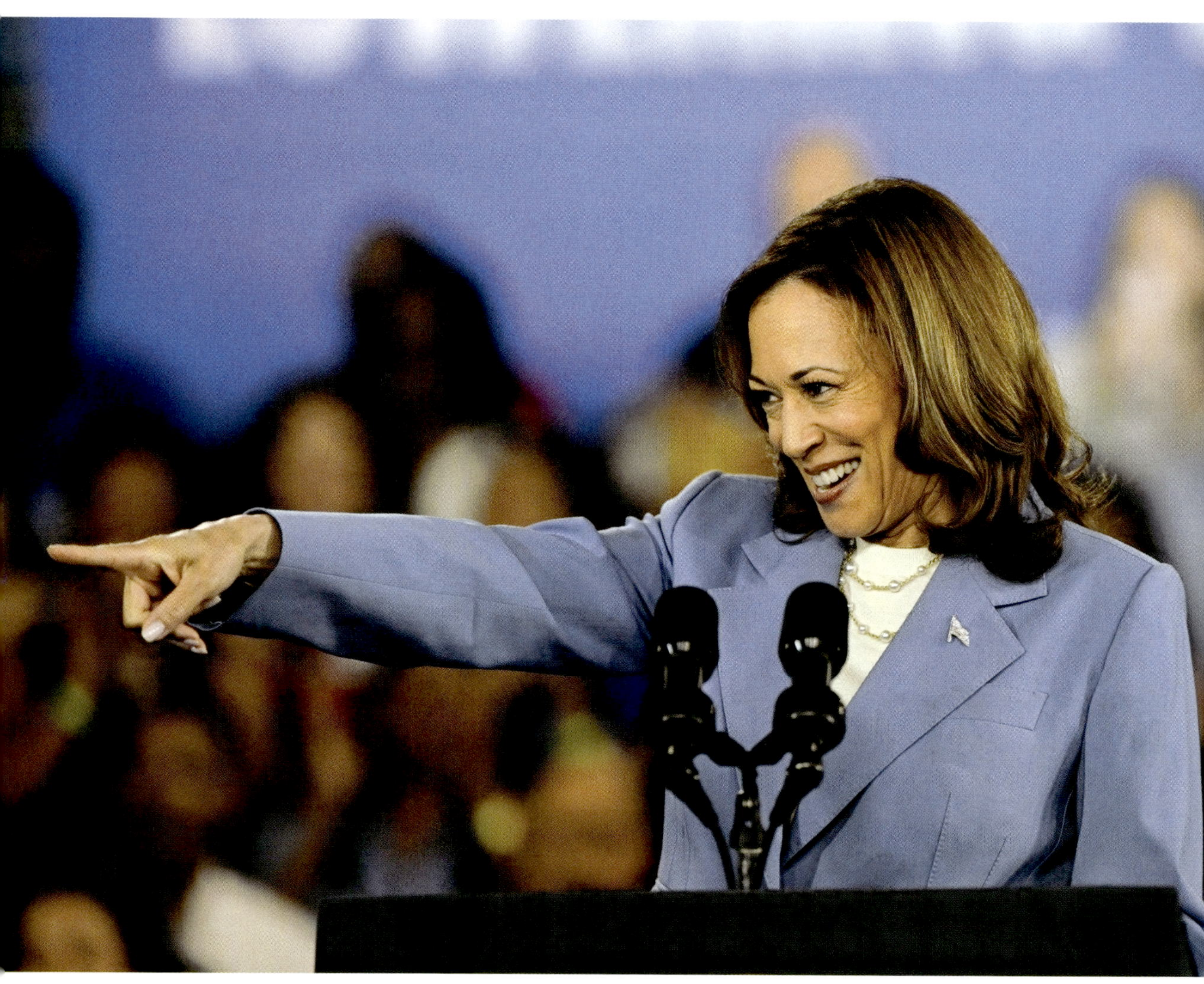

HARRIS IS known to single out people in the crowd—pointing to them, smiling at them—like they're the only ones in the building. Here, she is at the Hendrick Center for Automotive Excellence in Raleigh, North Carolina, on August 16, 2024. This was her first major policy speech since accepting the Democratic Party nomination.

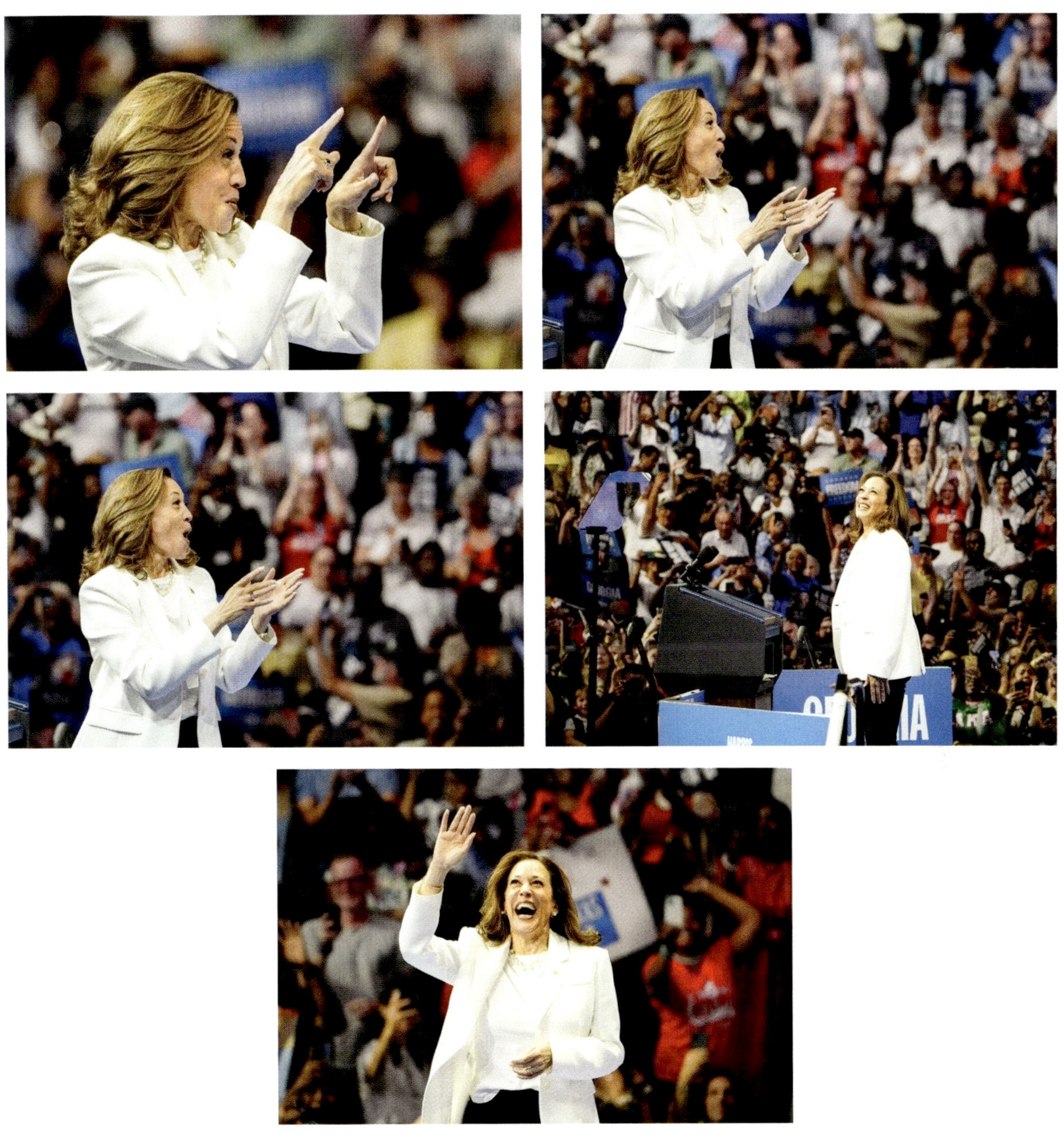

VICE PRESIDENT HARRIS appears onstage during her campaign rally at Enmarket Arena in Savannah, Georgia, on August 29, 2024.

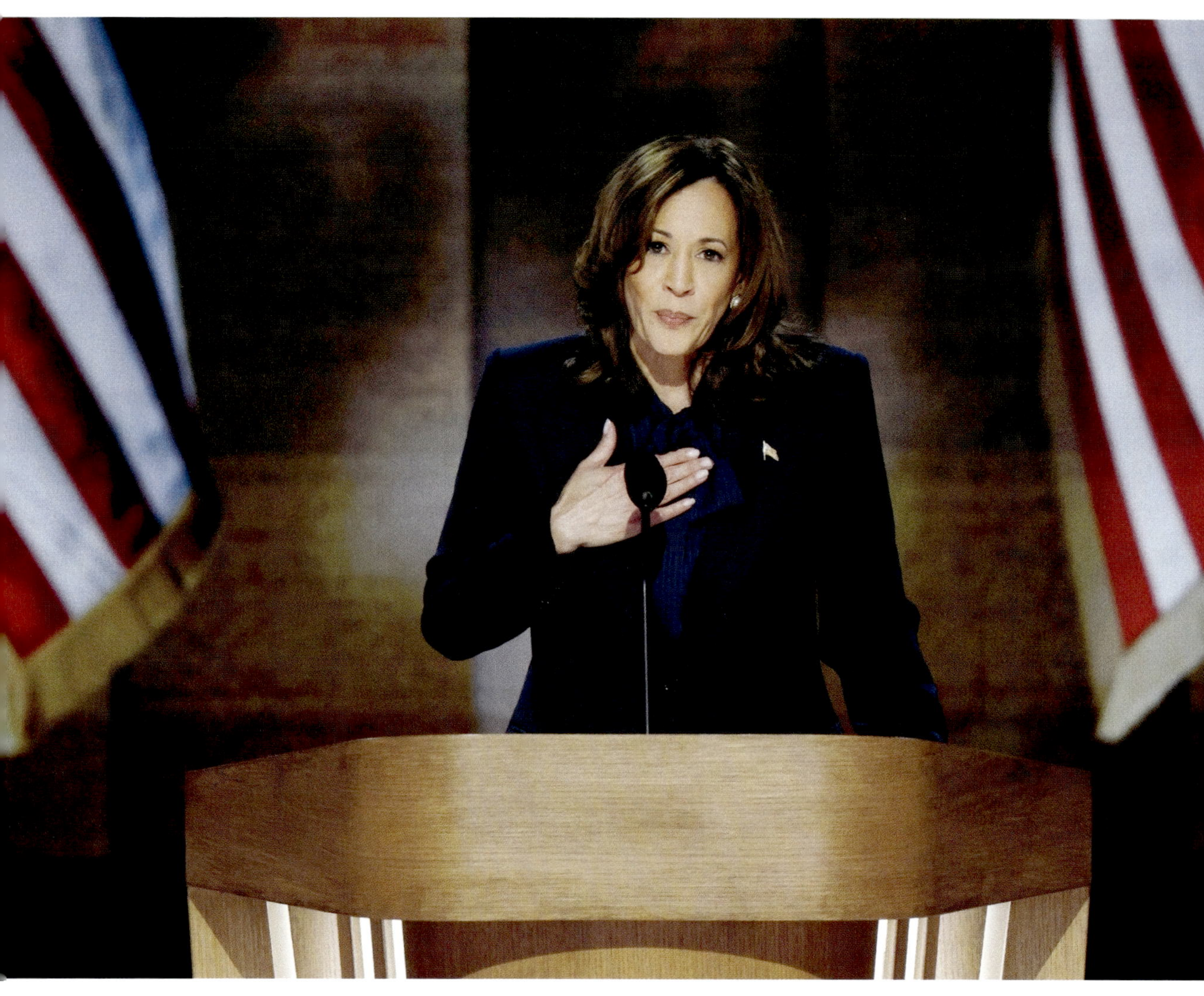

HARRIS DELIVERS her acceptance speech—the most important speech of her political career—on the final night of the Democratic National Convention, at the United Center in Chicago, on August 22, 2024.

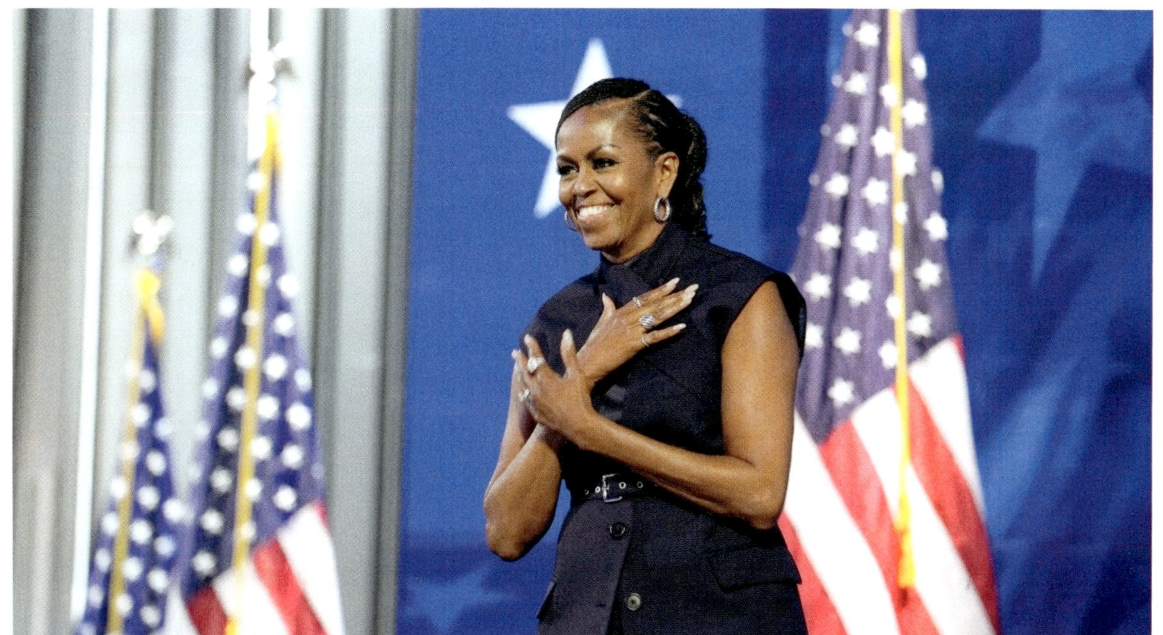

MICHELLE OBAMA gave an inspiring, mic-drop speech that was hard to top during the second day of the Democratic National Convention.

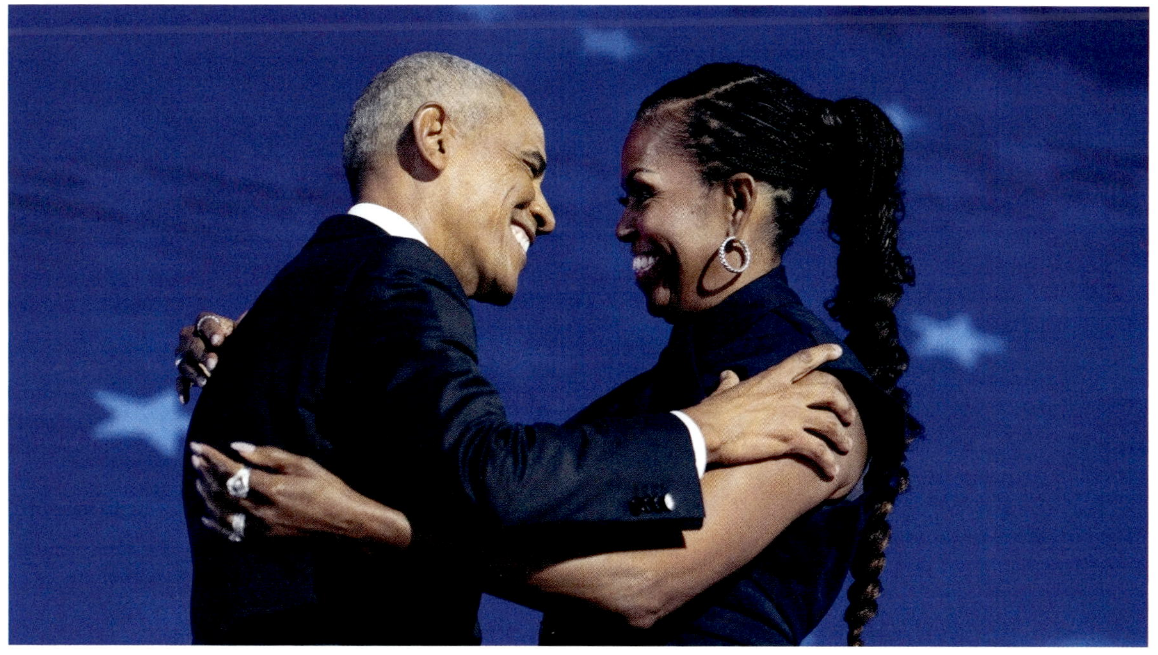

FORMER PRESIDENT BARACK OBAMA hugs his wife as he is introduced during the Democratic National Convention. He later wondered: Who scheduled him to speak after Michelle Obama?

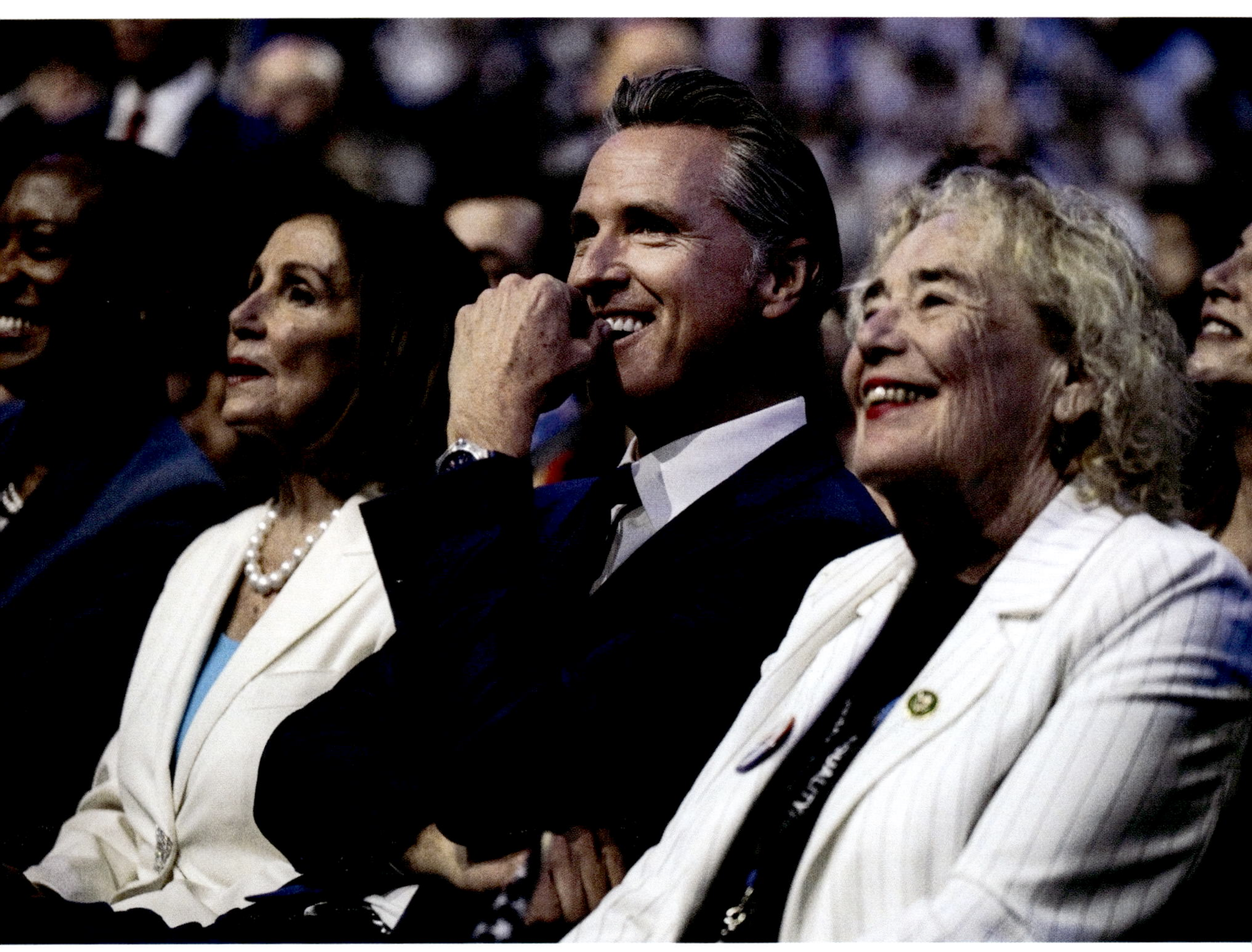

CALIFORNIA GOVERNOR GAVIN NEWSOM, a longtime friend and political ally of Harris's, was enjoying himself at the Democratic National Convention. But he had a tricky, uncertain role to play as a surrogate for Harris going forward, well aware that Californians like him were not popular in some crucial areas of the country. "I just want to be helpful and not hurtful," he told the *Los Angeles Times*.

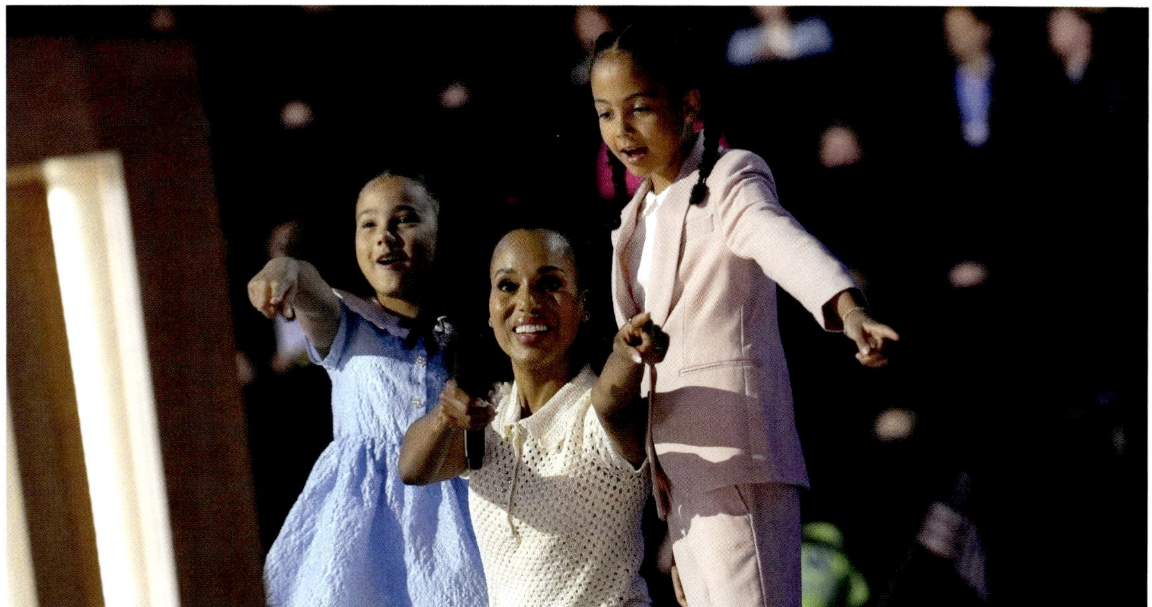

ACTOR KERRY WASHINGTON speaks onstage with the grandnieces of Kamala Harris, Amara Ajagu (*right*) and Leila Ajagu (*left*), during the final day of the Democratic National Convention.

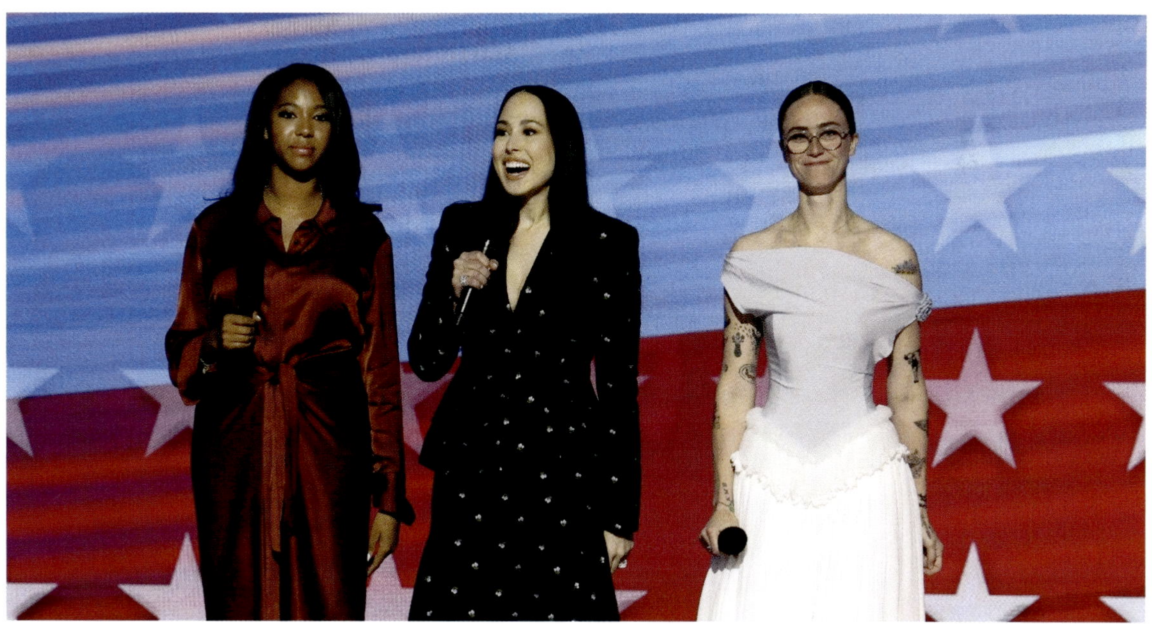

Left to right: Helena Hudlin, goddaughter of Vice President Kamala Harris; Meena Harris, Kamala's niece; and Ella Emhoff, daughter of Second Gentleman Doug Emhoff, who calls Harris "Momala," speak onstage during the final day of the Democratic National Convention.

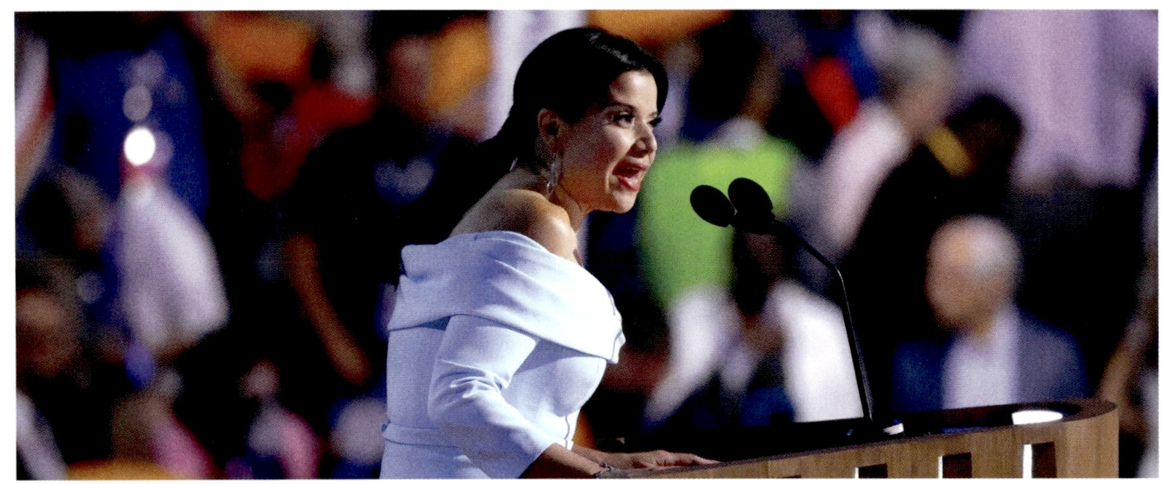

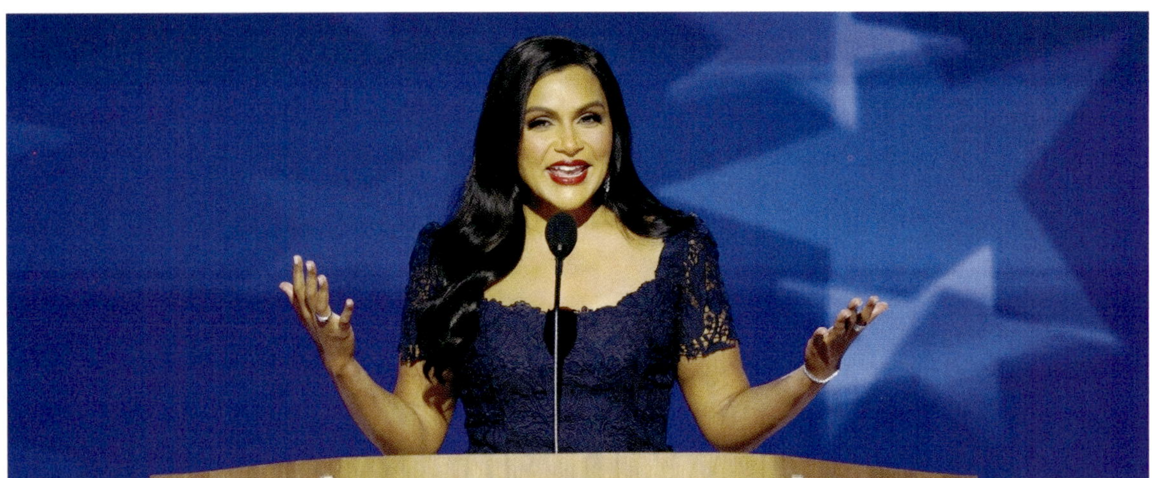

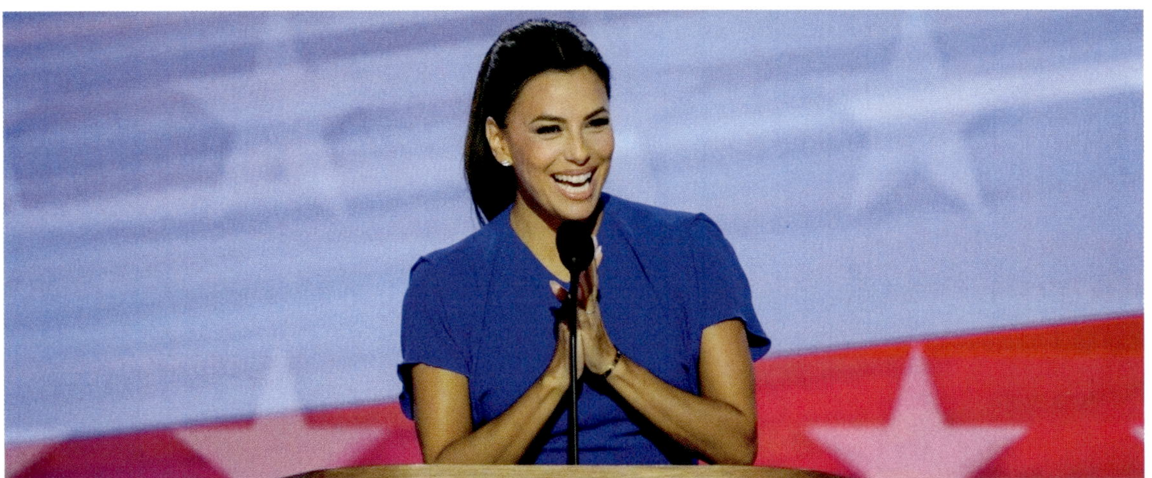

Top to bottom: Ana Navarro, Mindy Kaling, and Eva Longoria give impassioned speeches at the DNC.

THE DEMOCRATIC NATIONAL CONVENTION always features a concert lineup of big-name performances. This year's featured Stevie Wonder, Patti LaBelle, Pink, John Legend and Sheila E., Common and Jonathan McReynolds, and many more. Rapper Lil Jon even took the microphone to help the Georgia delegation with its roll call vote. Support from the entertainment industry was seen as a Harris advantage.

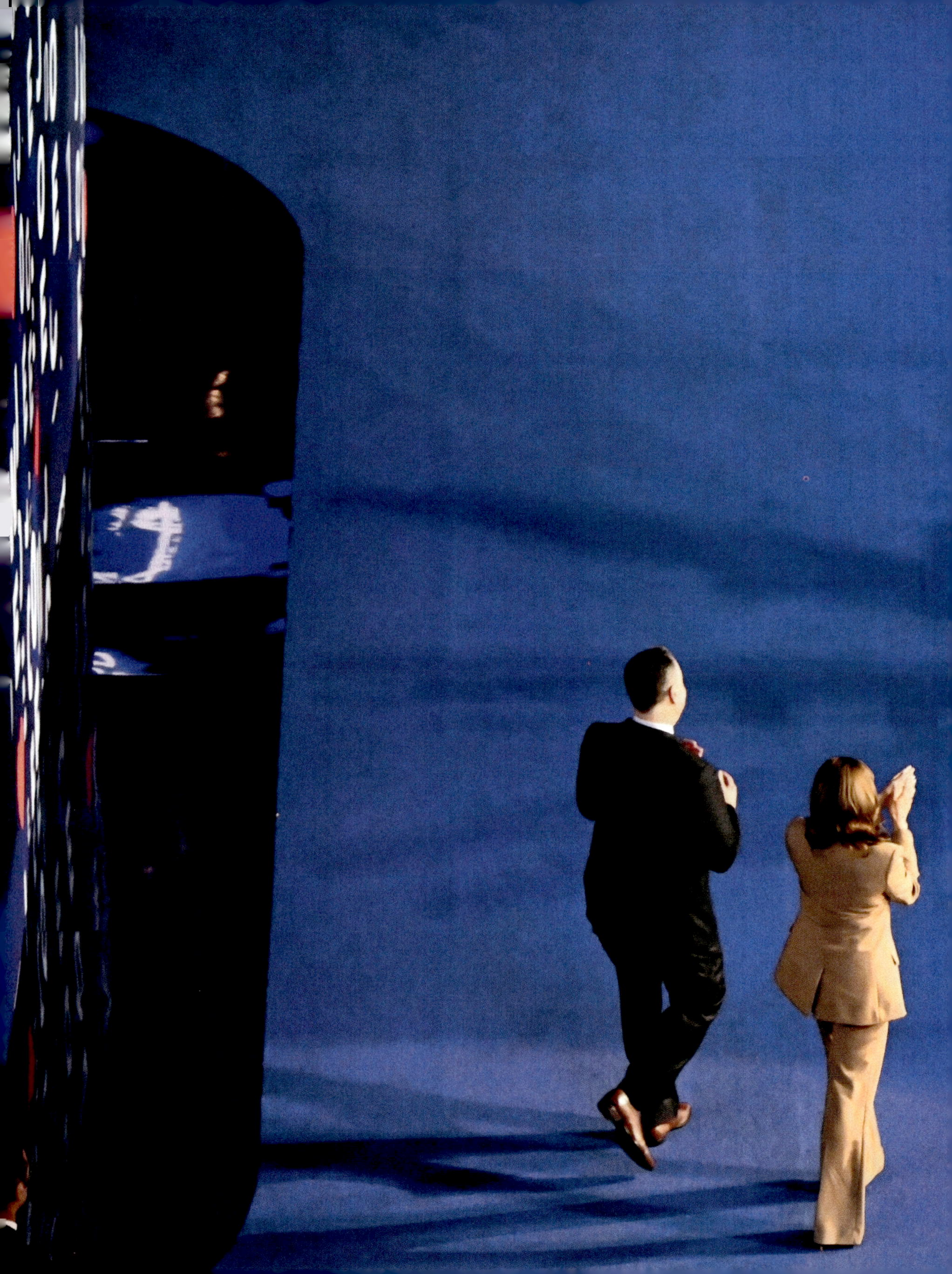

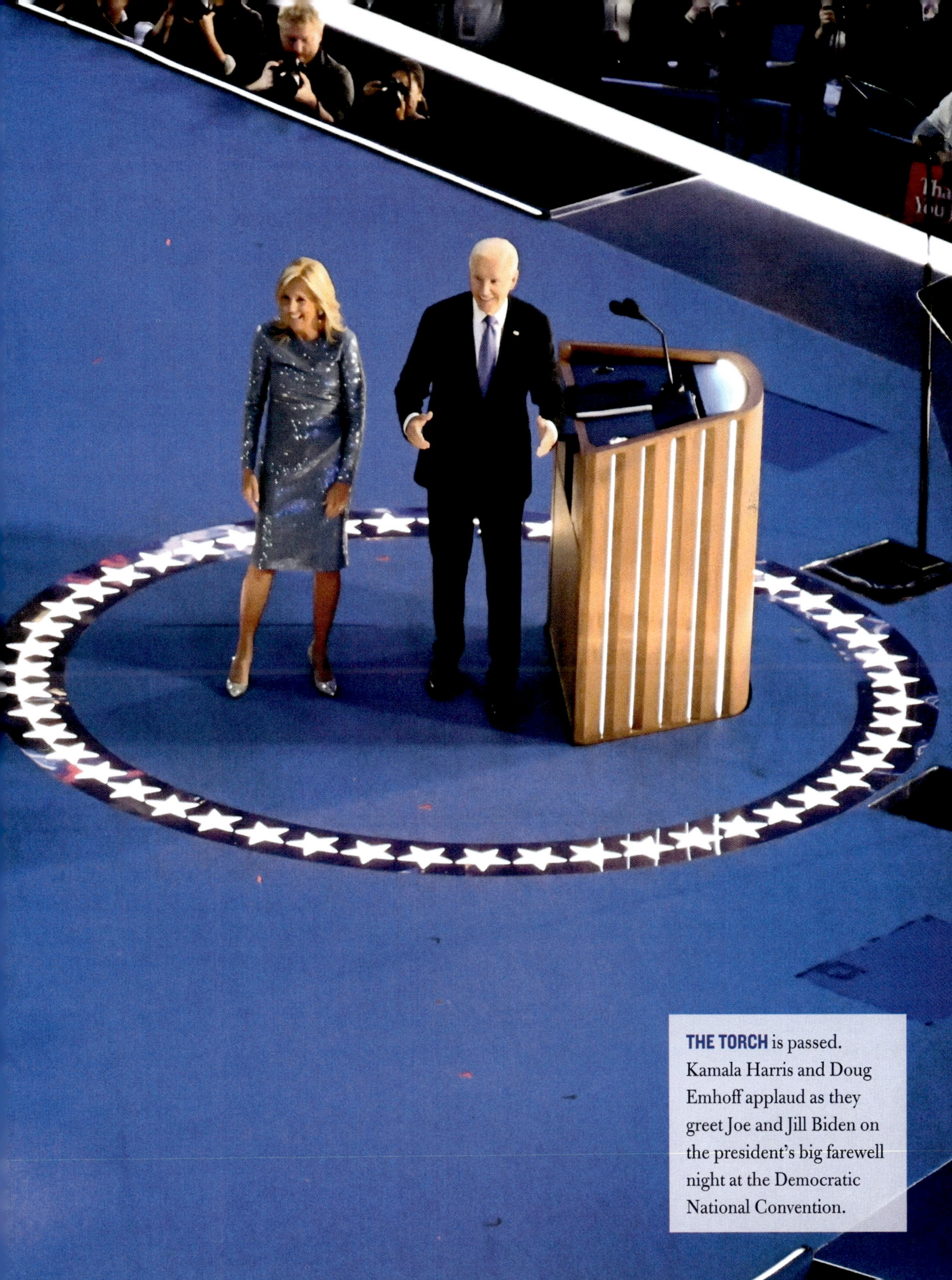

THE TORCH is passed. Kamala Harris and Doug Emhoff applaud as they greet Joe and Jill Biden on the president's big farewell night at the Democratic National Convention.

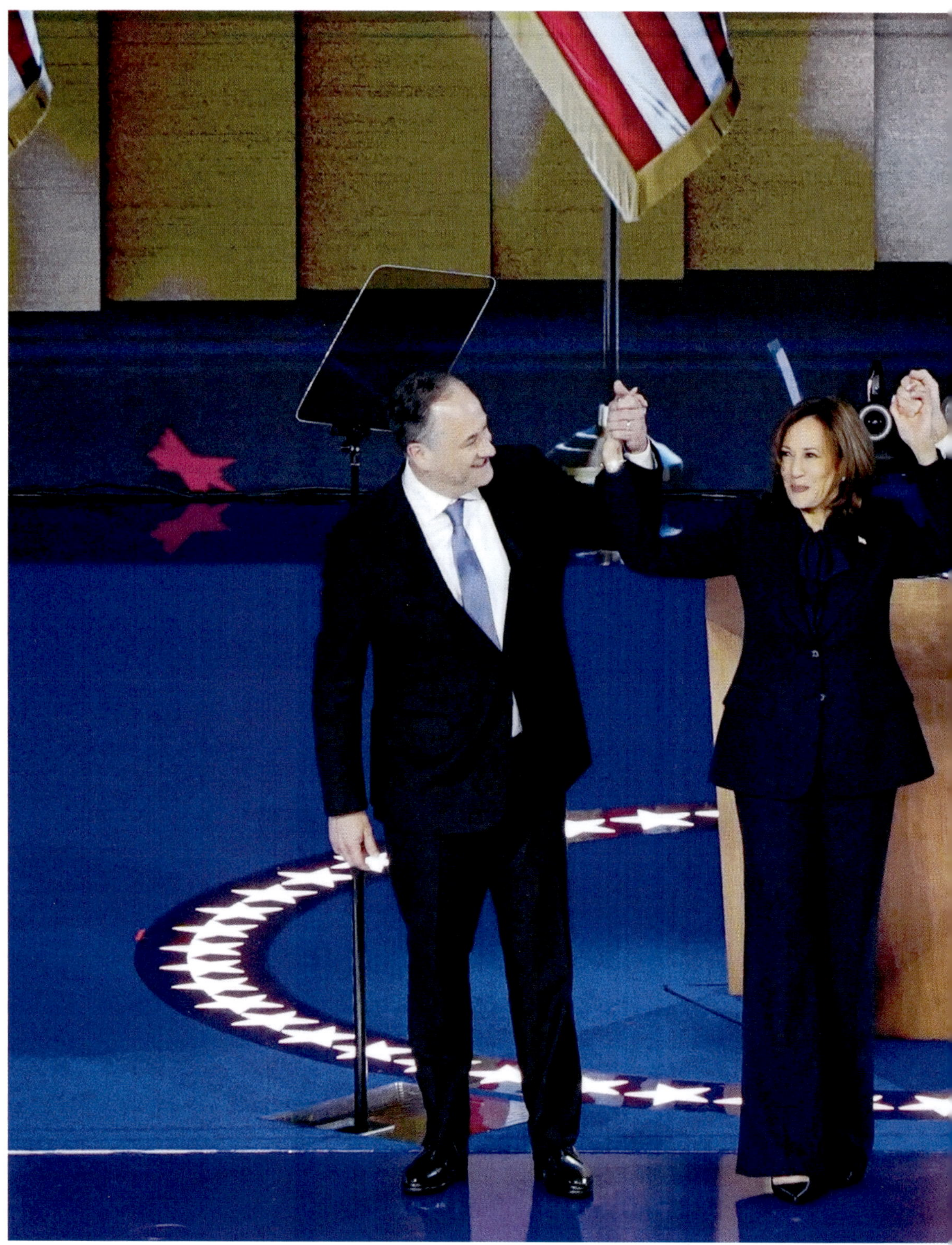

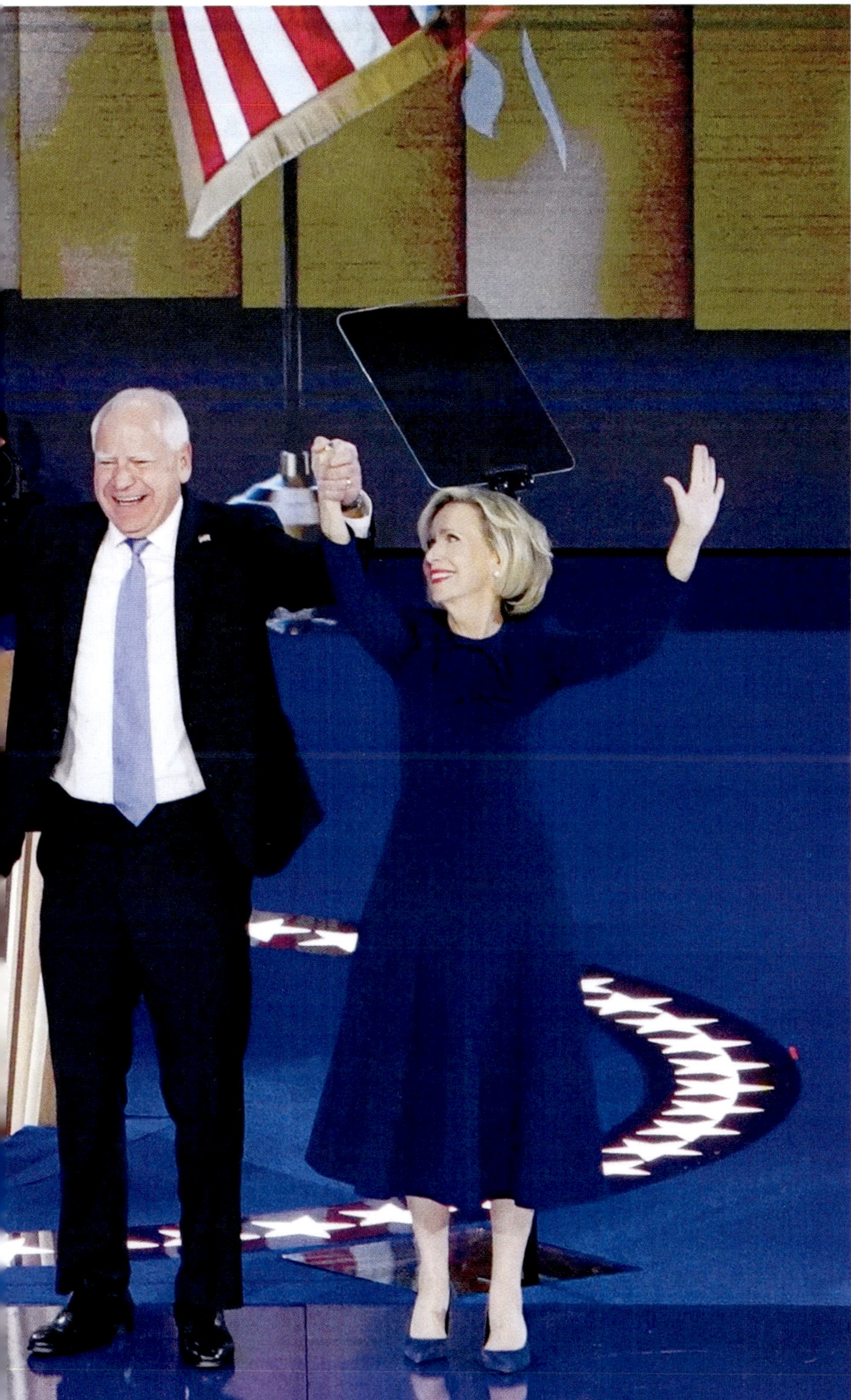

THE TICKET is made. Doug Emhoff, Kamala Harris, Tim Walz, and Gwen Walz onstage on the final night of the Democratic National Convention.

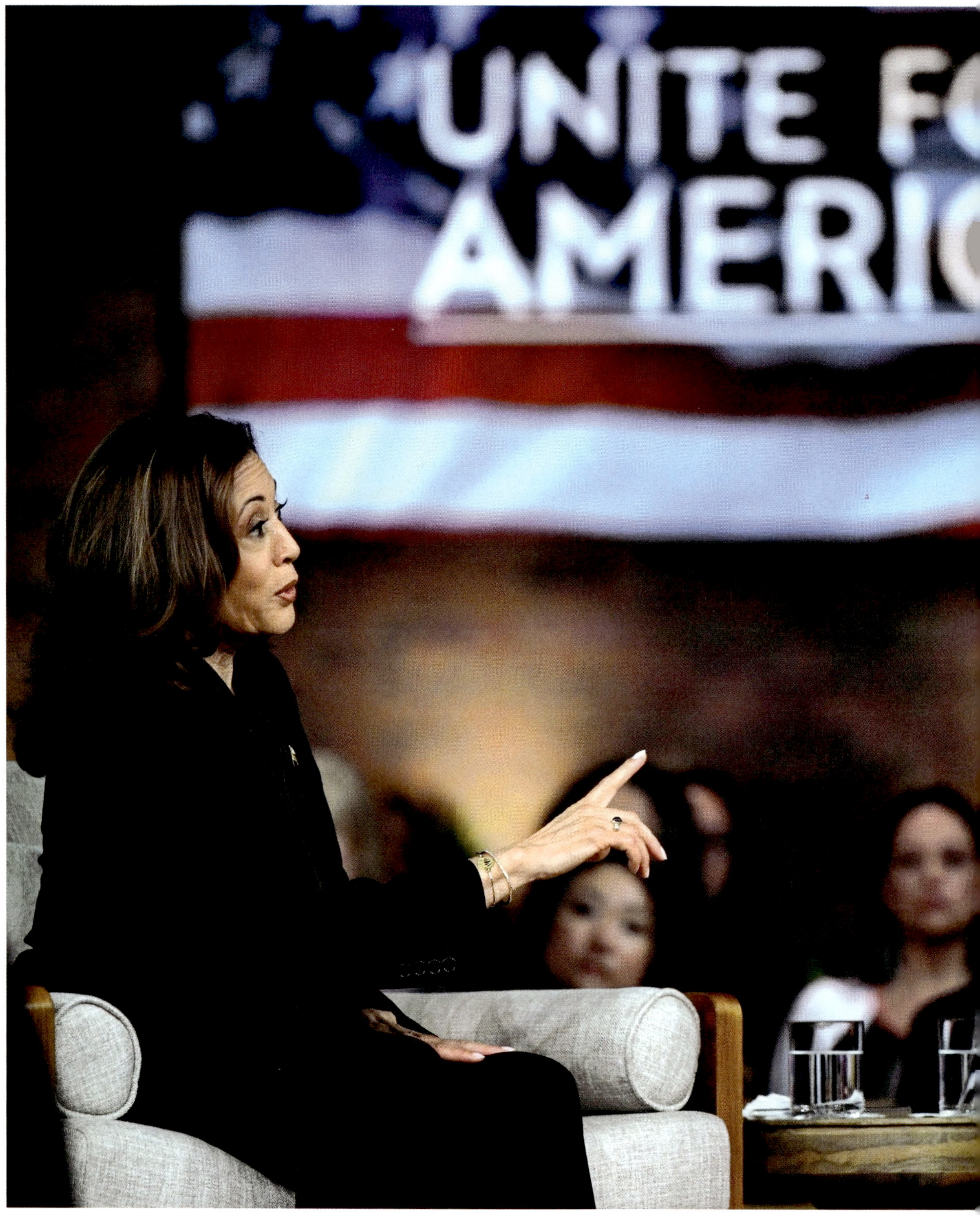
UNITE FO
AMERIC

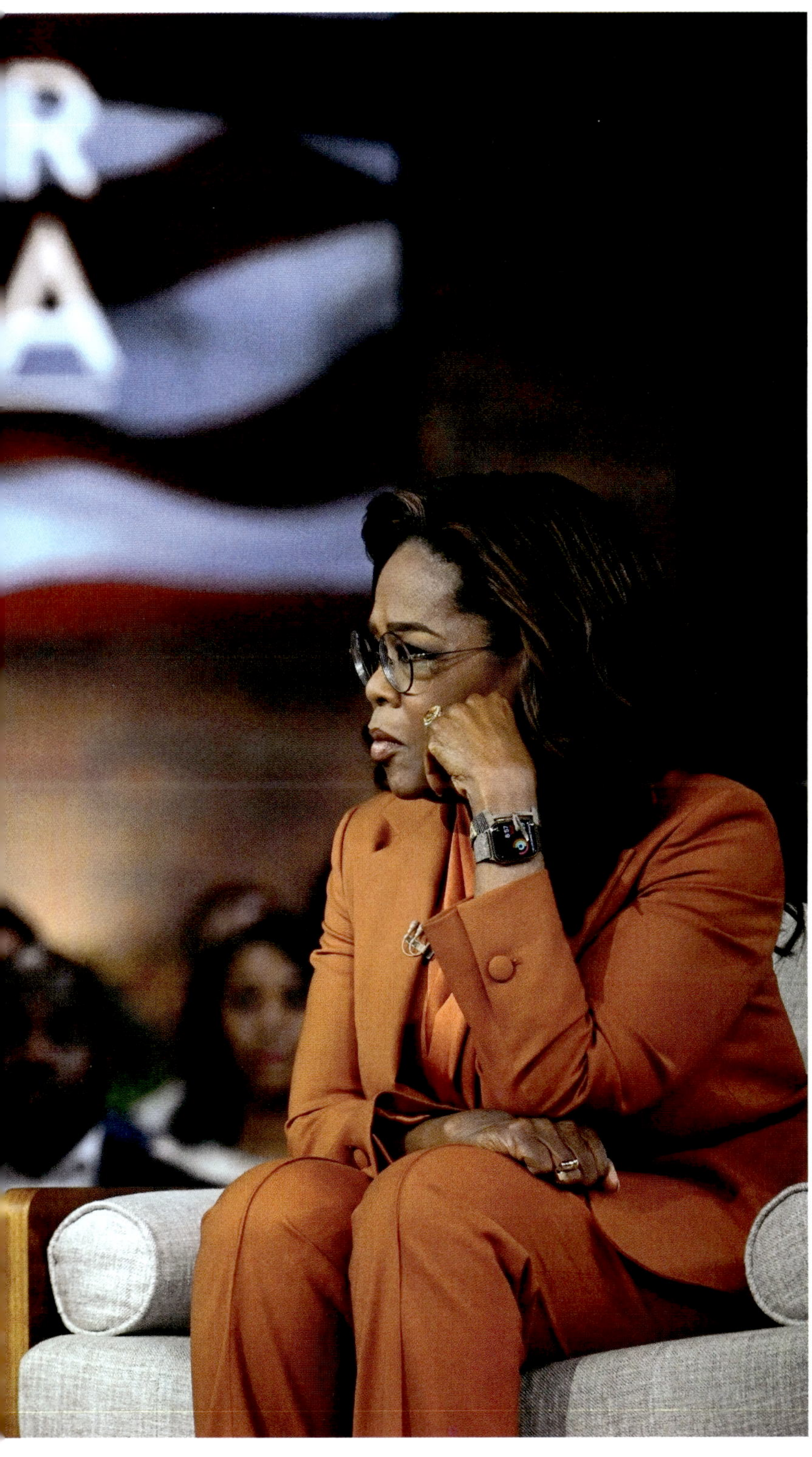

DEMOCRATIC PRESIDENTIAL NOMINEE KAMALA HARRIS attends a town hall–style forum, "Unite for America," hosted by Oprah Winfrey in Michigan on September 19, 2024. The event streamed to hundreds of thousands and featured celebrities from Chris Rock to Meryl Streep. Harris received questions on most of the campaign cycle's top issues, including guns and immigration. But the most emotional moment came when a mother told the story of her daughter dying after a delay in hospital treatment related to Georgia's restrictive abortion laws, a testimony that moved many in the audience to tears. "I'm just so sad," said Harris, "and the courage you all have shown is extraordinary." Oprah emerged in the campaign as one of Harris's biggest supporters.

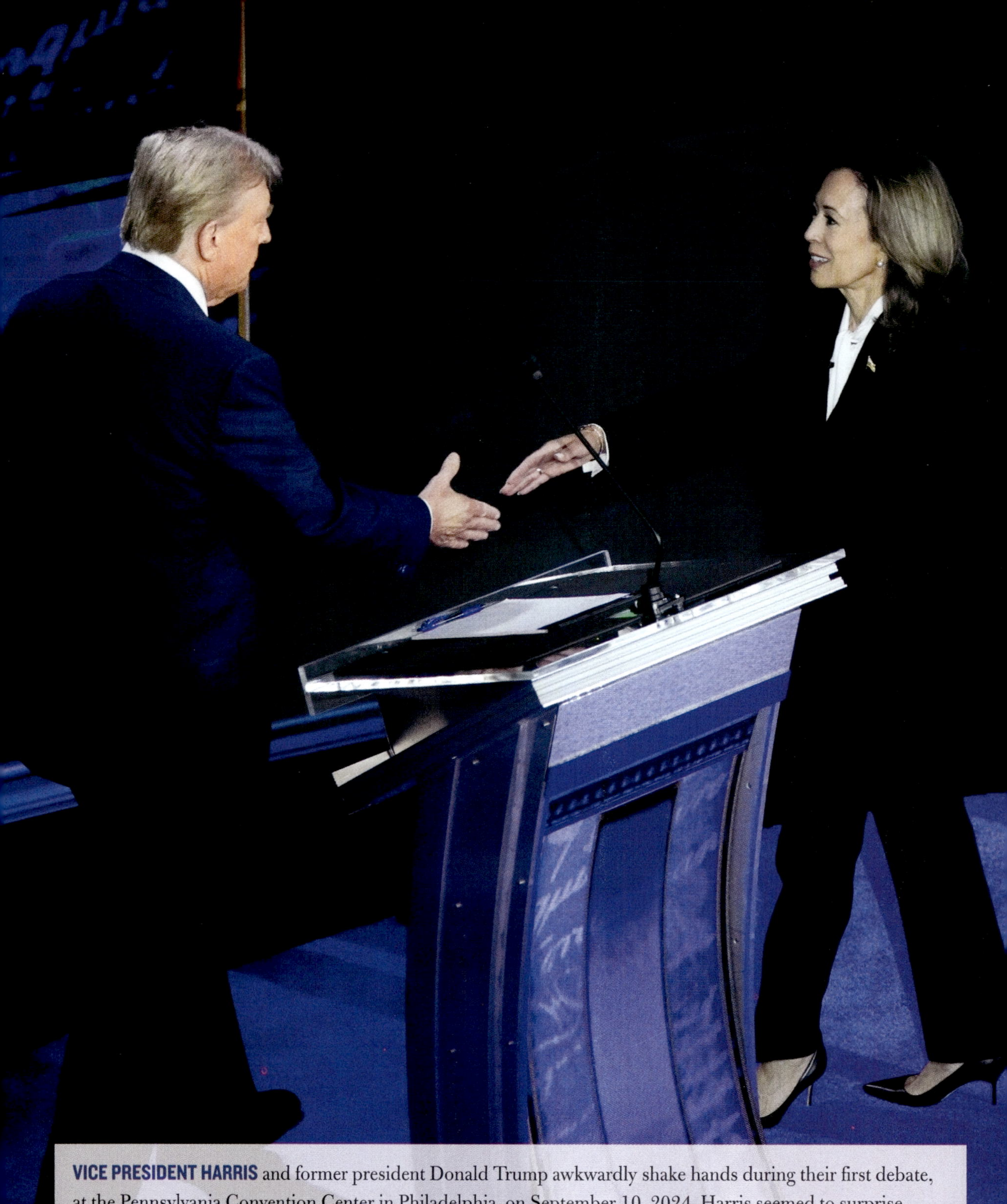

VICE PRESIDENT HARRIS and former president Donald Trump awkwardly shake hands during their first debate, at the Pennsylvania Convention Center in Philadelphia, on September 10, 2024. Harris seemed to surprise Trump by initiating the handshake, and she kept him off-balance throughout the debate, which most analysts said she won decisively.

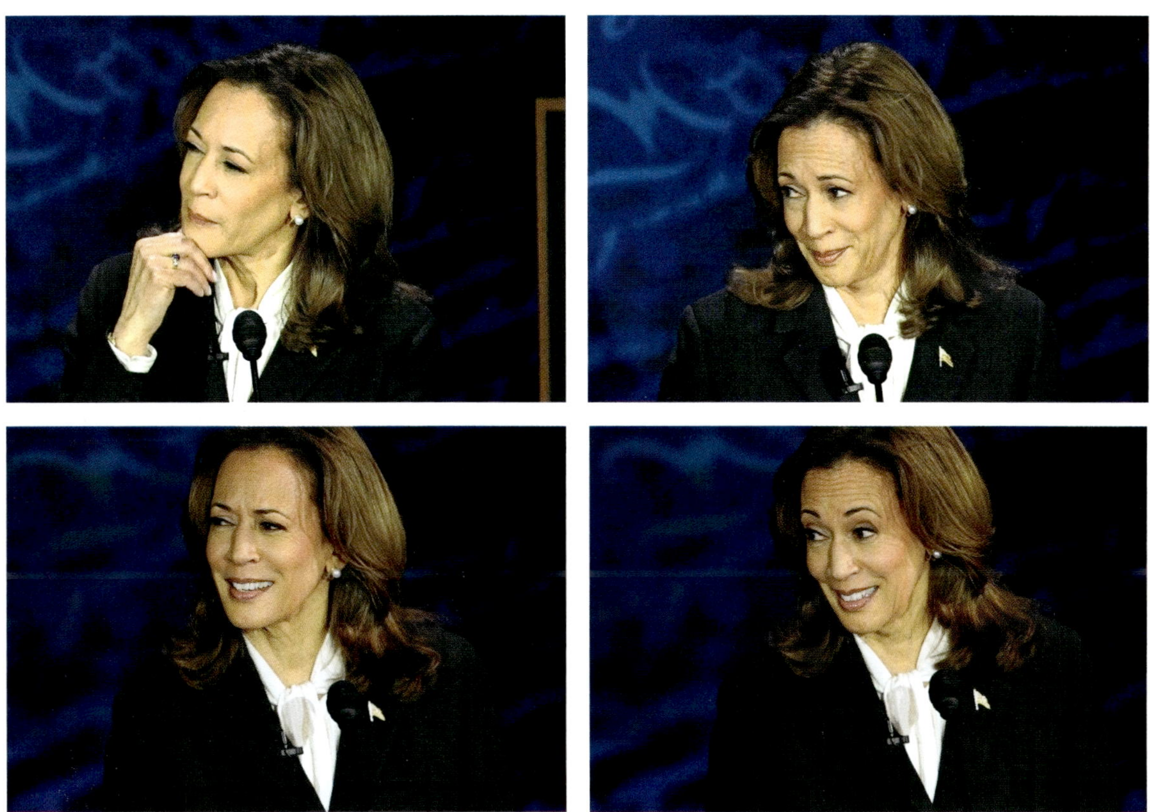

THE CHIN STROKE, the furrow, the syrup-scented "Bless his heart," the side-eye.

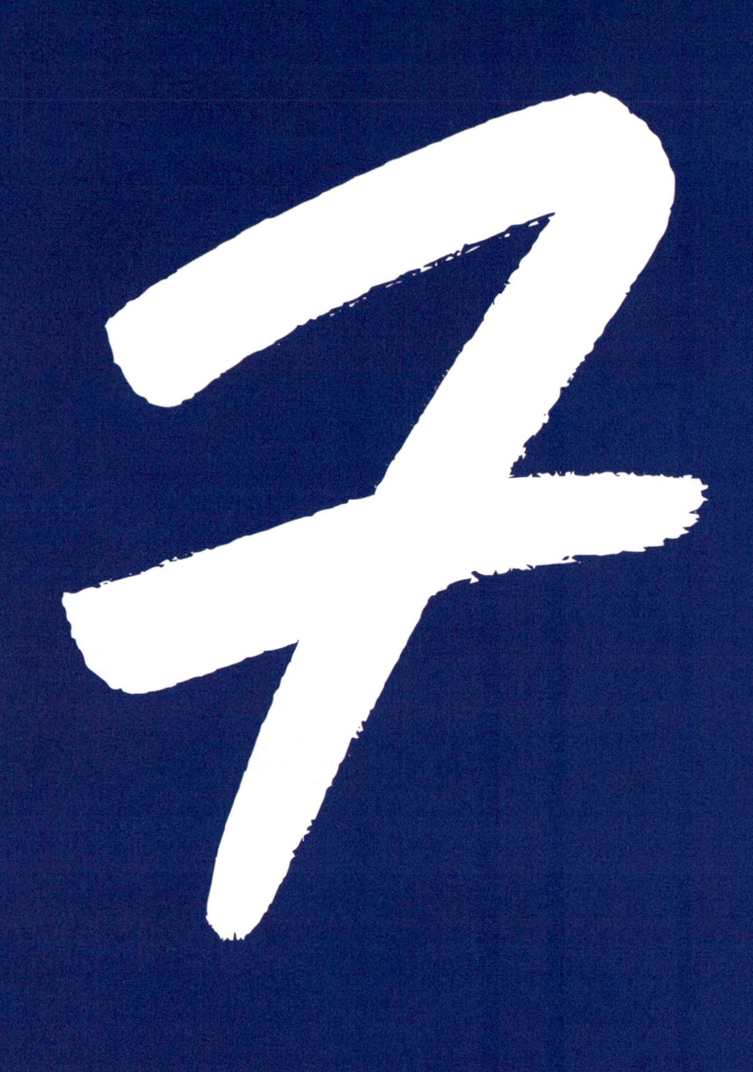

COVER STORIES

"Kamala Harris is on the cover of Vogue *again. The picture is beautiful, yes, but more importantly, it is a crisp, clear presentation of a candidate who has until recently, according to detractors and ambivalent voters, resisted being known. In her uniform of big-shouldered pantsuit and wrap-neck blouse, she looks formal, but also, finally, familiar."*

—RACHEL TASHJIAN, *THE WASHINGTON POST*

In an age of Instagram and visual expression everywhere on digital platforms, there is one prize that even the biggest names in politics, sports, and entertainment can't resist: the magazine cover. But negotiations over cover images can be fraught and drawn out, and not always end well.

Such was the case with the February 2021 print *Vogue* cover that featured Harris in a full body shot, looking casual, hands clasped in front, wearing a Donald Deal blazer with white tee, black pants, and black Converse sneakers. It was widely debated online as to whether the image was befitting this historic vice president. Was it respectful enough? There were reports that the Harris team also was not happy with the image. The criticism was surprising to some. The cover was shot by Tyler Mitchell, who made fashion history in 2018 as the first Black photographer to shoot a *Vogue* cover, and both the writer of the cover story and the editor overseeing the shoot were Black as well. Weighing in on the 2024 election, *Vogue* published a digital cover featuring the vice president wearing a more traditional look with the cover line "The Candidate For Our Times." Now almost everyone was happy.

The photos in this section show a creative range of Harris depictions—from covers of *Time* to a portrait from *Rolling Stone.*

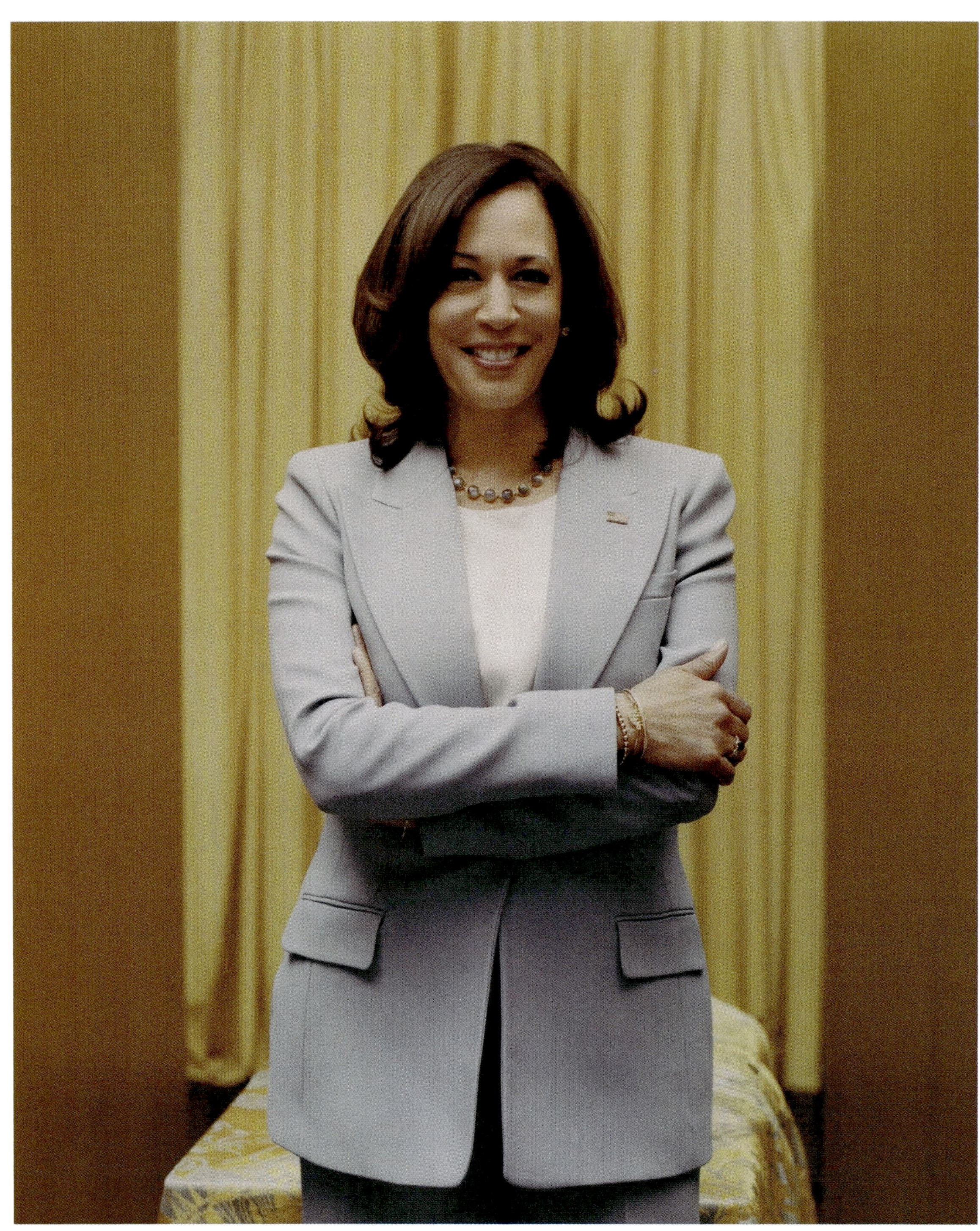

VICE PRESIDENT KAMALA HARRIS on the digital cover of the February 2021 issue of *Vogue*.

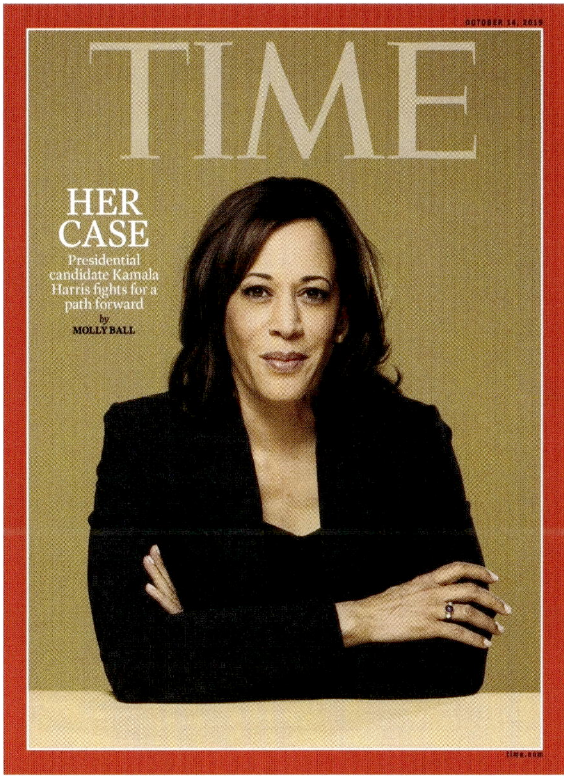

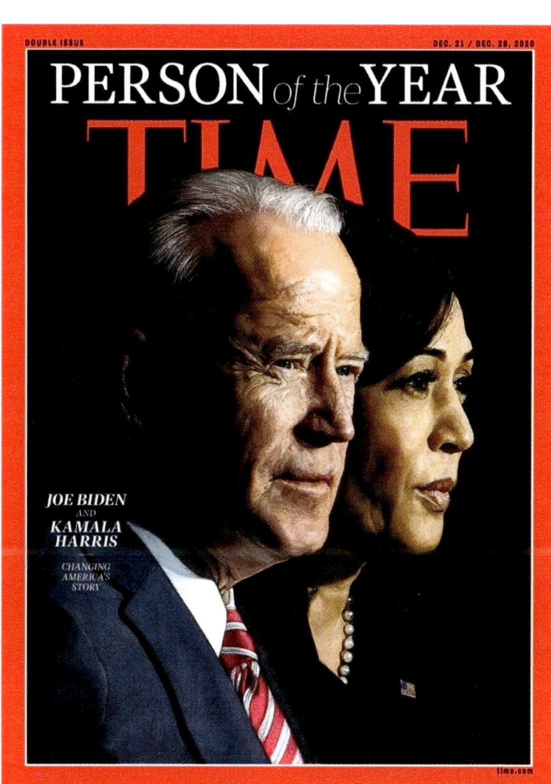

TIME has featured Harris on its cover several times, often pictured or illustrated in some manner of contemplation.

"The only thing [my parents] fought about was who got the books."

—KAMALA HARRIS

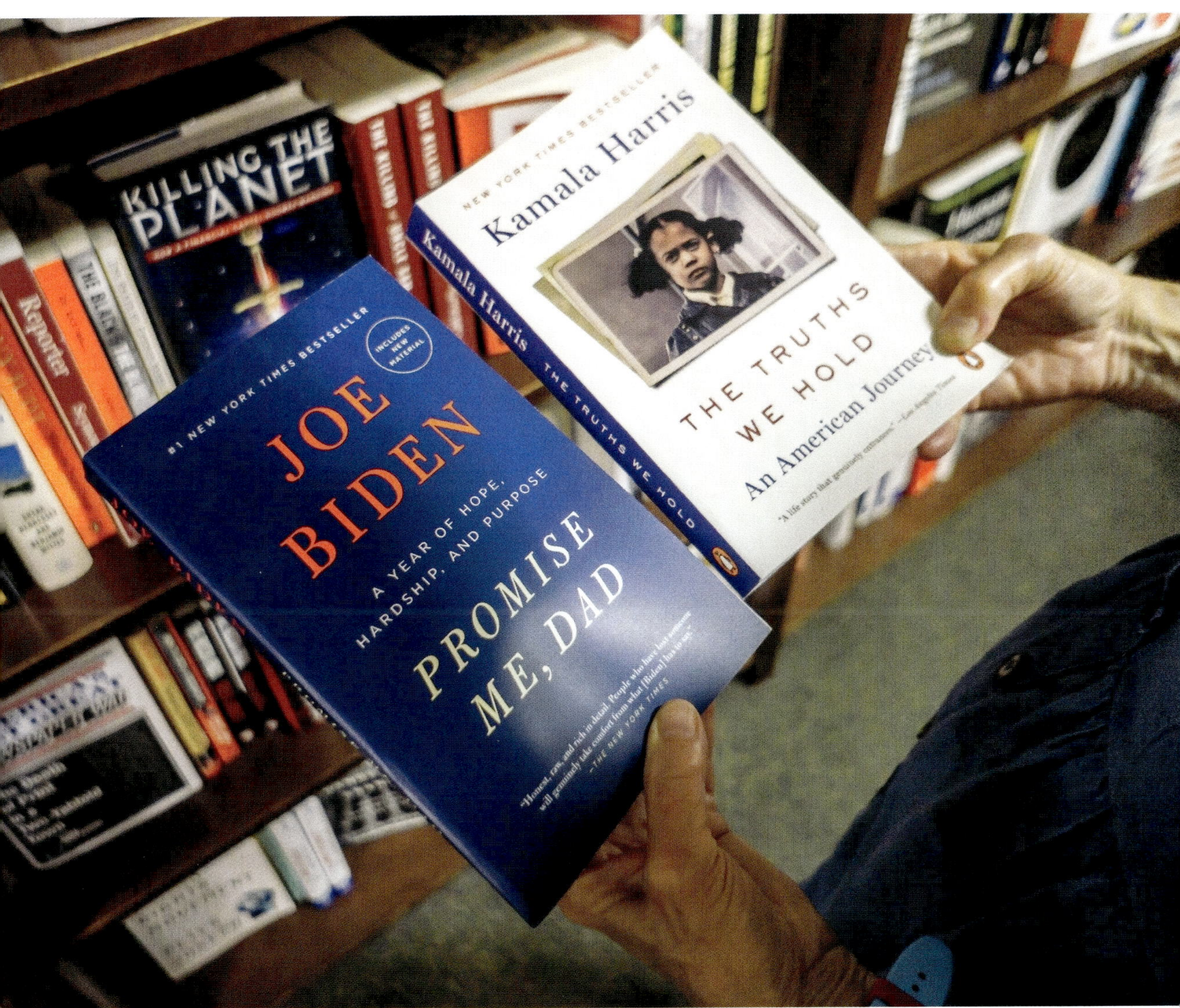

A READER chooses copies of Joe Biden's *Promise Me, Dad* and Kamala Harris's *The Truths We Hold* in a bookstore in New York in August 2020.

"All the News That's Fit to Print"

The New York Times

Late Edition
Today, sunshine, showers or thunderstorms, high 88. **Tonight,** partly cloudy, showers or thunderstorms, low 74. **Tomorrow,** thunderstorms, high 84. Weather map, Page C8.

VOL. CLXIX . . . . No. 58,783 © 2020 The New York Times Company NEW YORK, WEDNESDAY, AUGUST 12, 2020 $3.00

HARRIS JOINS BIDEN TICKET, ACHIEVING A FIRST

Political Warrior Shaped by Life In 2 Worlds

By MATT FLEGENHEIMER and LISA LERER

Kamala Harris's first act as a political candidate was knocking out a former boxer: the progressive San Francisco district attorney who had been her boss.

Her freshman Senate term has been defined by committee performances so lacerating that Trump administration officials have complained of her lawyerly velocity. "I'm not able to be rushed this fast," a flustered Jeff Sessions once said to her. "It makes me nervous."

And in Ms. Harris's most memorable turn as a presidential contender, speaking with practiced precision to the man who on Tuesday chose her as his running mate, she began with a less than charitable disclaimer — "I do not believe you are a racist" — before flattening him with the "but . . ."

"It was a *debate*," she has said repeatedly since then, offering no apology for campaign combat.

That is San Francisco politics, friends say. That is Kamala Devi Harris.

In announcing Ms. Harris, 55, as his vice-presidential nominee, Joseph R. Biden Jr. told supporters she was the person best equipped to "take this fight" to President Trump, making space in a campaign premised on restoring American decency for a willing brawler who learned early in her career that fortune would not favor the meek among Black women in her lines of work.

"She had to be savvy to find a way," said Senator Cory Booker of New Jersey, who has known Ms. Harris for more than two decades. "There was no path laid out for her. She had to find her way through the kind of set of obstacles that most people in the positions that she's held have not had to ever deal with."

It is this dexterity, people close to her say, that has most powered Ms. Harris's rise — and can be most frustrating to those who wish her electoral fearlessness were accompanied by policy audacity to match.

Caustic when she needs to be but cautious on substantive issues

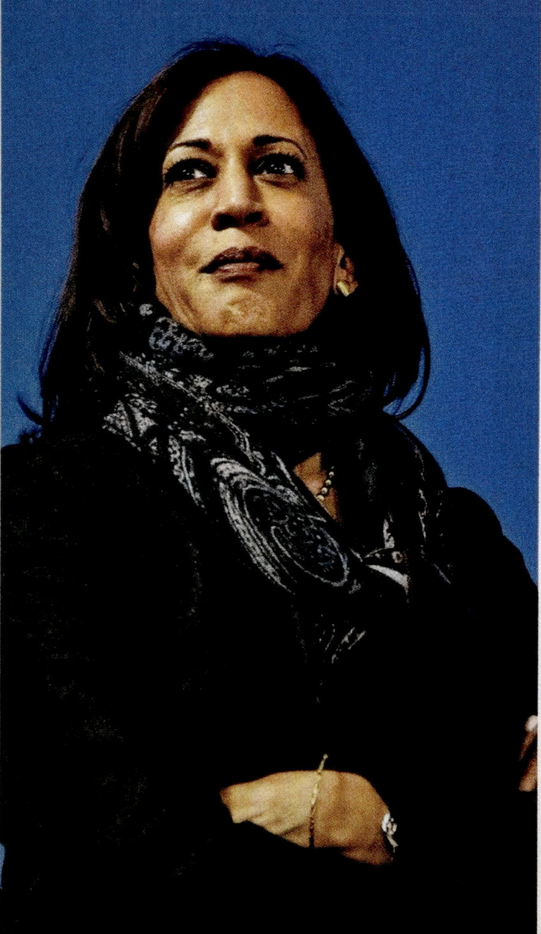

NEWS ANALYSIS

Pick Seen as Safe but Energizing

By JONATHAN MARTIN and ASTEAD W. HERNDON

WASHINGTON — In naming Kamala Harris as his running mate, Joseph R. Biden Jr. made a groundbreaking decision, picking a woman of color to be vice president and, possibly, a successor in the White House someday. Yet in some ways, Mr. Biden made a conventional choice: elevating a senator who brings generational and coastal balance to the Democratic ticket and shares his center-left politics at a time of progressive change in the party.

Unlike Barack Obama and George W. Bush, who selected veteran Washington hands as their vice presidents, Mr. Biden, 77, is opting for a time-honored model in which running mates are not just governing partners but political understudies of sorts. Pegged as a rising star for a decade, but with less than four years of experience in the Senate — she was 8 years old when Mr. Biden was first elected to the chamber — Ms. Harris, 55, reflects a traditional archetype in an election year that has been anything but normal.

She is also a thoroughly establishment-friendly figure, as is Mr. Biden: Both have hewed closely to their party's mainstream for years, shifting left with the times but always with an eye on the broader electorate and higher office. He long said he wanted someone "simpatico" with him and, in Ms. Harris, he found that person, at least when it comes to ideology.

Progressive Democrats now find themselves led by two moderates with relatively cautious political instincts, even as activist energy courses through the party and left-wing challengers unseat some incumbents. The mostly young protesters filling the streets of nearly every American city to decry police brutality and President Trump are represented by two figures who have offered sympathetic words and proposals but whose careers have been shaped by their relationship with law enforcement.

"She's not of the far left of the

Woman of Color in No. 2 Slot of Major Party

By ALEXANDER BURNS and KATIE GLUECK

Joseph R. Biden Jr. selected Senator Kamala Harris of California as his vice-presidential running mate on Tuesday, embracing a former rival who sharply criticized him in the Democratic primaries but emerged after ending her campaign as a vocal supporter of Mr. Biden's and a prominent advocate of racial-justice legislation after the killing of George Floyd in late May.

Ms. Harris, 55, is the first Black woman and the first person of Indian descent to be nominated for national office by a major party, and only the fourth woman in U.S. history to be chosen for a presidential ticket. She brings to the race a far more vigorous campaign style than Mr. Biden's, including a gift for capturing moments of raw political electricity on the debate stage and elsewhere, and a personal identity and family story that many find inspiring.

Mr. Biden announced the selection over text message and in a follow-up email to supporters: "Joe Biden here. Big news: I've chosen Kamala Harris as my running mate. Together, with you, we're going to beat Trump." The two are expected to appear together in Wilmington, Del., on Wednesday.

After her own presidential bid disintegrated last year, many Democrats regarded Ms. Harris as all but certain to try for another run for the White House in the future. By choosing her as his political partner, Mr. Biden, if he wins, may well be anointing her as the de facto leader of the party in four or eight years.

A pragmatic moderate who spent most of her career as a prosecutor, Ms. Harris was seen throughout the vice-presidential search as among the safest choices available to Mr. Biden. She has been a reliable ally of the Democratic establishment, with flexible policy priorities that largely mirror Mr. Biden's, and her supporters argued that she could reinforce Mr. Biden's appeal to Black voters and women with-

THE FRONT PAGE of *The New York Times* after Joe Biden selected Kamala Harris as his vice-presidential running mate.

Facing page:
A PHOTO from *Rolling Stone*'s June 11, 2024, interview with Kamala Harris.

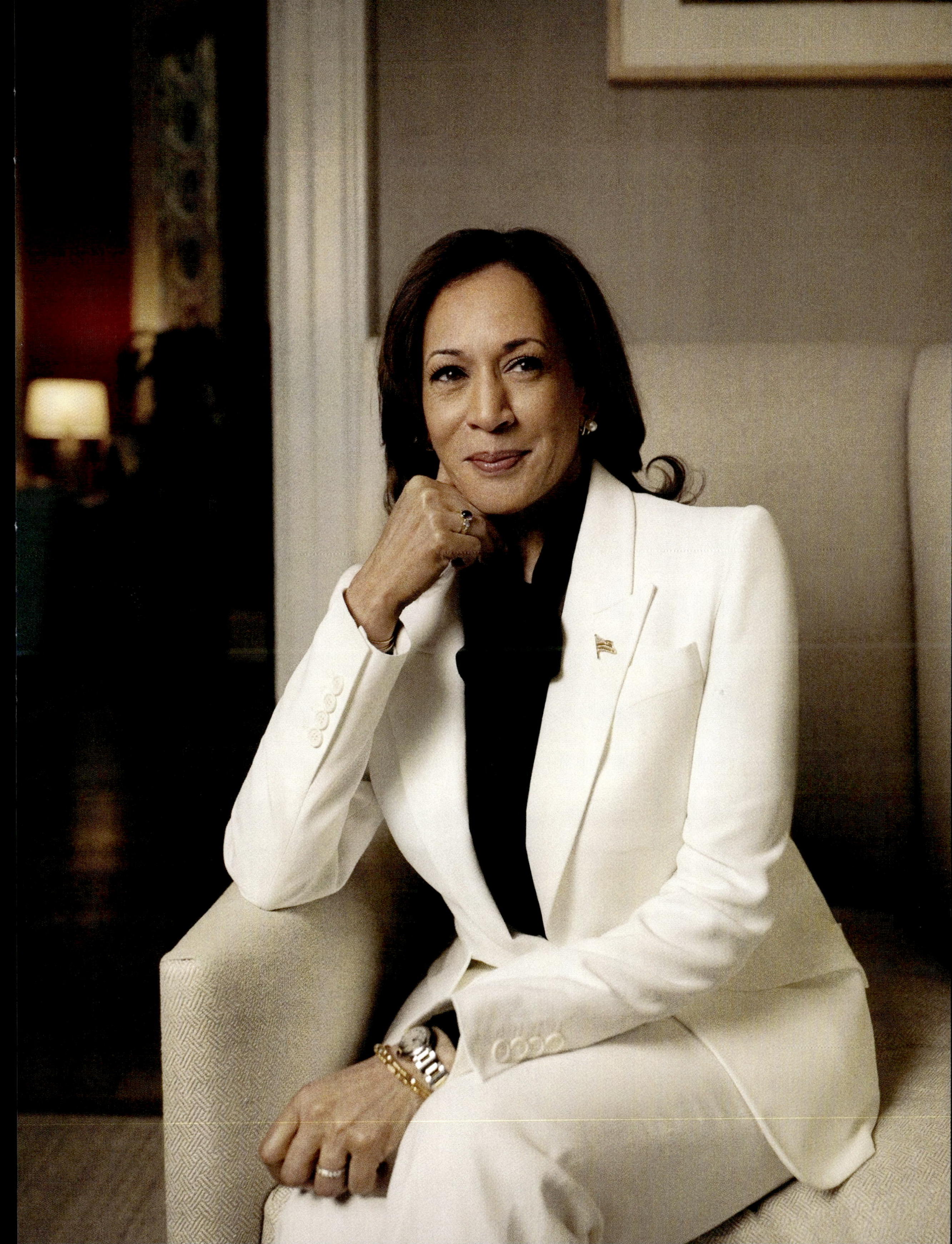

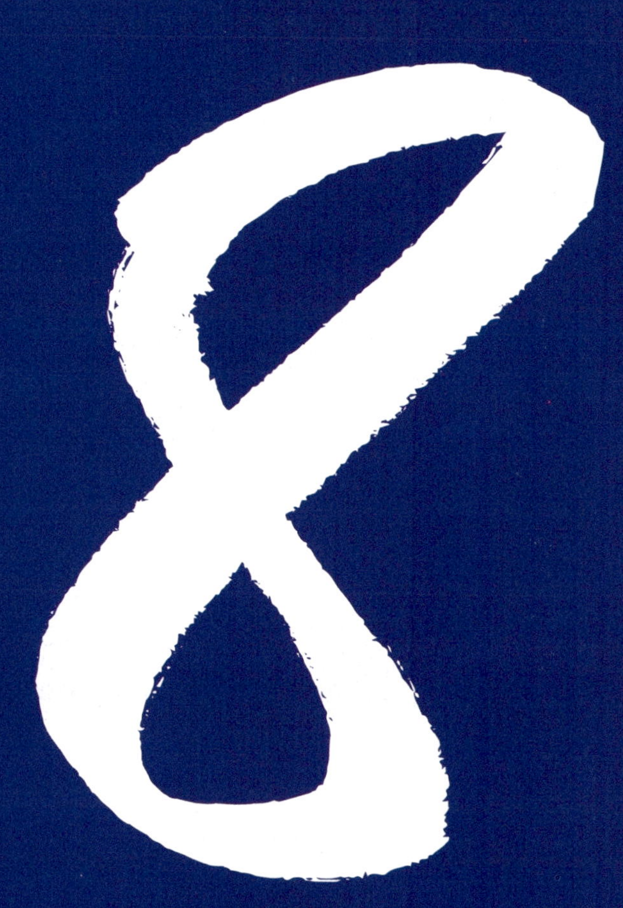

THE SELFIE

“Bringing back the joy—

one selfie at a time.”

—KAMALA HARRIS, AUGUST 15, 2024

Kamala Harris posted that quote on X after taking a selfie with running mate Tim Walz. She is a big selfie fan. On National Selfie Day—yes, there is such a day, June 21—Harris posted on her Facebook page during her first presidential race: "I love taking selfies with people I meet on the campaign trail—but I don't always get to see how they turn out!"

She then invited anyone who had taken a selfie with her to share it in the comments.

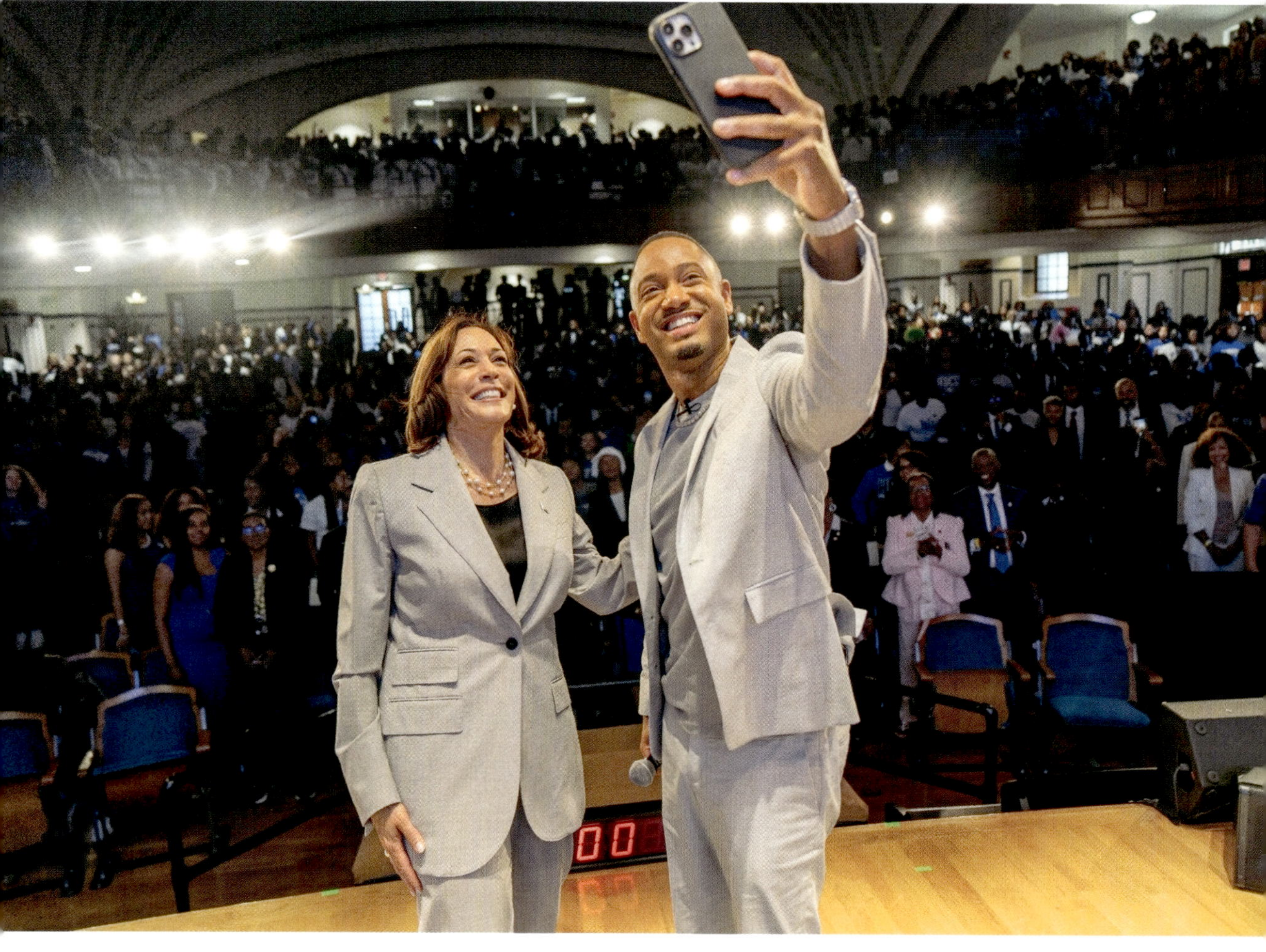

VICE PRESIDENT KAMALA HARRIS poses for a selfie after participating in a conversation with students moderated by actor Terrence J in Ogden Hall at Hampton University on September 14, 2023, in Hampton, Virginia.

Facing page:

KAMALA HARRIS AND TIM WALZ take their first selfie together.

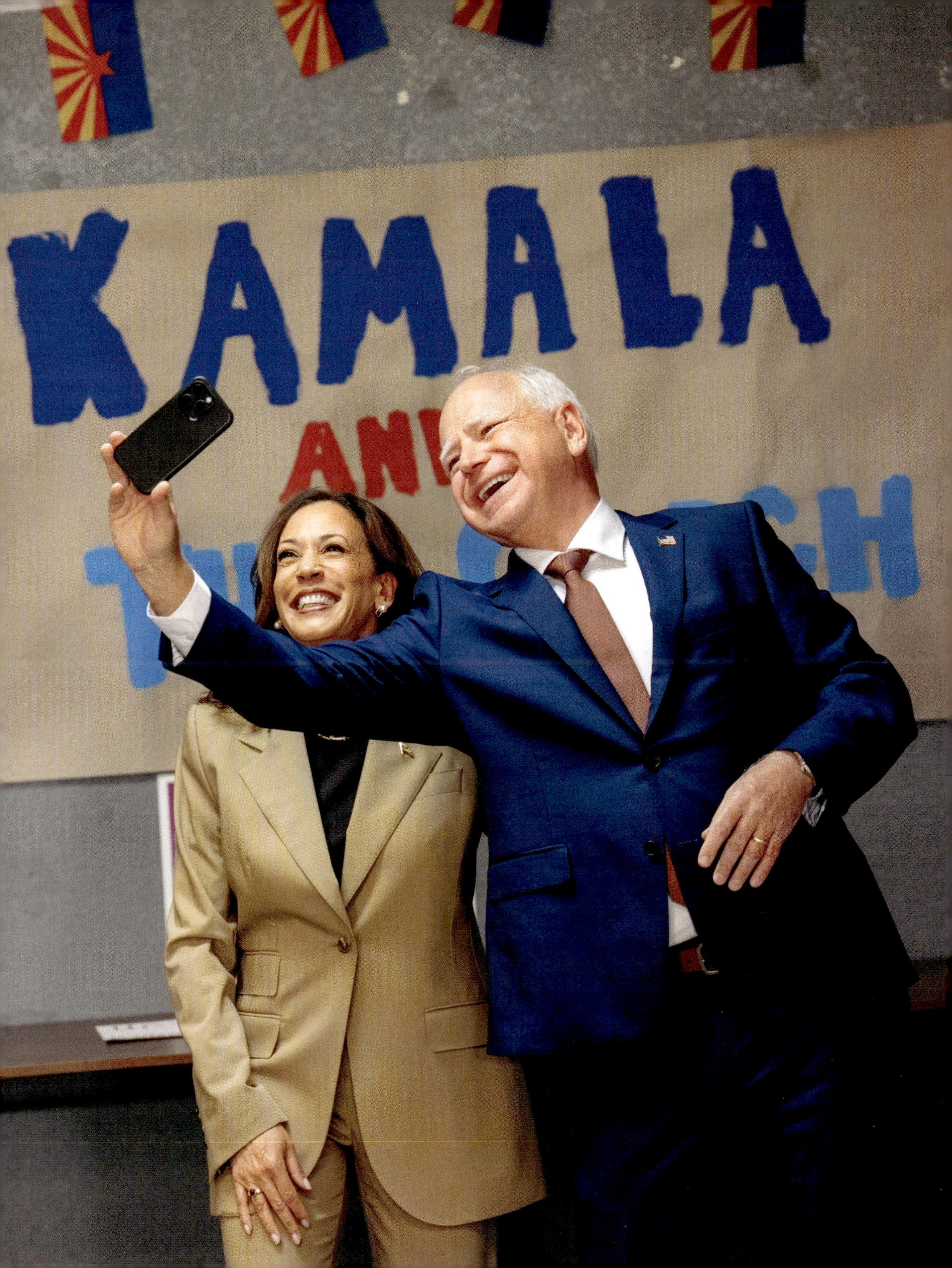
KAMALA

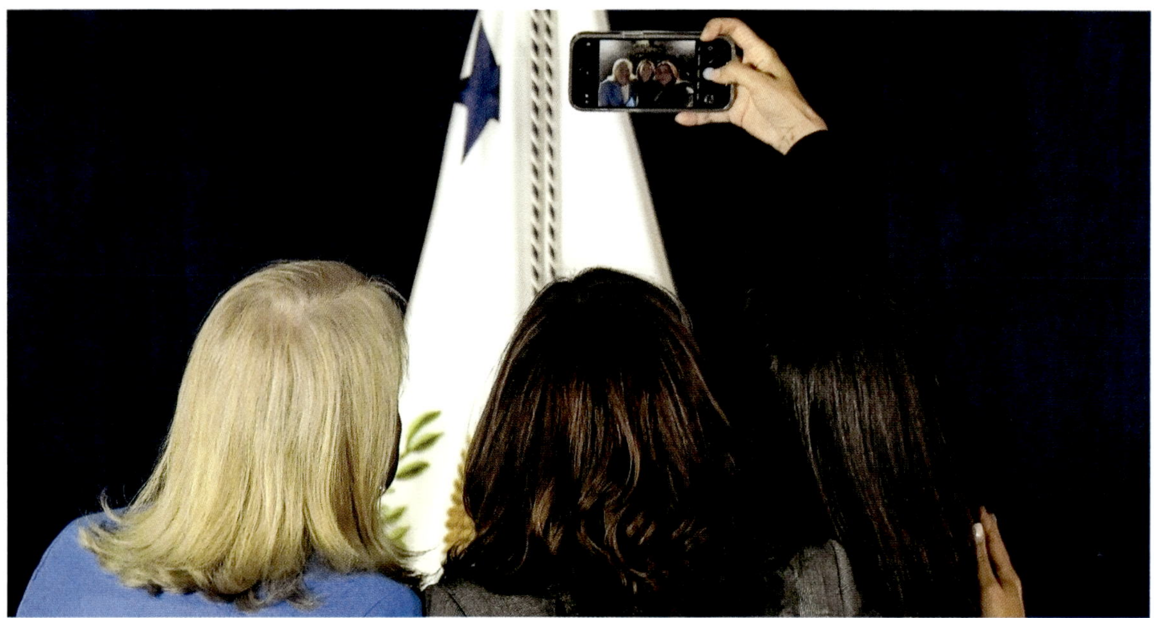

REPRESENTATIVE SYLVIA GARCIA OF TEXAS (*left*), Vice President Harris, and Representative Nanette Barragán of California take a selfie after Harris spoke at a community forum in Houston organized by the Congressional Hispanic Caucus on November 27, 2023. It was part of the caucus's "On the Road" series to engage Latino communities about the accomplishments of the Biden-Harris administration.

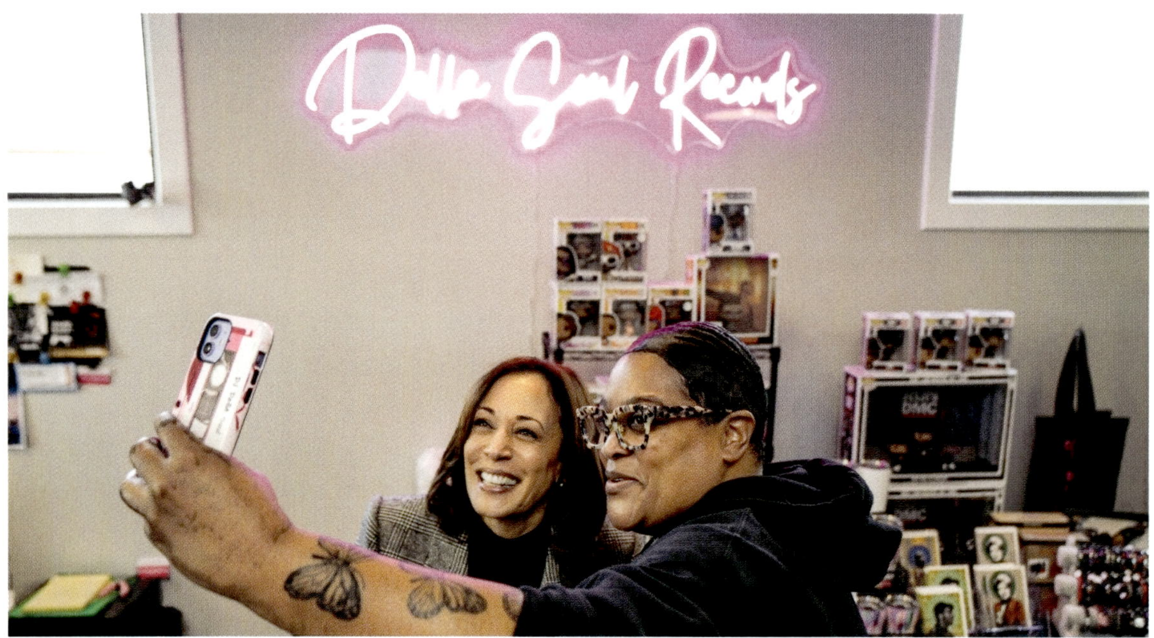

VICE PRESIDENT HARRIS poses for a photo with Della Marie Levi, owner of Della Soul Records, the first Black woman–owned vinyl record store in Grand Rapids, Michigan, on February 22, 2024.

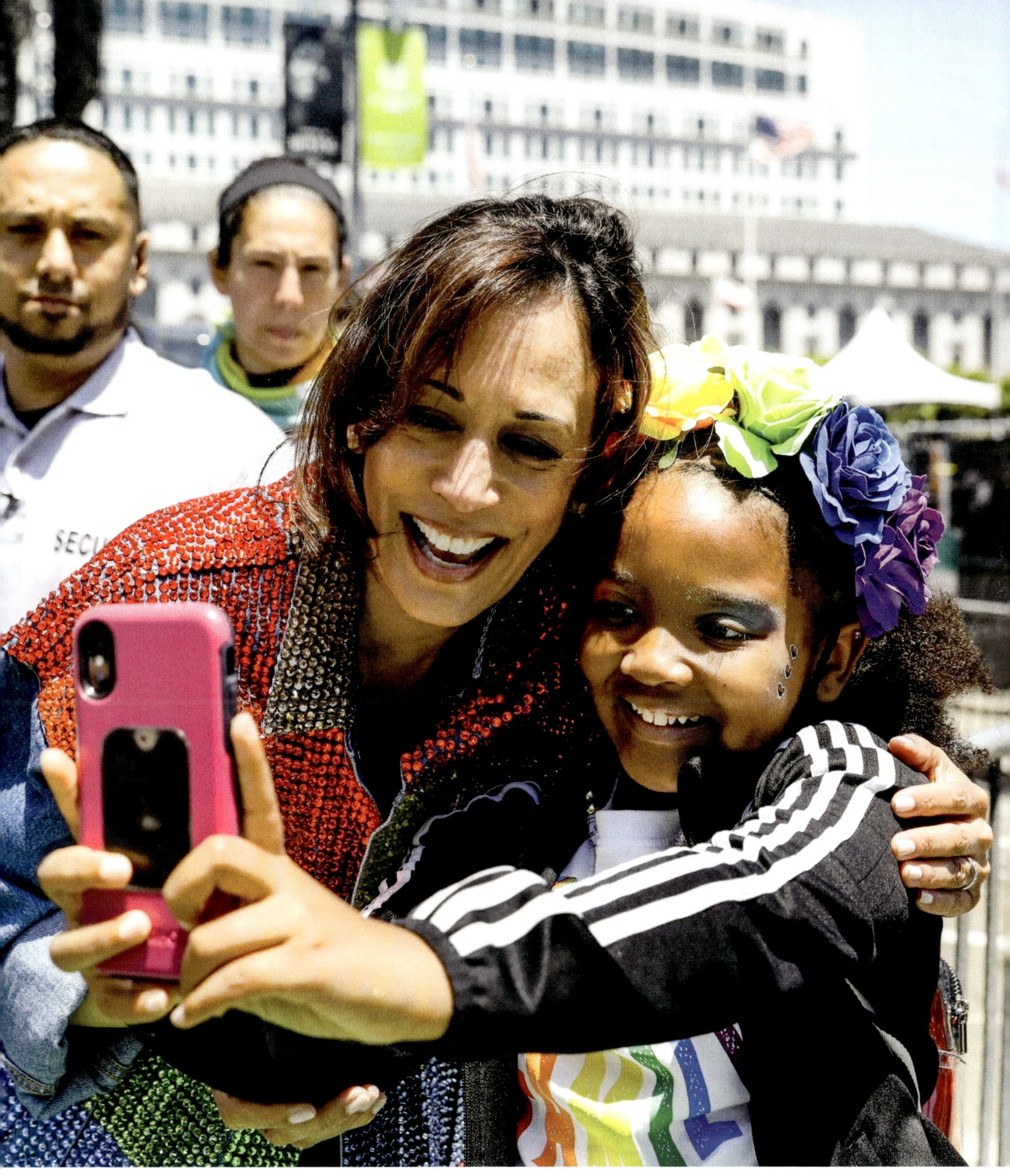

SENATOR KAMALA HARRIS takes a selfie with a young girl after participating in the annual Pride Parade in San Francisco on June 30, 2019.

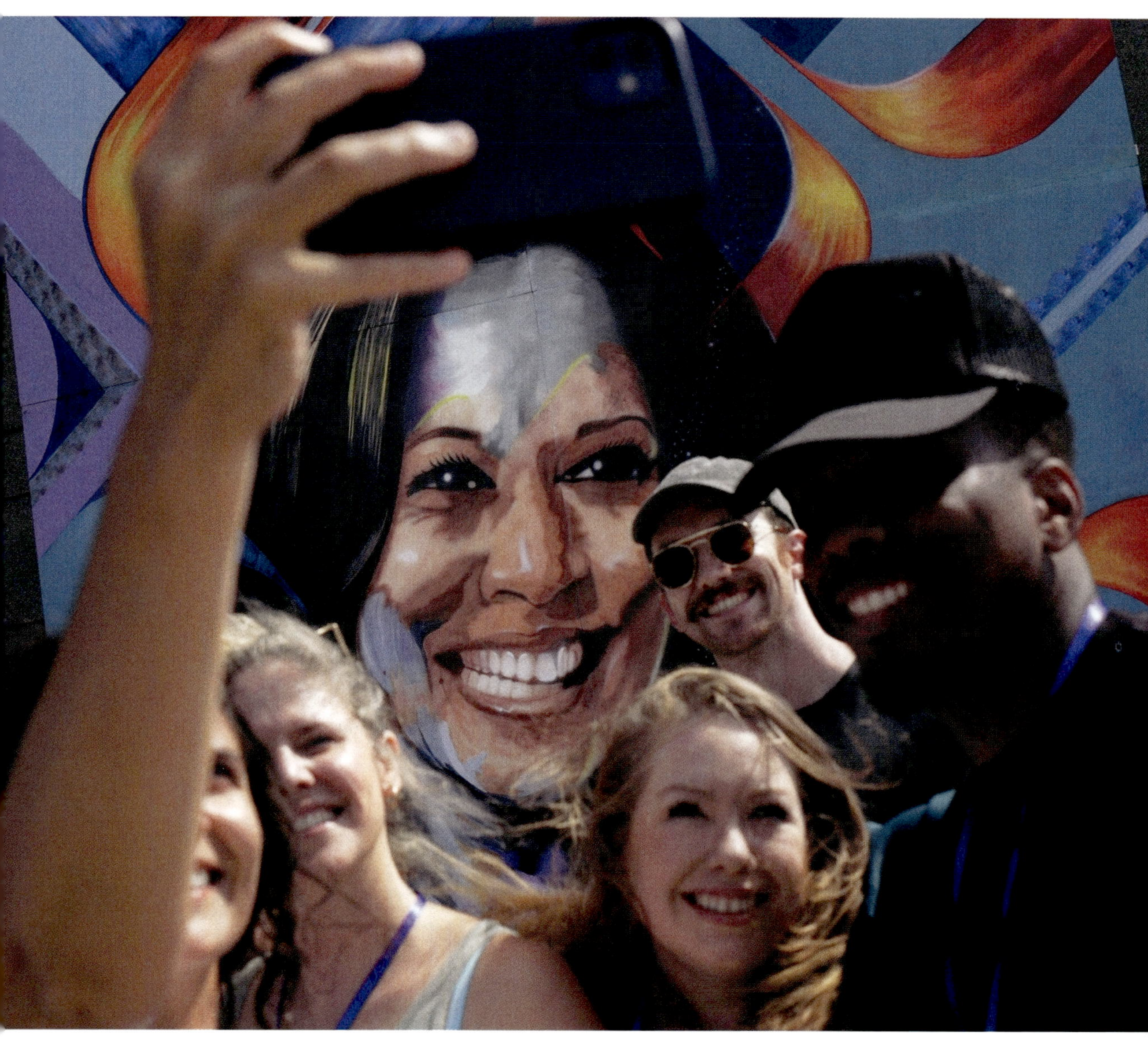

A VIVID MURAL of Harris in Chicago, created by EMILYs List, was a magnet for selfies. Here, people line up outside the United Center to take their snaps.

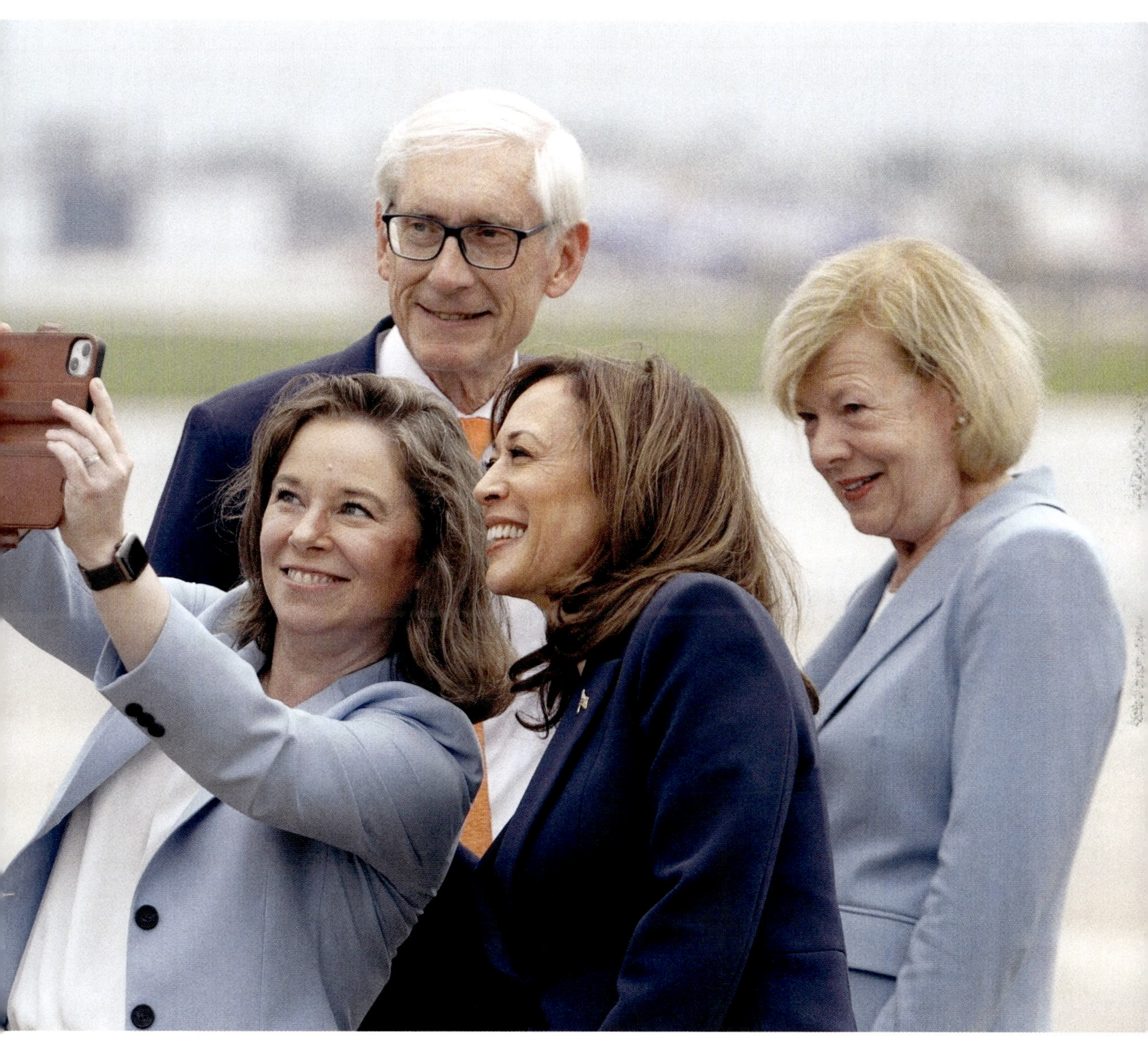

HARRIS GATHERS for a picture with Wisconsin Lieutenant Governor Sara Rodriguez (*left*), Wisconsin Governor Tony Evers (*second from left*), and U.S. Senator Tammy Baldwin, Democrat of Wisconsin, upon arrival at Milwaukee Mitchell International Airport on July 23, 2024.

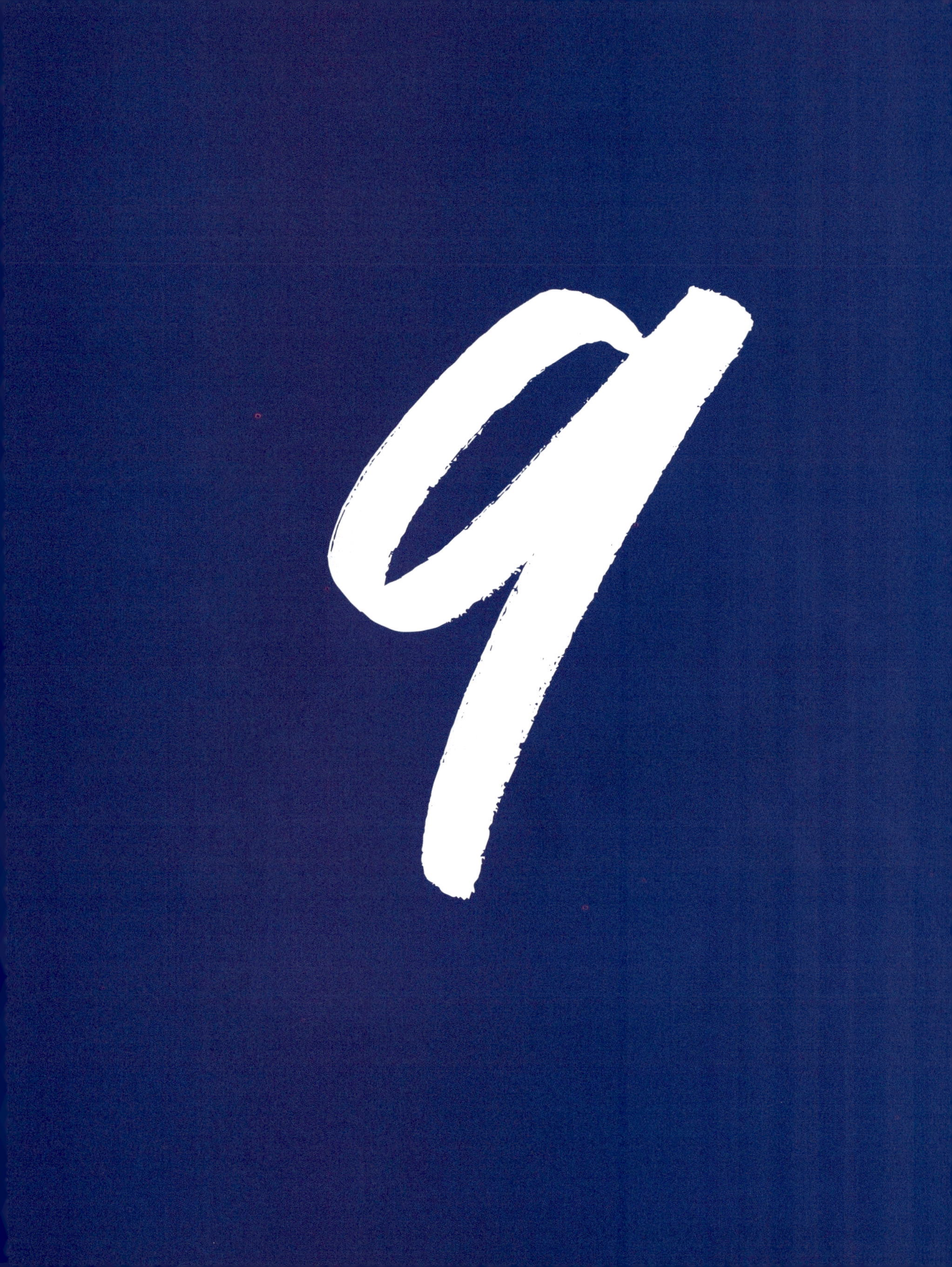
9

THE KIDS KNOW

"[Children's] fuel is their optimism; their fuel is that they believe something can get done to improve the condition of themselves, their communities, our country, and our world."

—KAMALA HARRIS

Sometimes children ask the best questions. In a "Kids Interview Kamala Harris" session during her first presidential campaign, one boy asked her: "What is your plan to make America nice again?" To which Harris replied: "As president, I am always going to reward people for being nice."

Harris clearly enjoys interacting with children of all ages and circumstances, as these photos indicate. Oddly, the campaign took an unexpected turn toward debating maternal status after a 2021 video resurfaced of JD Vance deriding Democrats in power as "childless cat ladies." He name-checked Harris, even though she has two stepchildren. Vance's remarks triggered a backlash from women who don't have biological children and from others concerned about the threats to reproductive health, including in vitro fertilization. For Harris, the episode gave her momentum—"Cat Ladies for Kamala" groups formed—and reminded her of all the children who deserve love. As she wrote in an essay for *Elle* about being a stepparent: "There's nothing worse than disappointing a child."

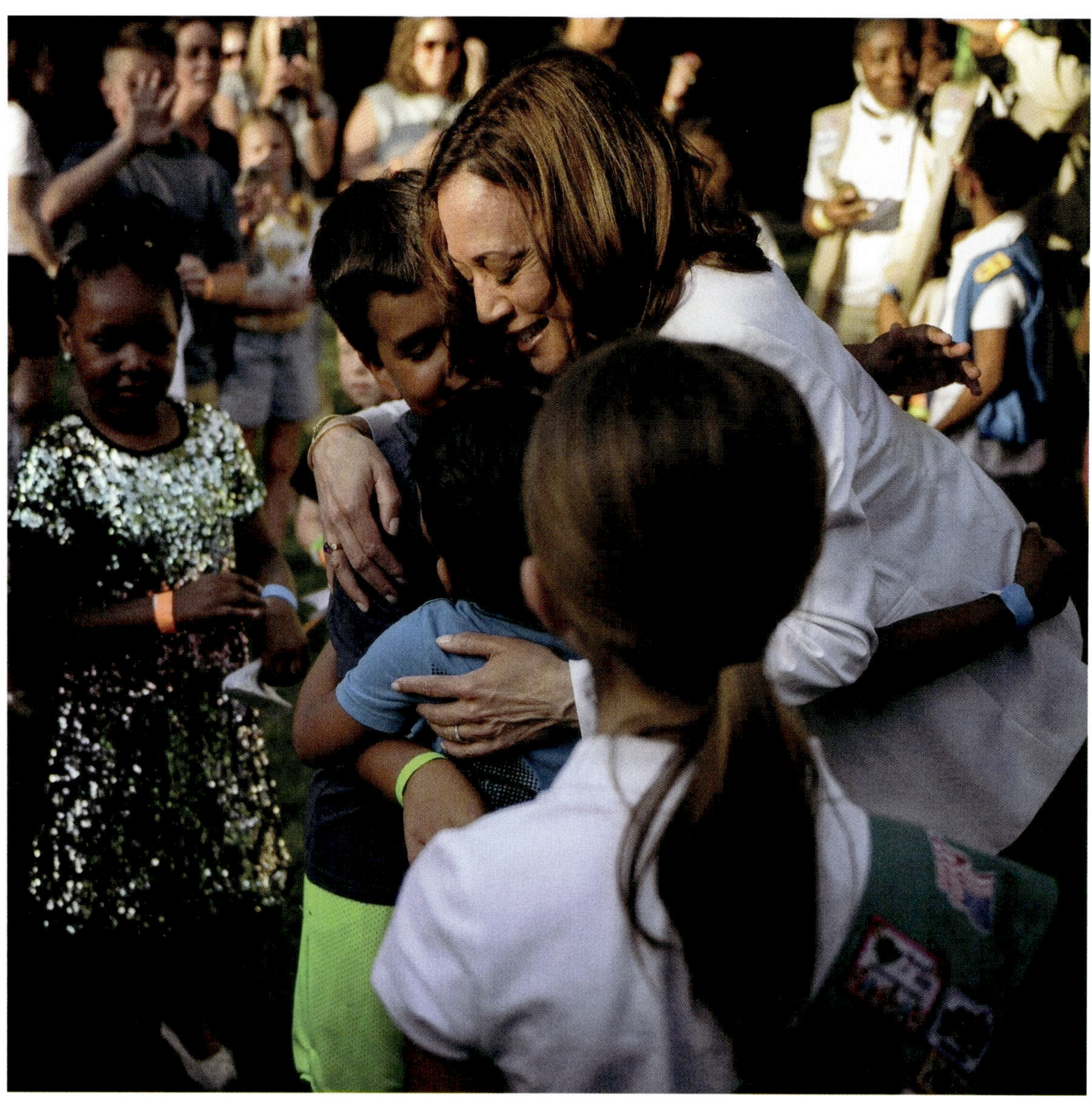

IN THIS handout image provided by NASA, Vice President Harris hugs children who participated in hands-on STEM activities on the grounds of the vice president's residence at the Naval Observatory on June 17, 2022, in Washington, DC. The vice president and Second Gentleman hosted an evening of activities for military families and local STEM students and their families, including a special screening of Disney Pixar's *Lightyear*.

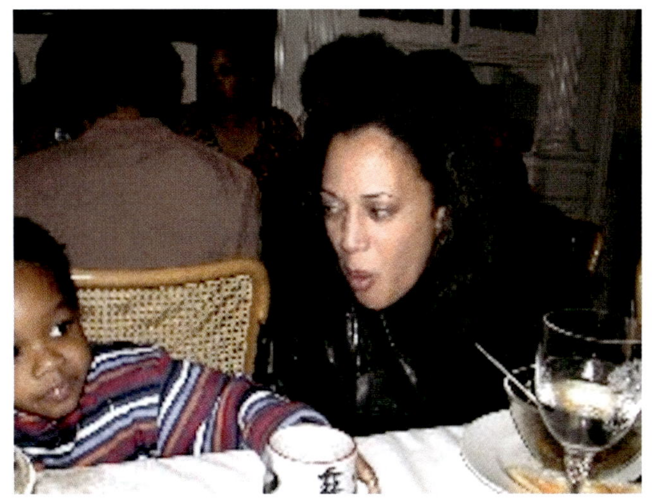

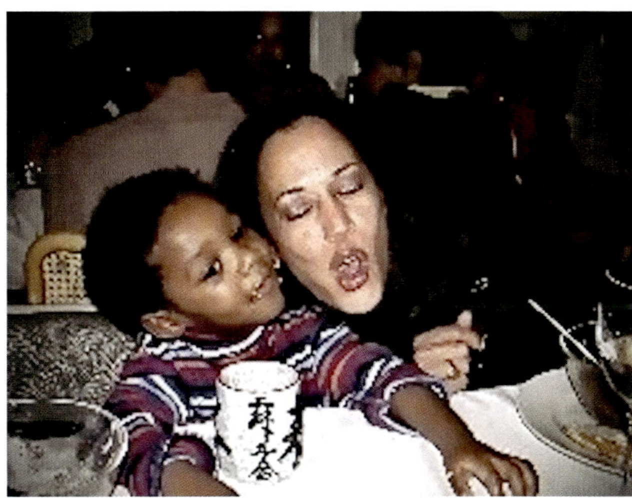

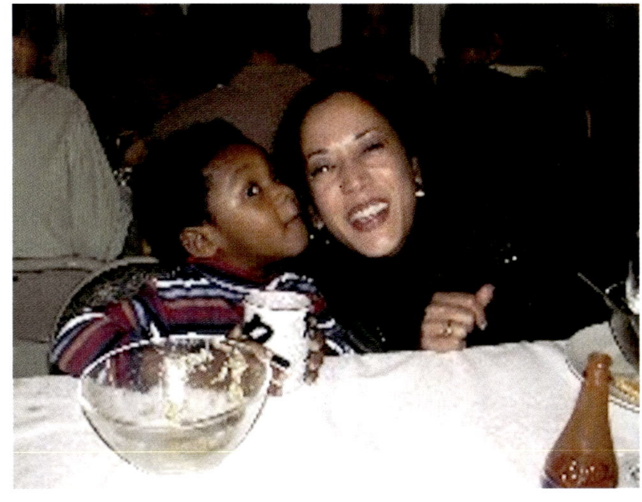

DAMIRI LINDO with Harris in San Francisco, 2003.

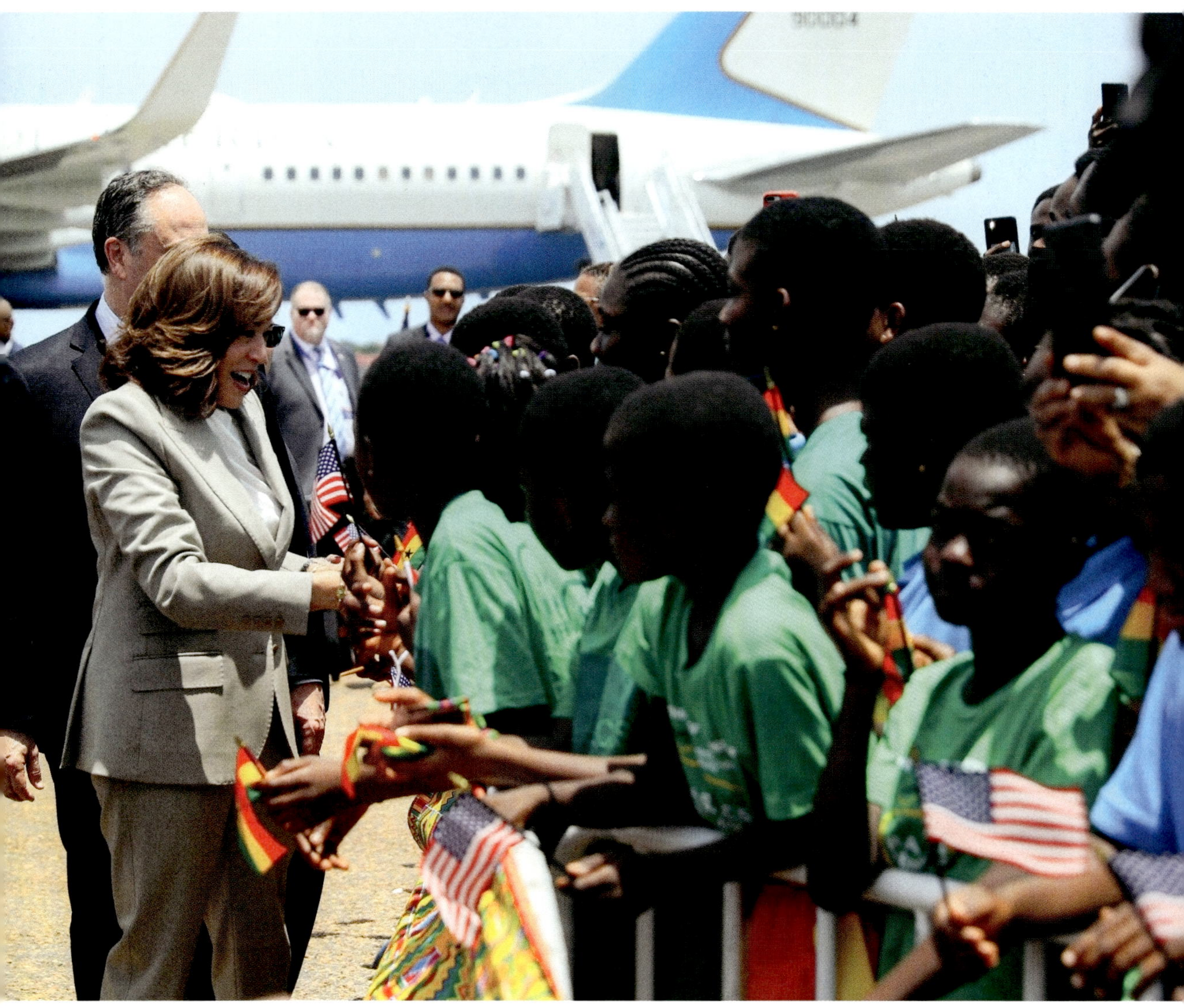

VICE PRESIDENT HARRIS greets children as she arrives at Kotoka International Airport in Accra, Ghana, on March 26, 2023. The vice president embarked on a three-country tour of Africa, promoting the White House's vision of the continent as the "future of the world." Harris's trip to Ghana, Tanzania, and Zambia was the latest salvo in deepening U.S. engagement with a continent largely ignored under Republican Donald Trump—and long viewed in Washington as more of a problem area than a land of opportunity.

Facing page:

KAMALA HARRIS visits an Oakland classroom to see students helped by the Vision To Learn program, which provides eye exams and glasses to kids in low-income communities at no cost to the children or their families.

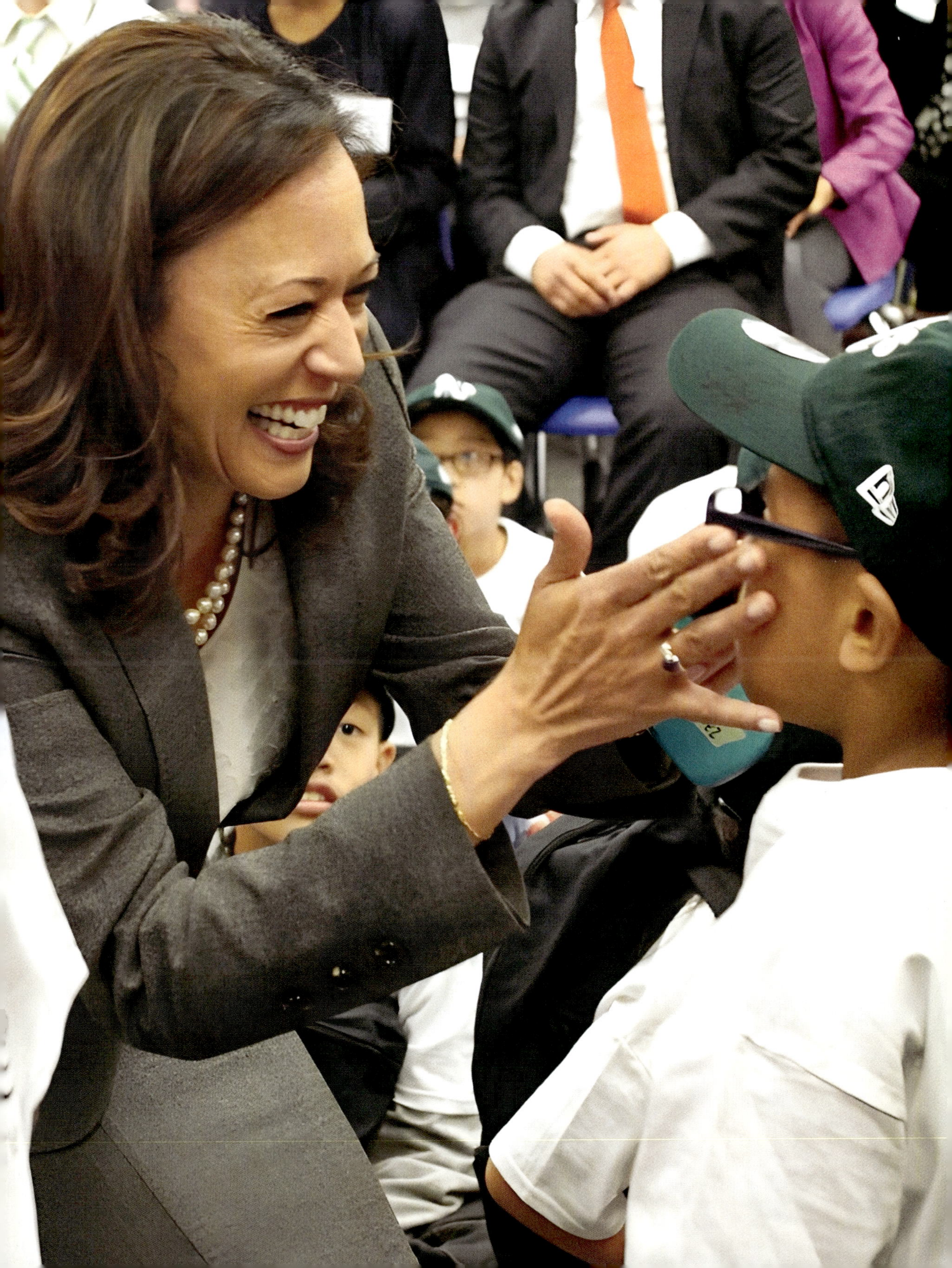

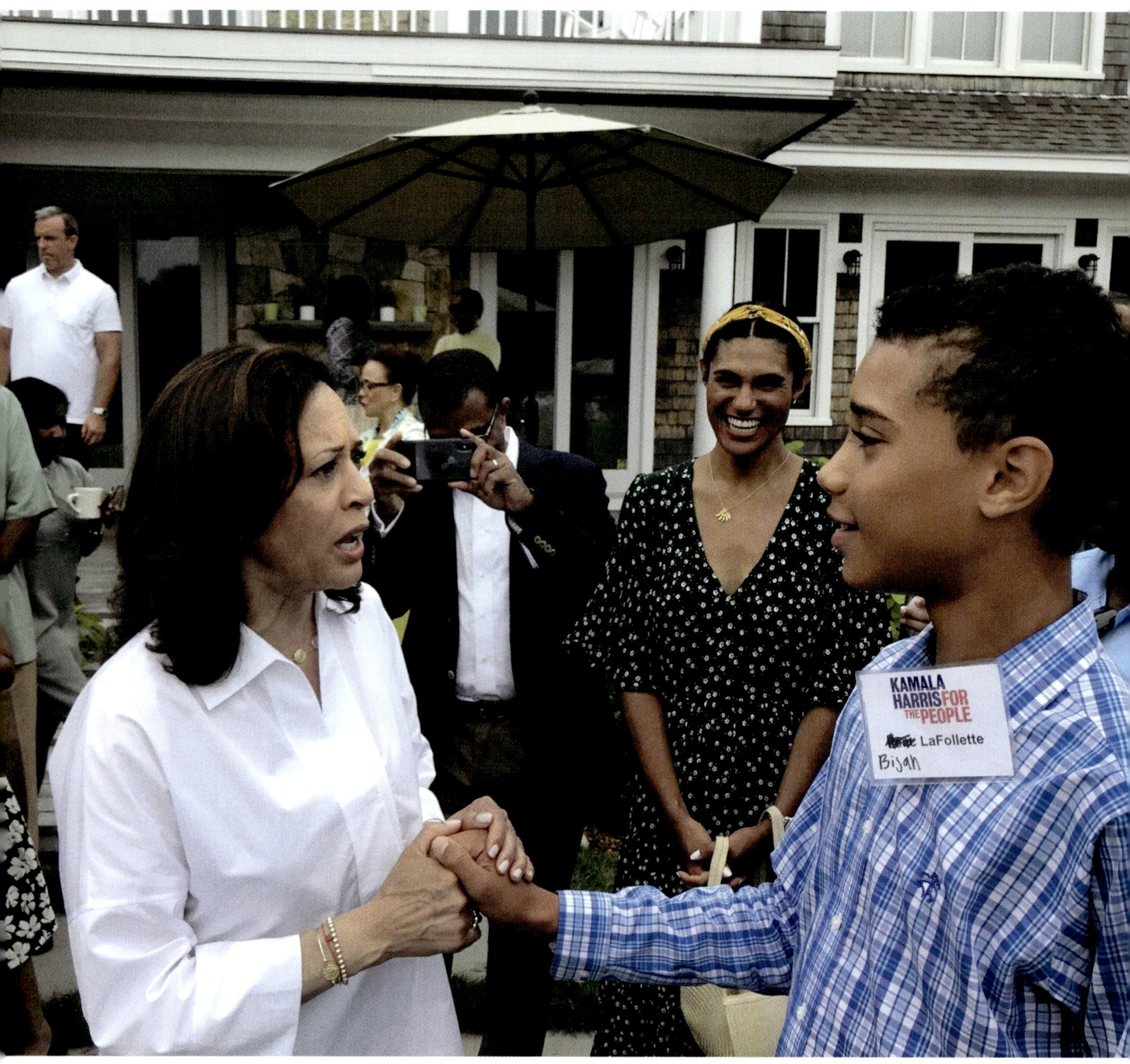

KAMALA HARRIS talks with a young student interested in politics at a fundraiser for her 2020 presidential campaign.

Facing page:

VICE PRESIDENT HARRIS shows Gianna Floyd, the daughter of George Floyd, the executive order that President Joe Biden signed during an event on federal policing reforms on May 25, 2022, in the East Room of the White House.

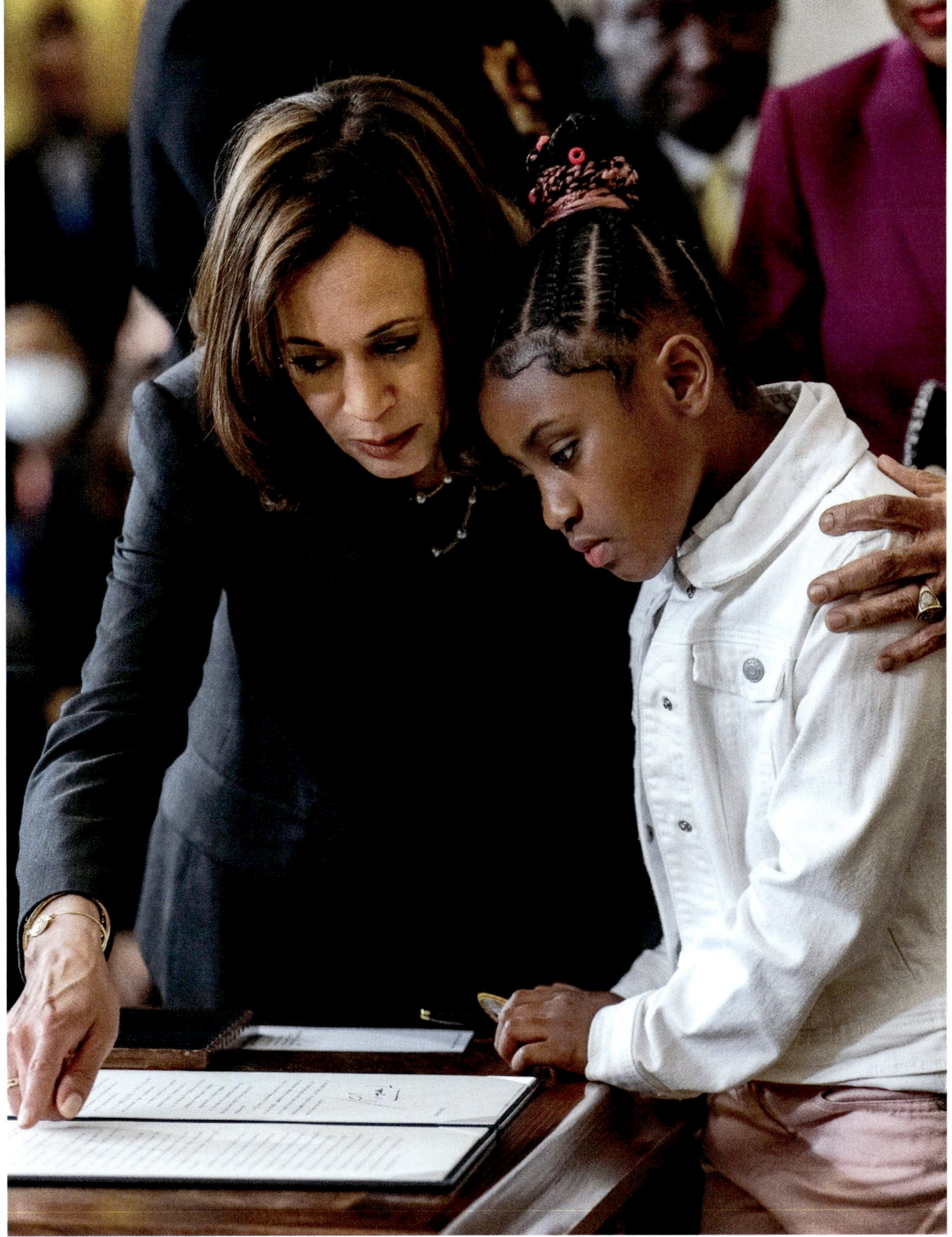

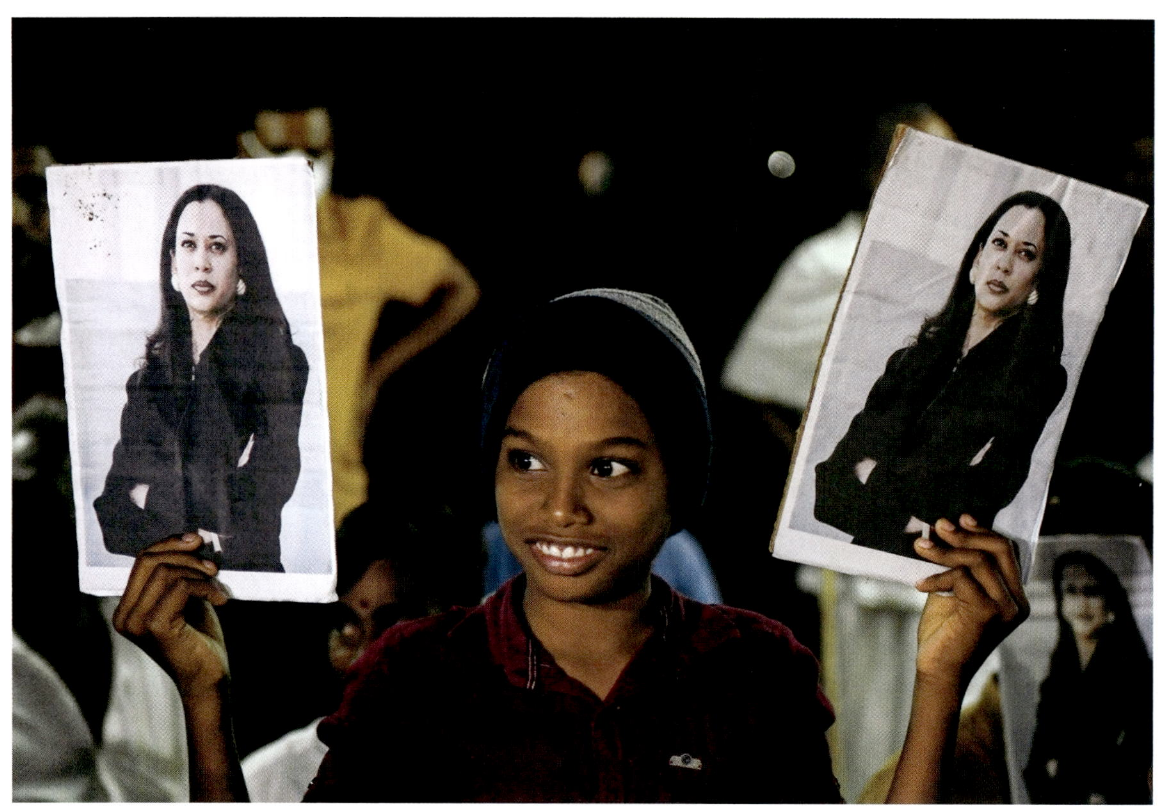

A BOY RESIDENT holds pictures of Vice President–Elect Kamala Harris as he attends a gathering to watch Harris's inaugural ceremony at her ancestral village of Thulasendrapuram, in the southern Indian state of Tamil Nadu, on January 20, 2021.

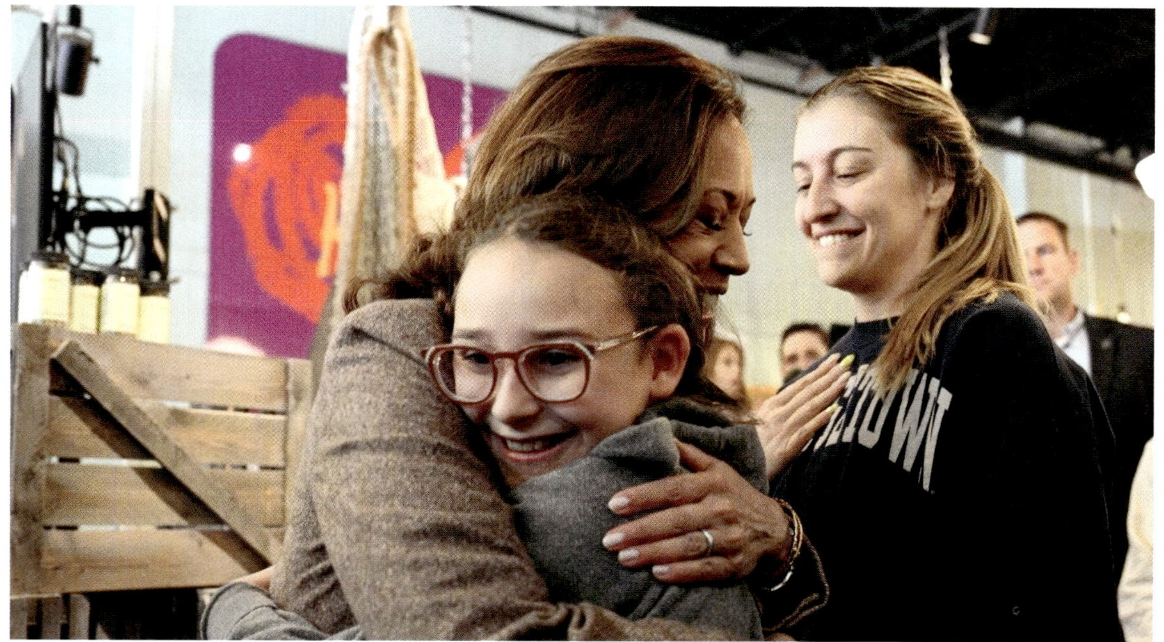

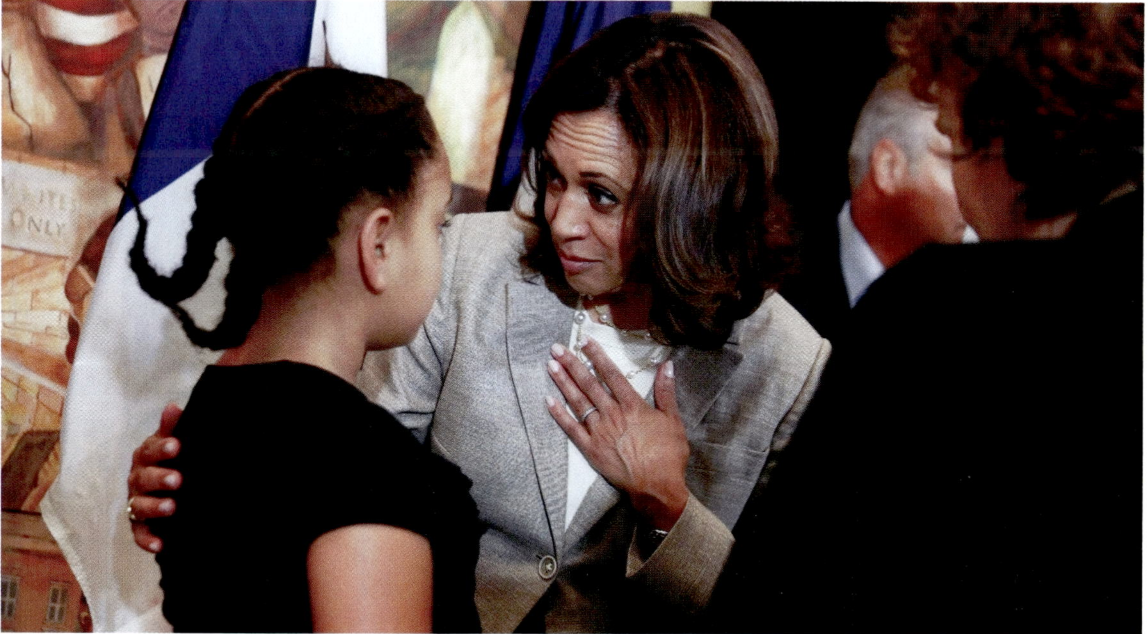

Top to botom:

KAMALA HARRIS hugs a young girl as they pose for a photo during a campaign stop at Penzeys Spices in Pittsburgh, Pennsylvania, on September 7, 2024.

SENATOR KAMALA HARRIS speaks to Kyrah Cortimiglia as she campaigns for president during the 2020 Democratic primary. She appeared at a roundtable discussion for women of color.

10

JOY & INTIMACY

"I looked at him, there on one knee, and burst into tears. Mind you, these were not graceful tears streaming down a glistening cheek. No, I'm talking about snorting and grunting, with mascara smudging my face."

—KAMALA HARRIS

Whether cooking dinners at home—which she loves!—supporting friends and changemakers, or strolling an Air National Guard base or museum with her husband, Harris lights up when she can just hang and be relaxed.

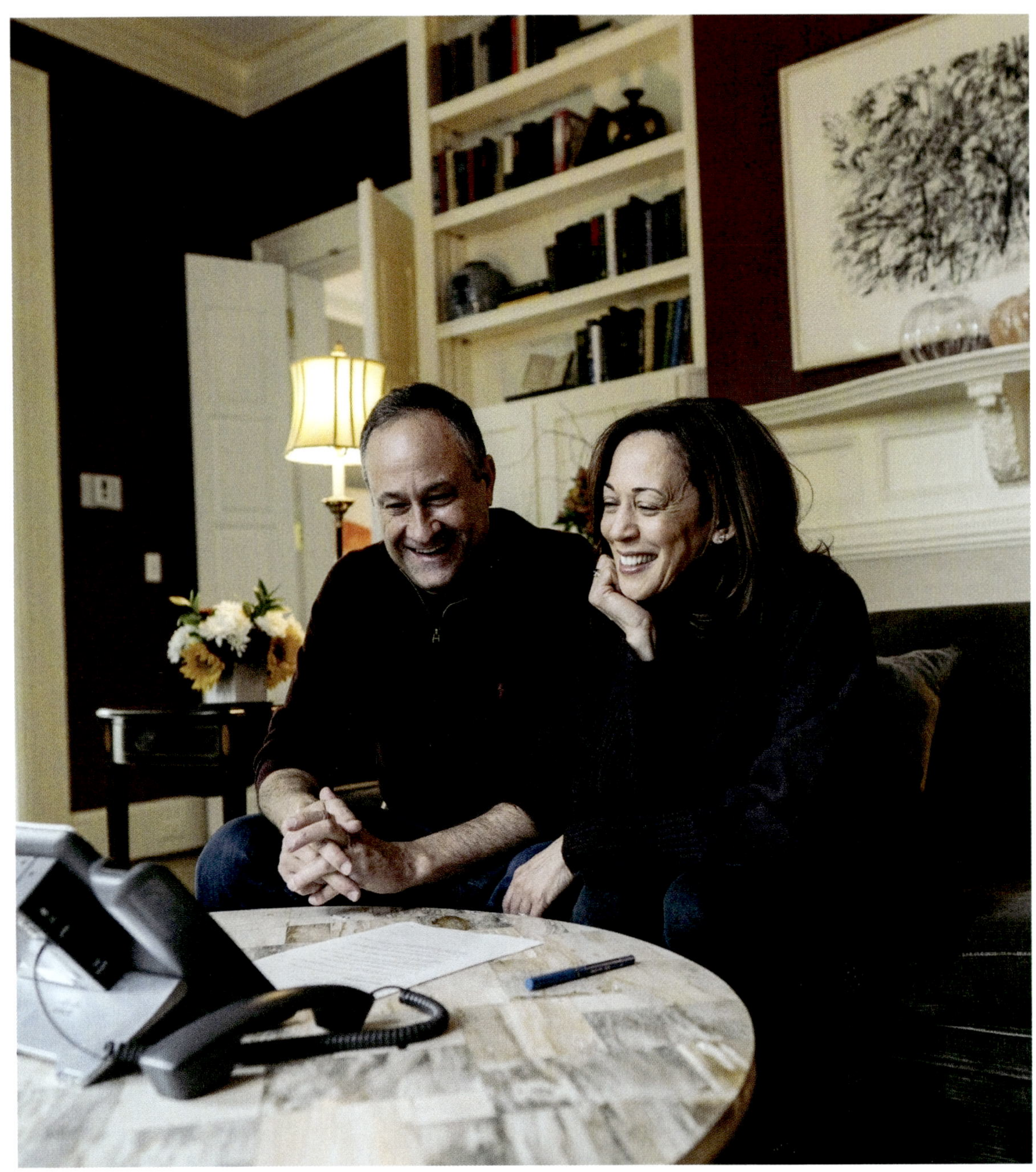

VICE PRESIDENT HARRIS and Second Gentleman Emhoff make phone calls to troops in Kuwait and San Diego to wish them a happy Thanksgiving from the vice president's residence in Washington, DC, on November 25, 2021.

Facing page:
VICE PRESIDENT Harris with her husband, Doug Emhoff, at the White House on May 9, 2024.

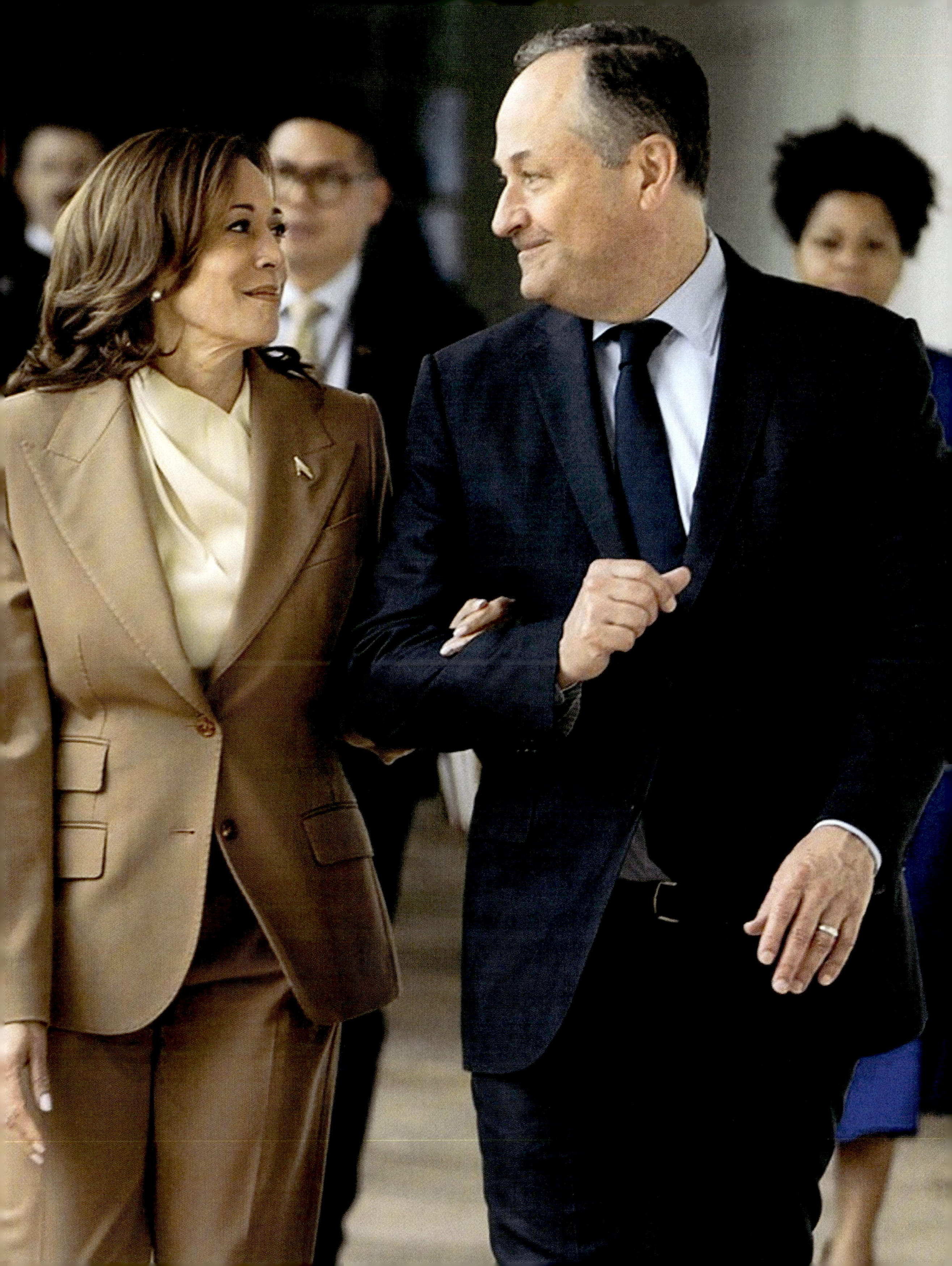

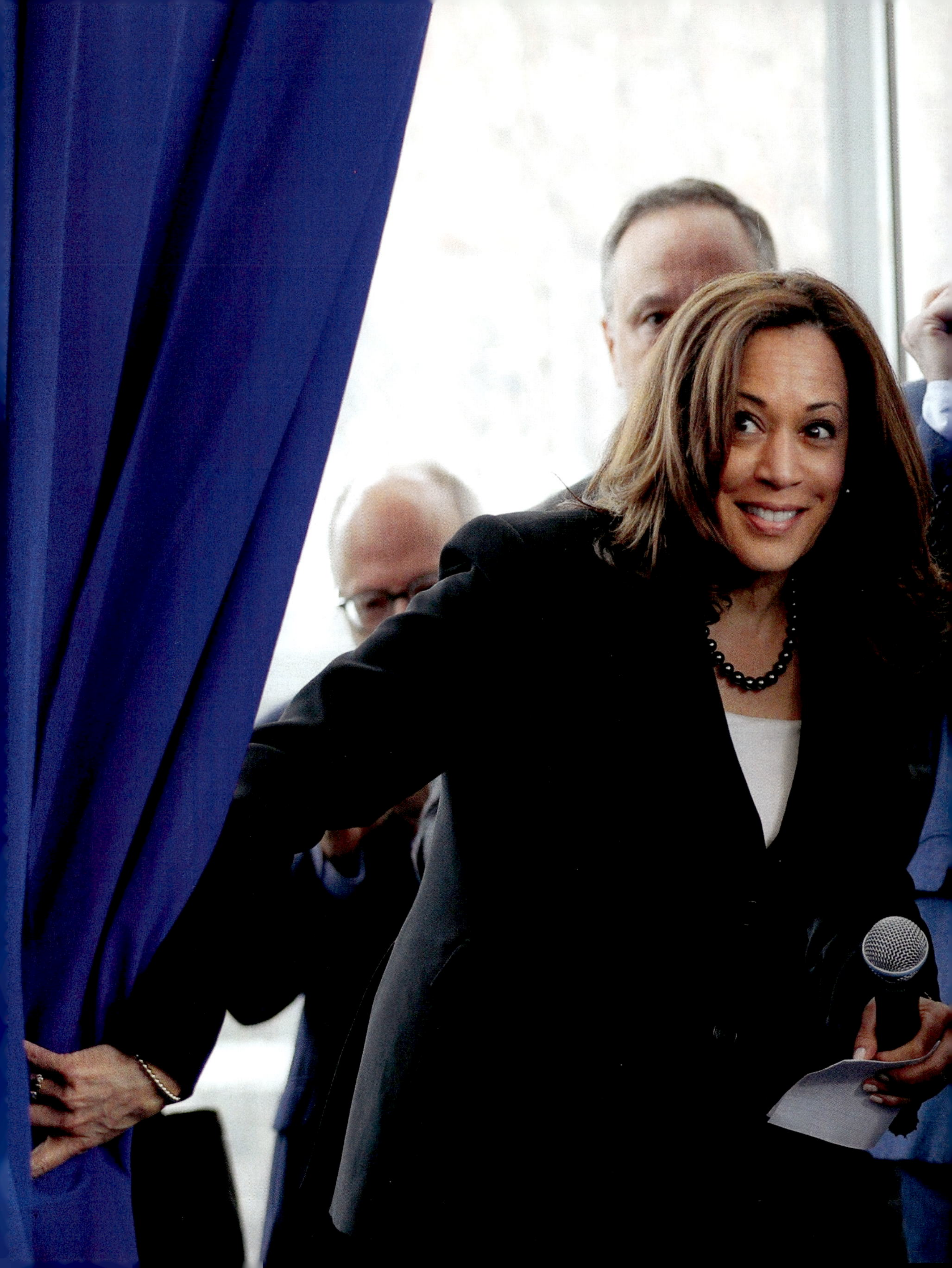

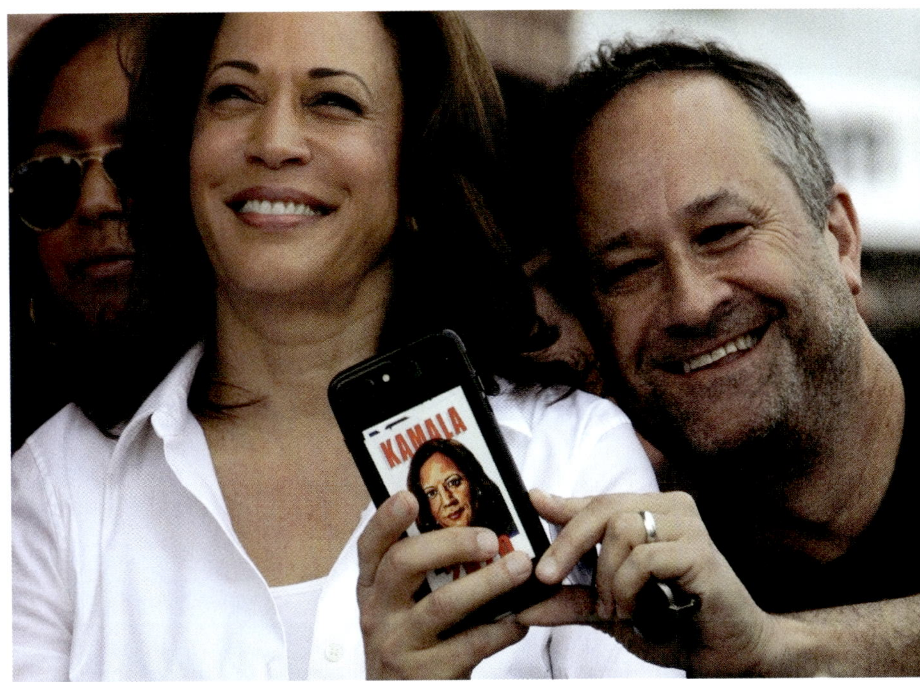

DOUG EMHOFF takes a selfie before Kamala Harris delivers a campaign speech at the Iowa State Fair in Des Moines on August 10, 2019.

SENATOR HARRIS takes the stage at a campaign stop at Keene State College in Keene, New Hampshire, in April 2019.

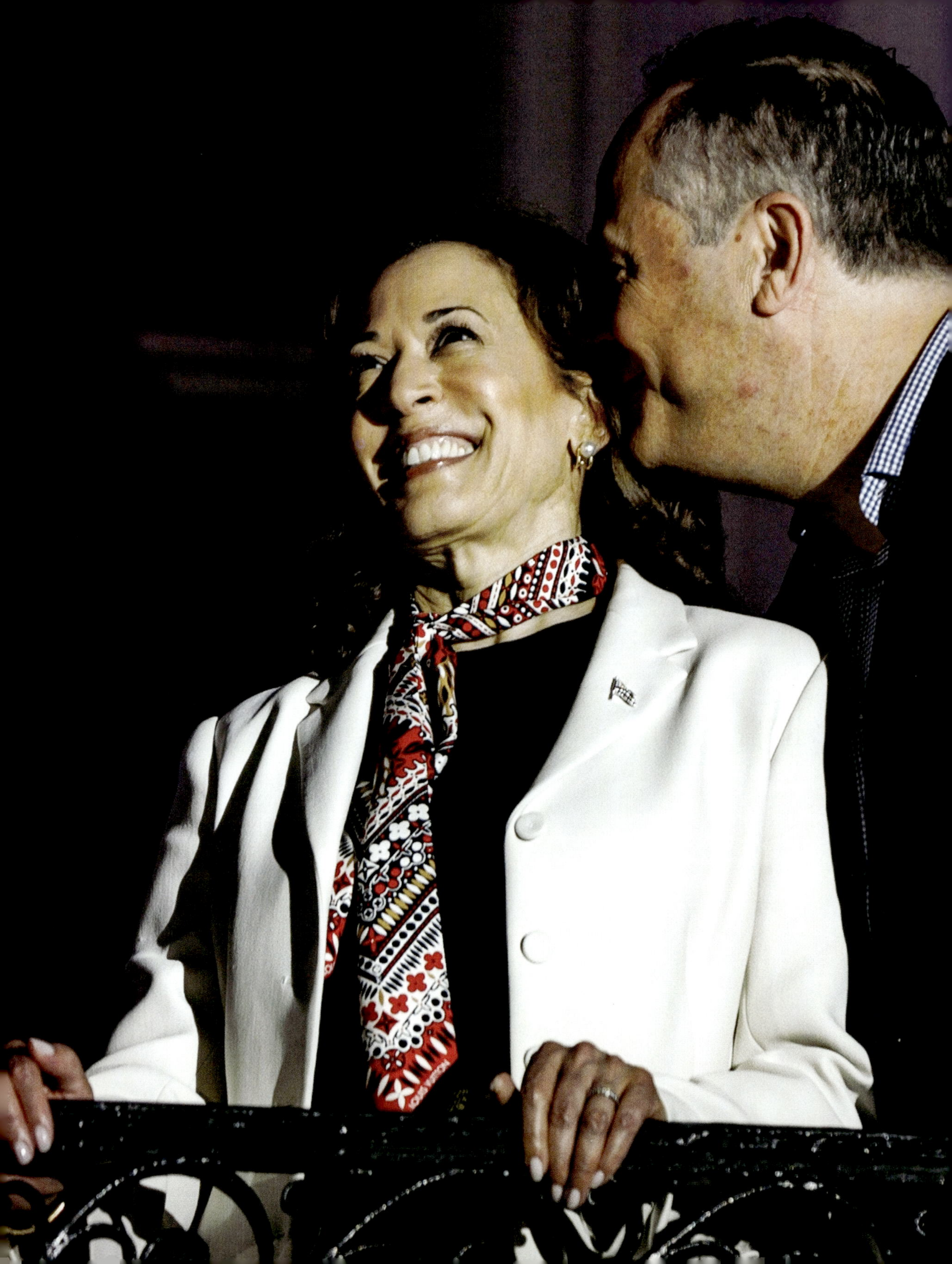

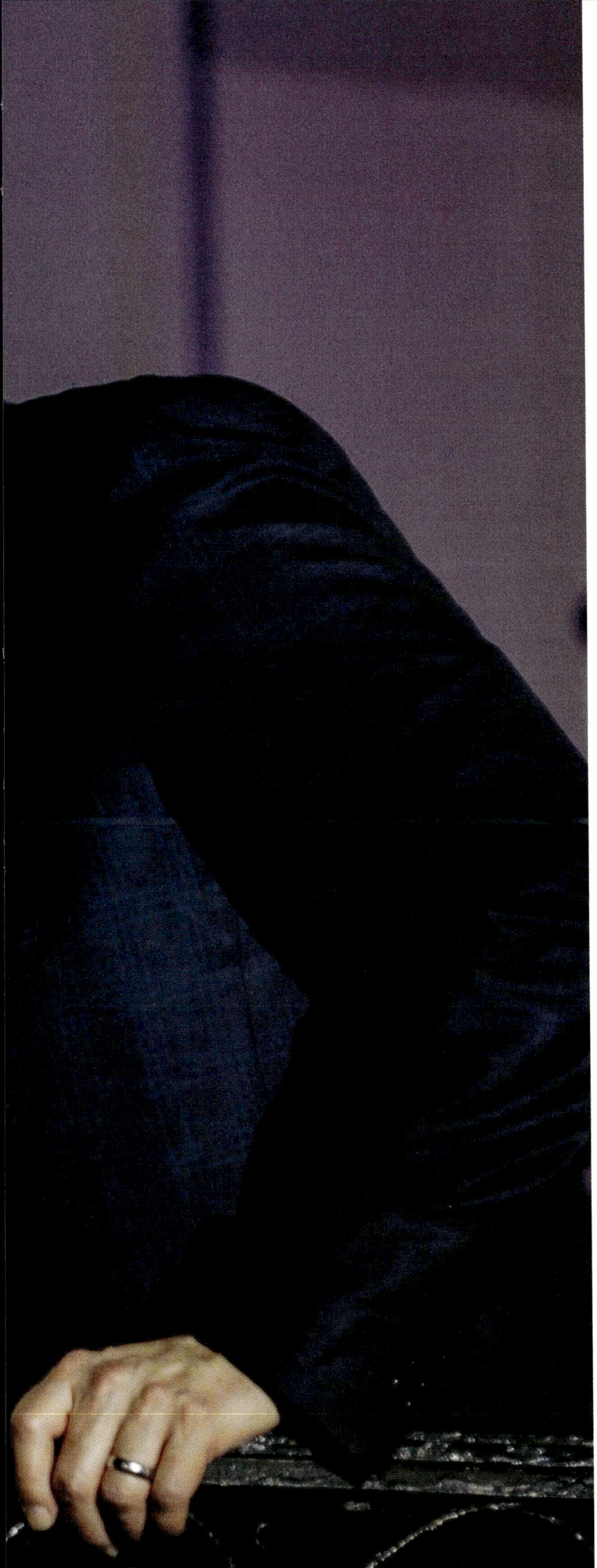

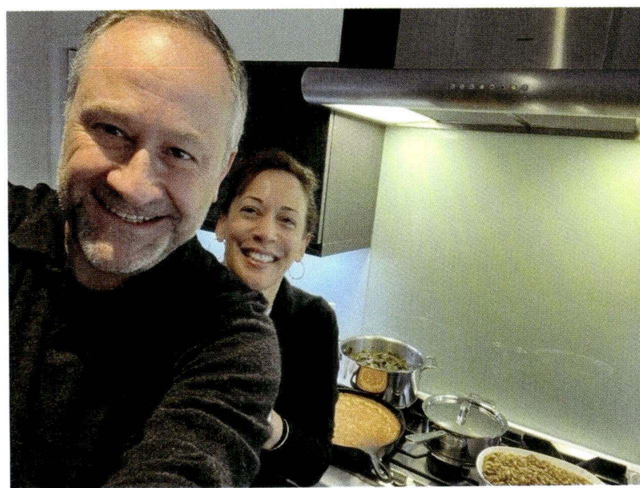

HARRIS AND EMHOFF in the kitchen cooking the traditional greens, black-eyed peas, and corn bread found in many Black households on New Year's Day.

WHAT ARE they talking about? Second Gentleman Doug Emhoff whispers to Vice President Kamala Harris in July 2024.

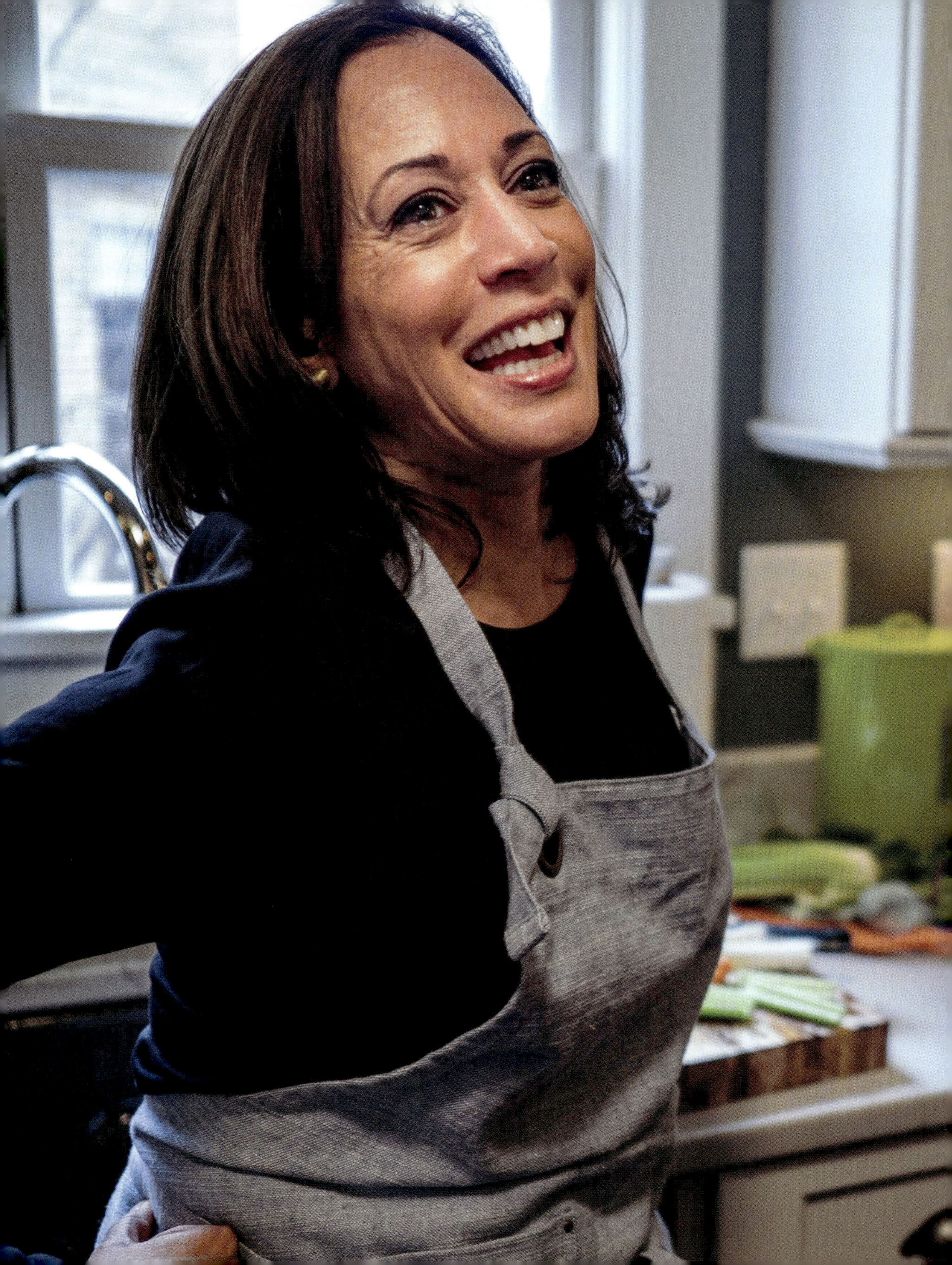

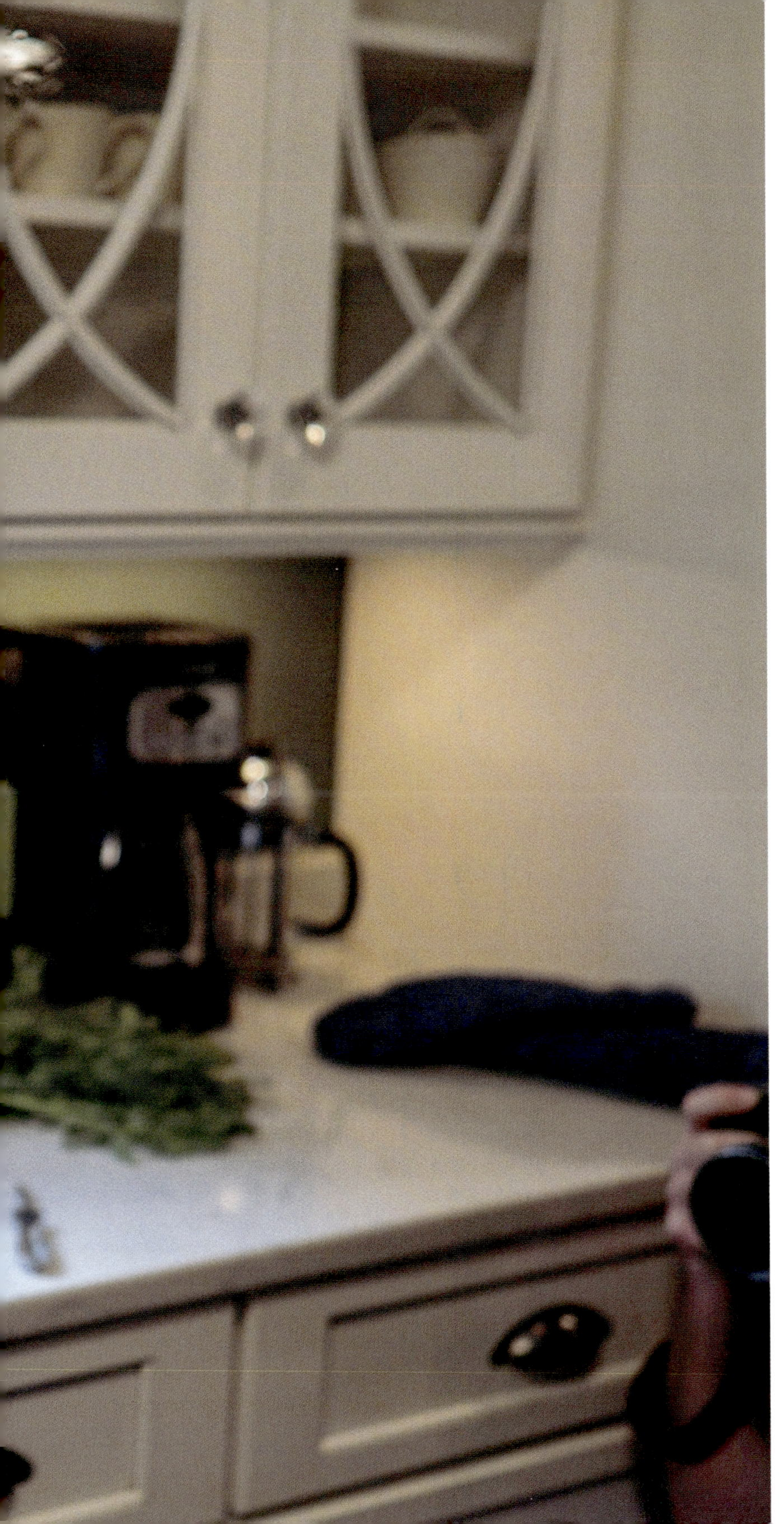

THE VICE PRESIDENT enjoys the art of cooking and family traditions. Among the foods she loves: gumbo, corn bread dressing, and chile relleno made with her mother's recipe.

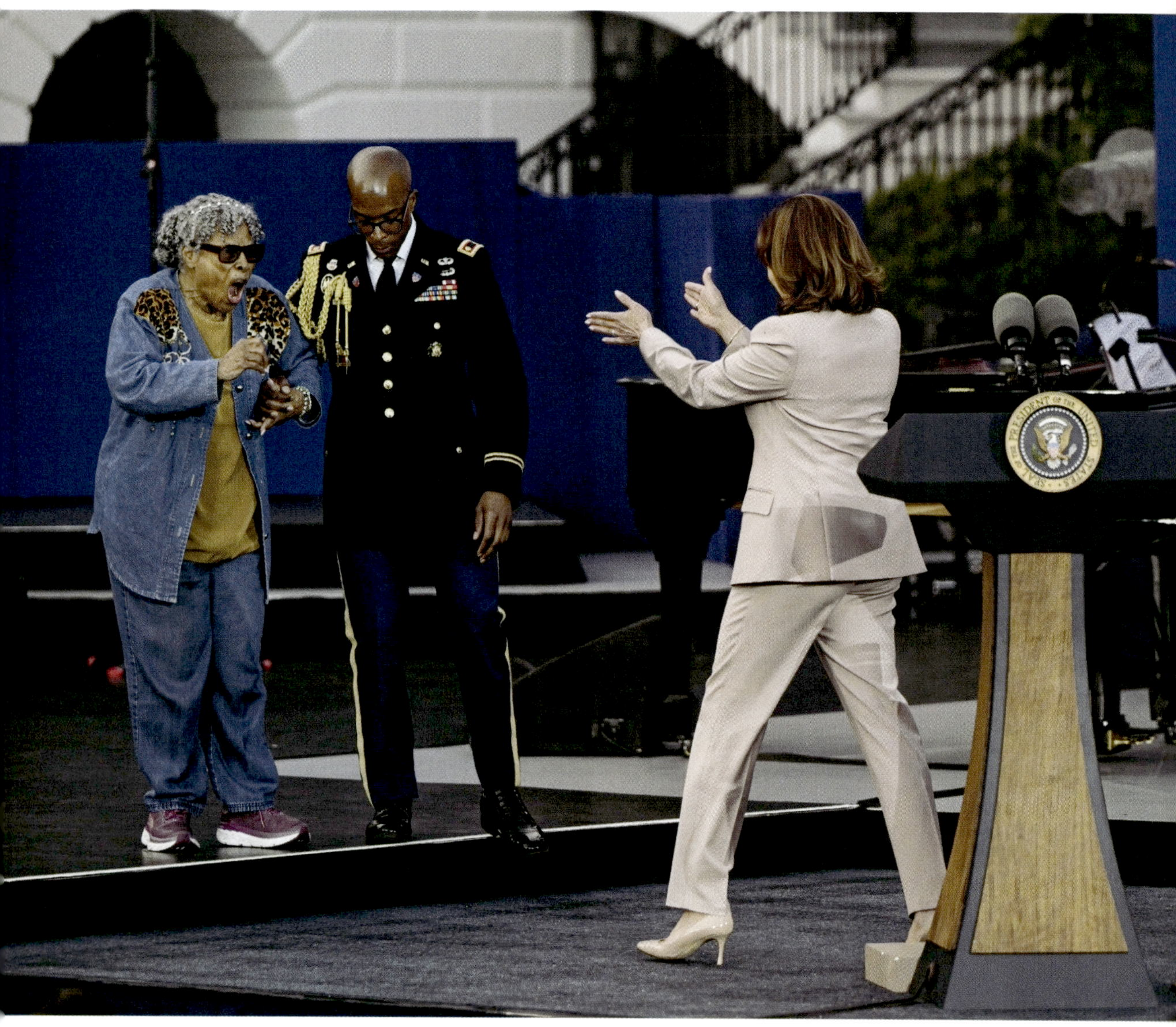

OPAL LEE (*left*), an activist known as the "grandmother of Juneteenth," arrives to make a speech as Vice President Harris (*right*) speaks during the Juneteenth concert on the South Lawn of the White House on June 13, 2023. The White House hosted the concert to mark the nation's newest federal holiday, established in 2021.

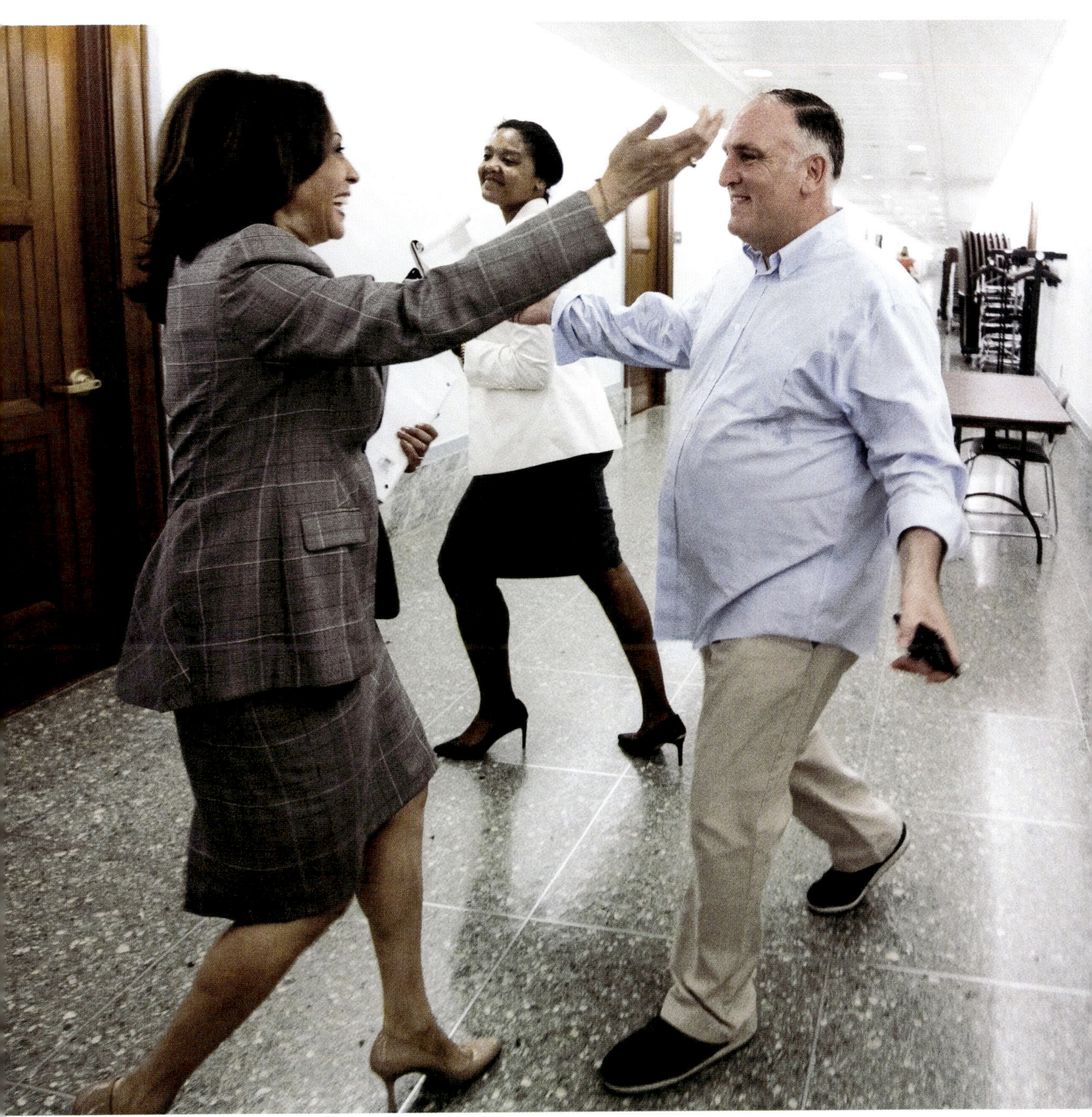

MS. HARRIS has long been a supporter of José Andrés and his efforts to feed the hungry and victims of disaster.

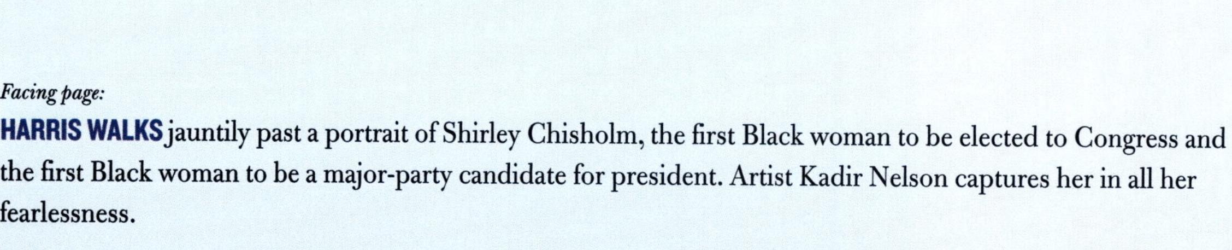

Facing page:

HARRIS WALKS jauntily past a portrait of Shirley Chisholm, the first Black woman to be elected to Congress and the first Black woman to be a major-party candidate for president. Artist Kadir Nelson captures her in all her fearlessness.

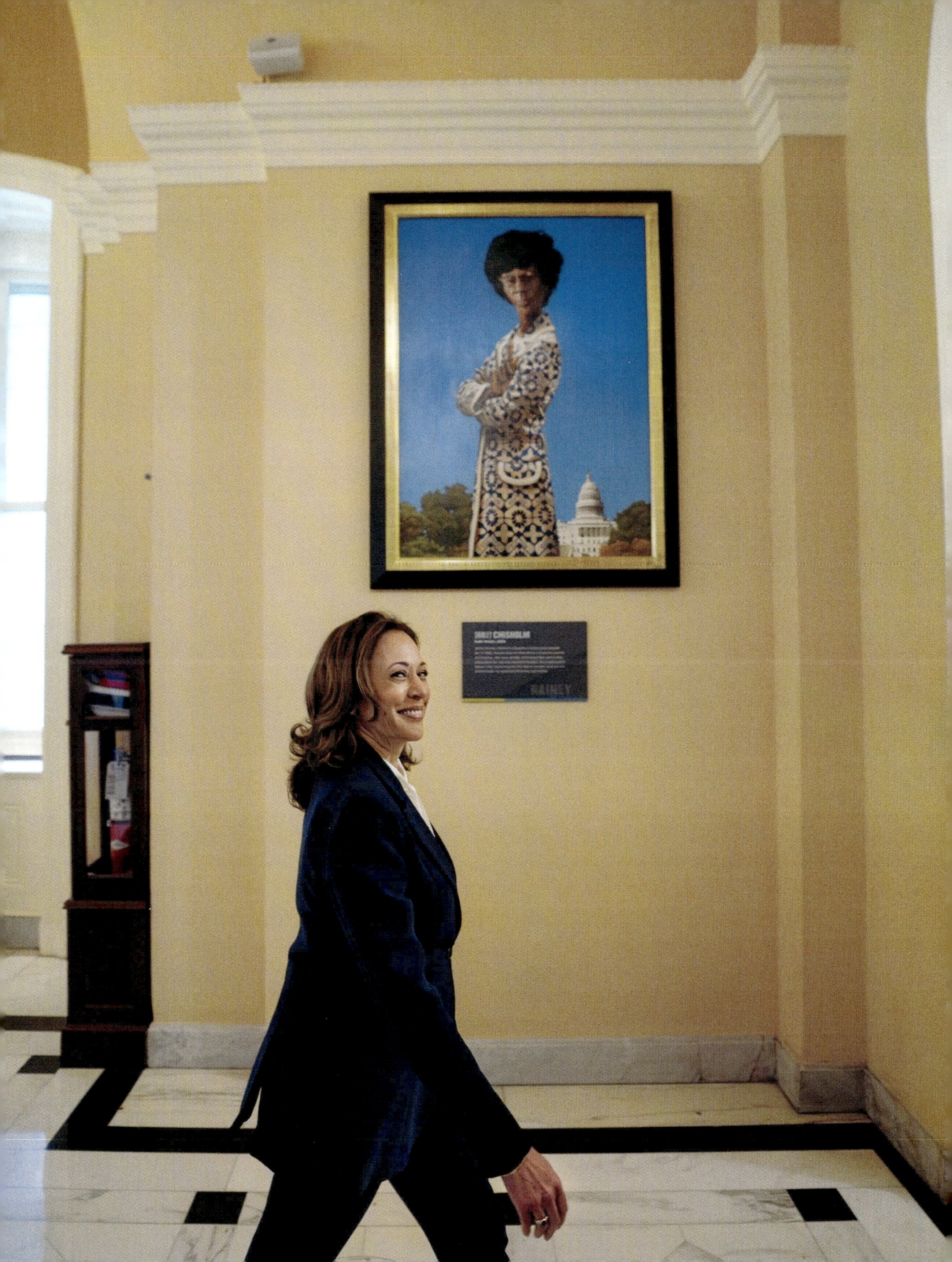

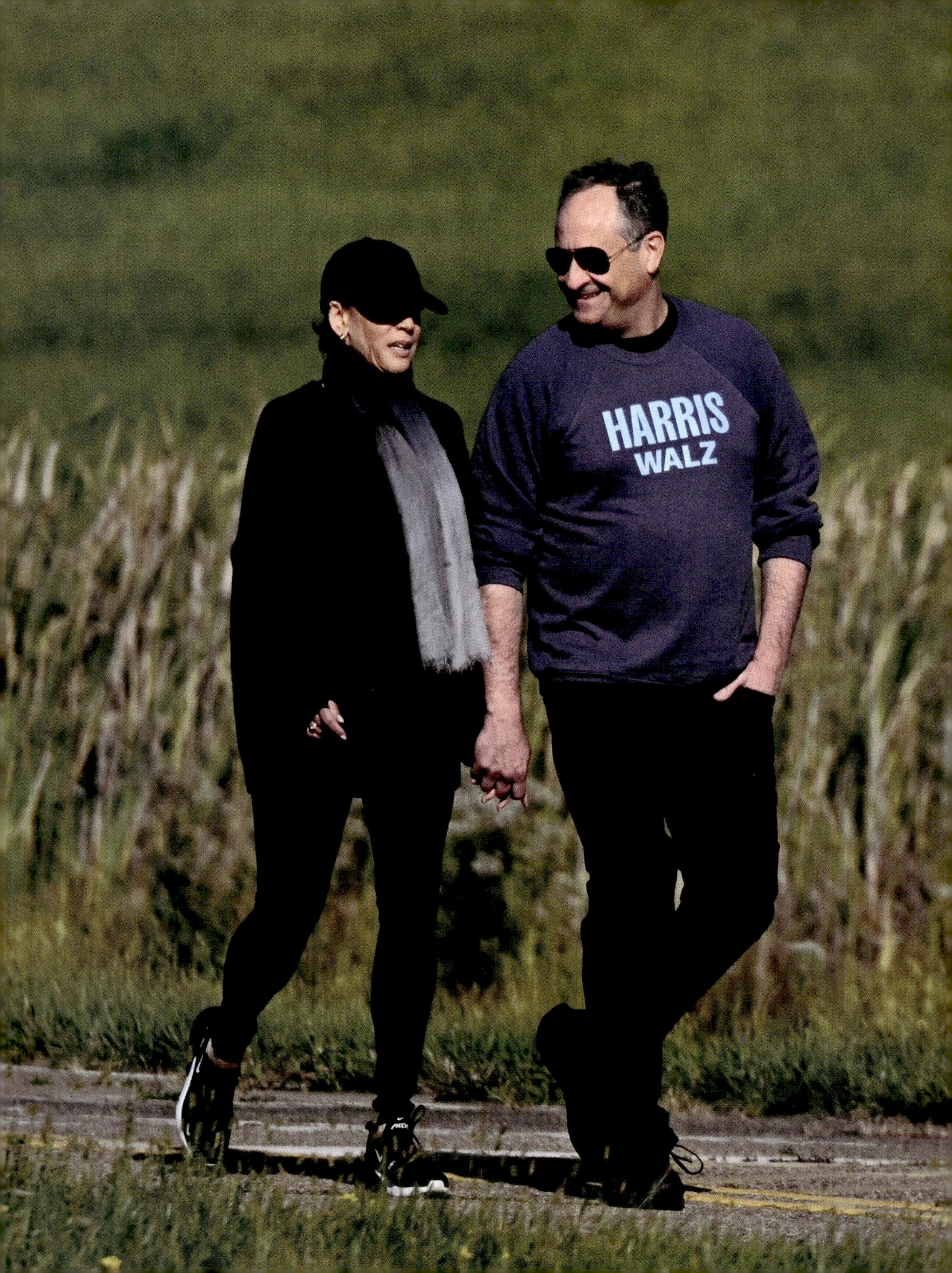
HARRIS
WALZ

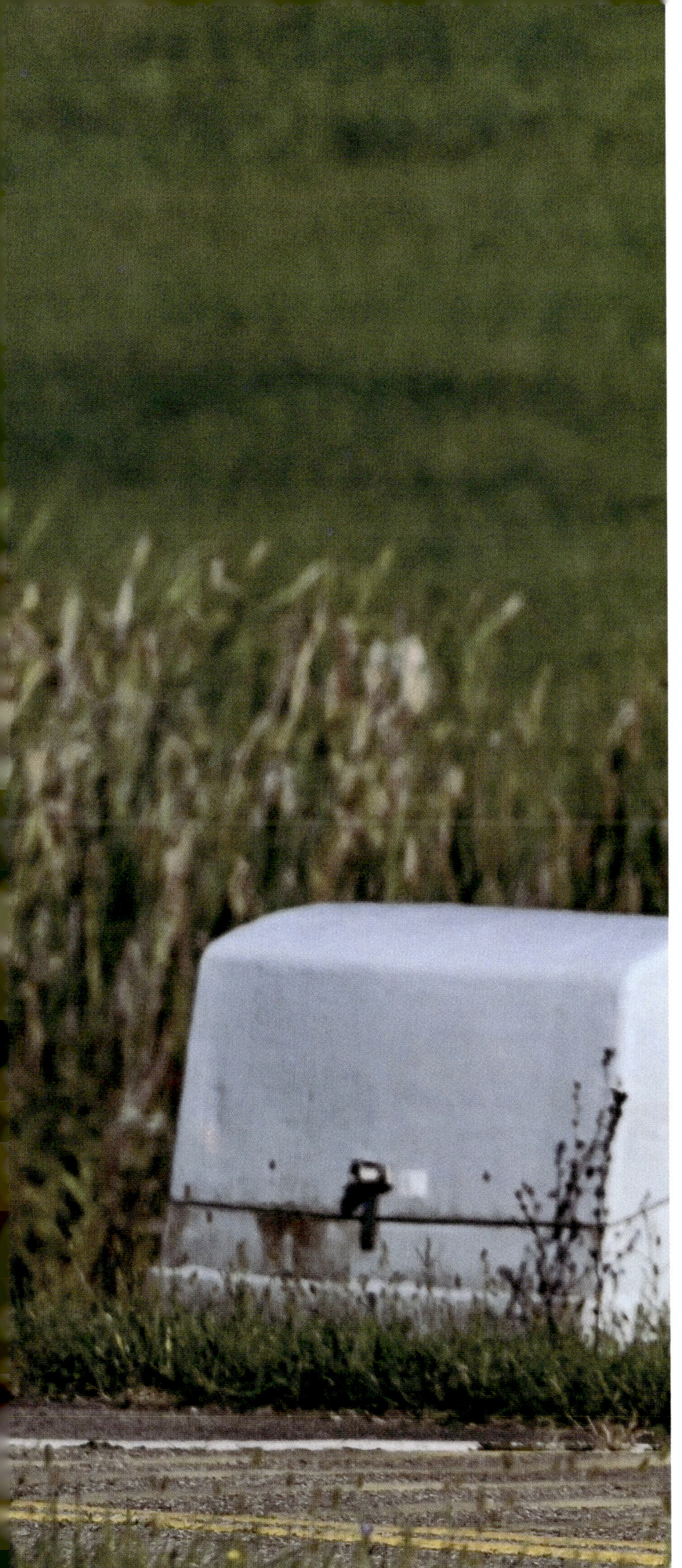

VICE PRESIDENT and Democratic presidential candidate Kamala Harris walks alongside her husband, Doug Emhoff, at a Pennsylvania Air National Guard base in Moon Township, Pennsylvania, on September 8, 2024.

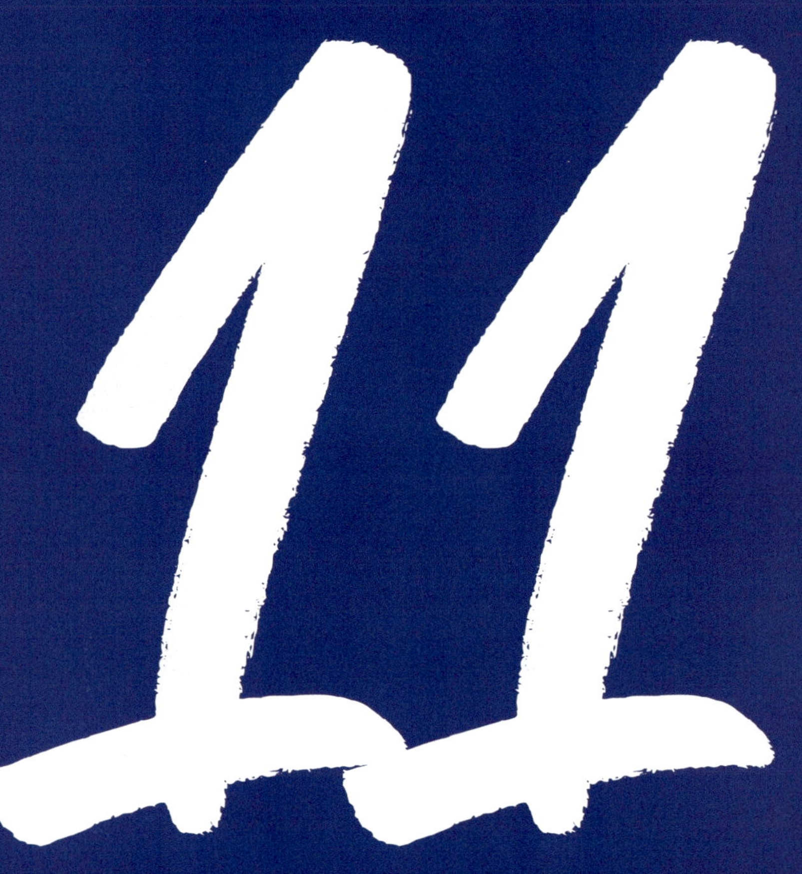
11

AKA & THE SISTERS

"Throughout our history, the leaders of Alpha Kappa Alpha have stood up, spoken out, and done the work to build a brighter future for our nation, including, of course, in 2020, when during the height of a pandemic, you helped elect Joe Biden president of the United States—and me as the first woman elected vice president of the United States."

—KAMALA HARRIS

Reflecting on a photo from the week when she was joining her sorority, Alpha Kappa Alpha (AKA), at Howard University, Harris said in 2020: "One of my names was 'C-Cubed,' for cool, calm, and collected."

Founded in 1908 at Howard, AKA is the oldest Greek-letter service organization in the country organized by Black college-educated women. The AKAs are incredibly important to Harris, and that sisterhood has energized her political campaigns and lifted her when she was down. These photos capture the warmth she has for her Howard friends and other Black women who are part of her network.

A big moment for Harris was her induction into The Links, Incorporated, one of the oldest and largest volunteer service organizations for women of African descent, with a membership of more than 17,000 professionals. During a 2018 ceremony in Los Angeles, Harris was visibly moved by her invitation to become the eleventh honorary member, a distinction offered to Condoleezza Rice, Rosa Parks, Leontyne Price, and Constance Baker Motley, among others, before her.

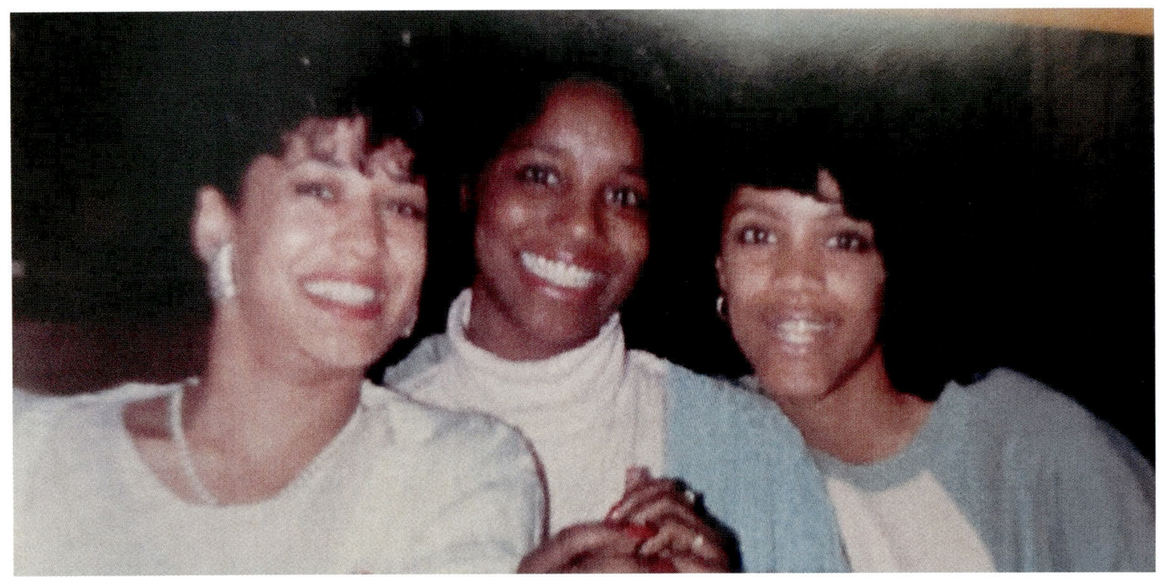

KAMALA HARRIS (*left*), Lisa Johnson Jackson (*center*), and Antoinette Smith in 1986, while they were students at Howard University.

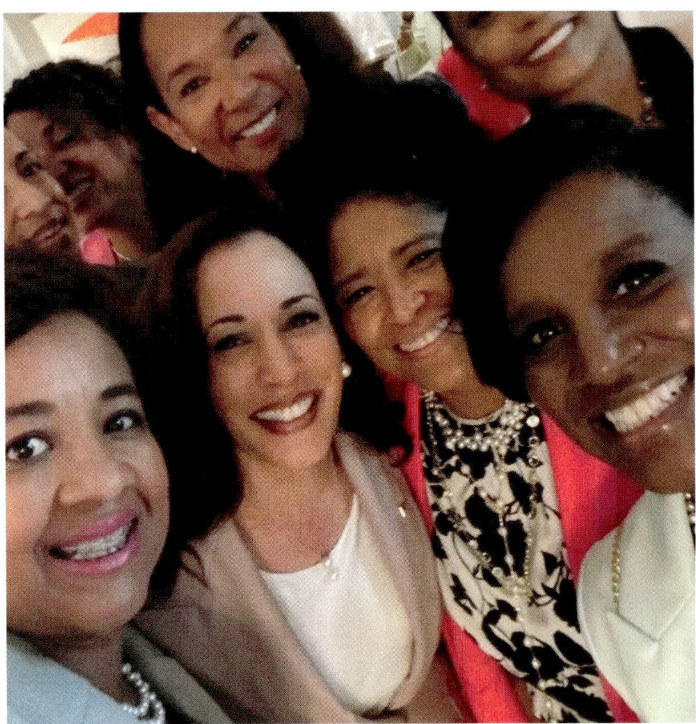

SELFIE with (*back to front, left to right*) Rhonda Pitts Cox, Jaye Wallace West, Jill Louis, Elaine Witter, Kuae Noel Kelch, Harris, Darla Washington, and Lisa Johnson Jackson.

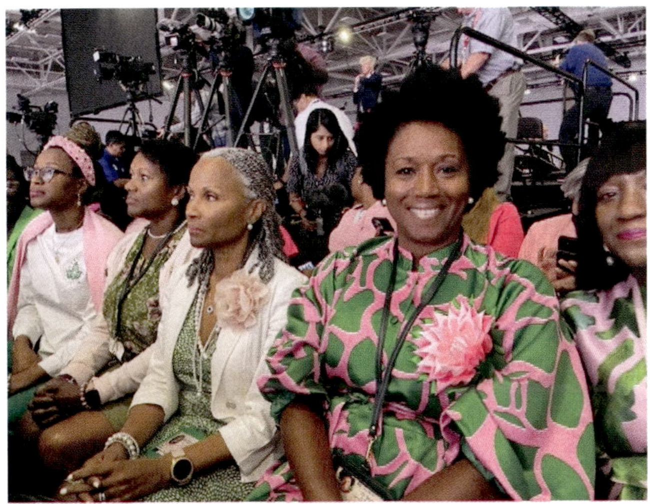

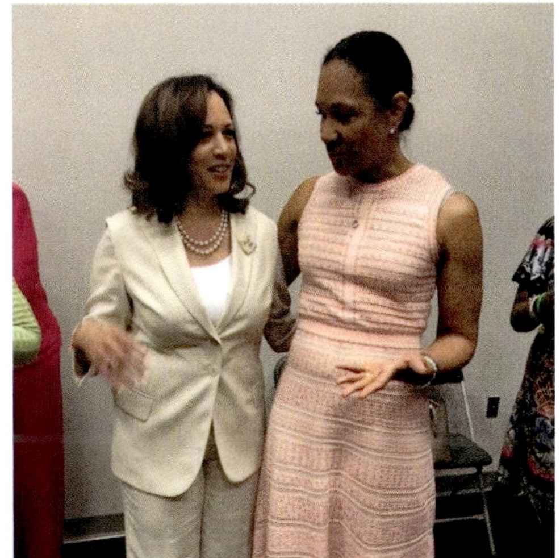

Left to right:

The VP's LINE SISTERS at the seventy-first annual meeting of the Boule, a Black sorority organization.

KAMALA HARRIS with sorority sister Jill Louis.

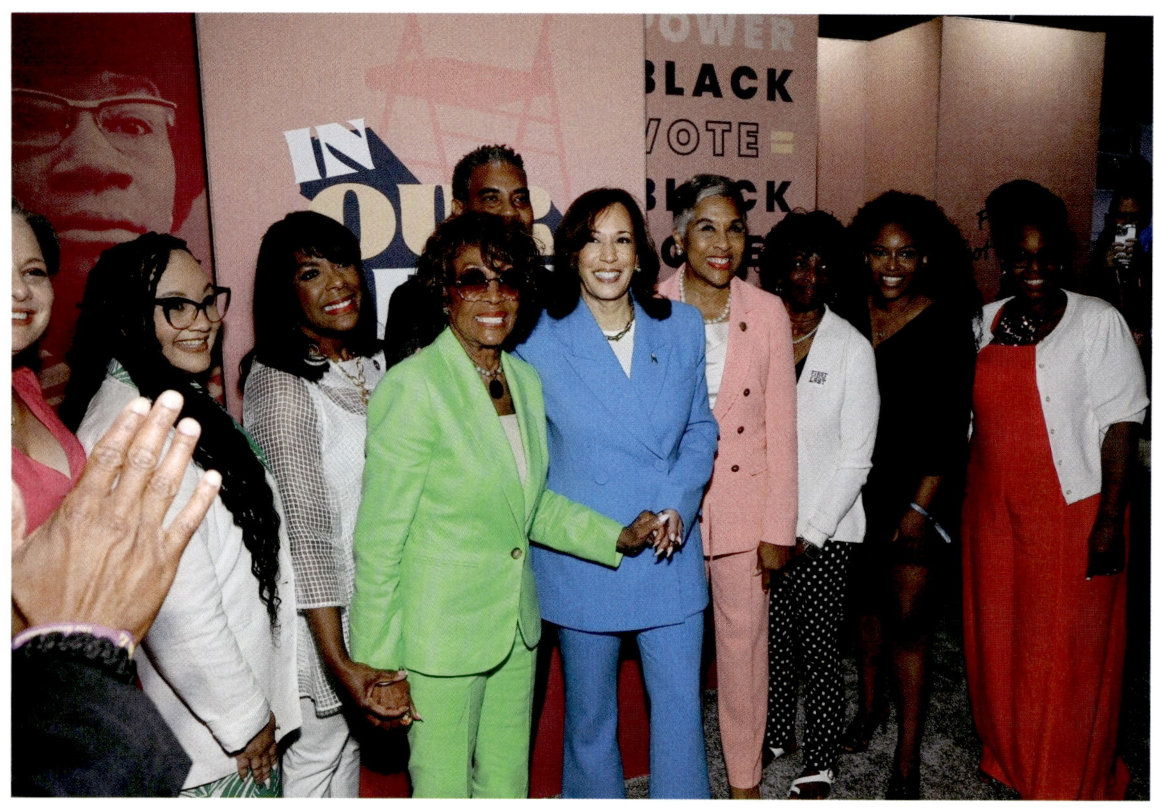

Left to right: Terri Sewell, Maxine Waters, Steven Horsford, Kamala Harris, Jasmine Crockett, and Nicole Austin-Hillery, and others attend the Essence Festival of Culture at Ernest N. Morial Convention Center on July 6, 2024, in New Orleans.

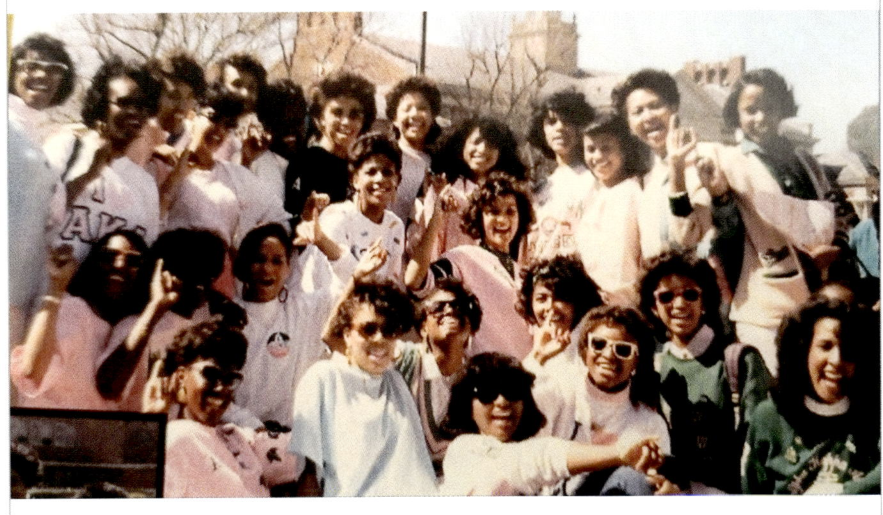

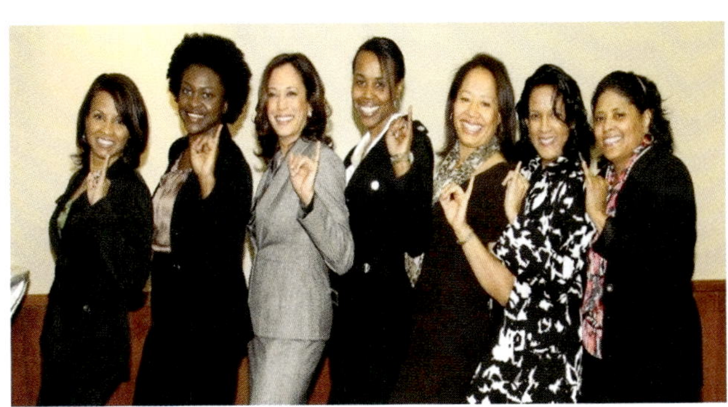

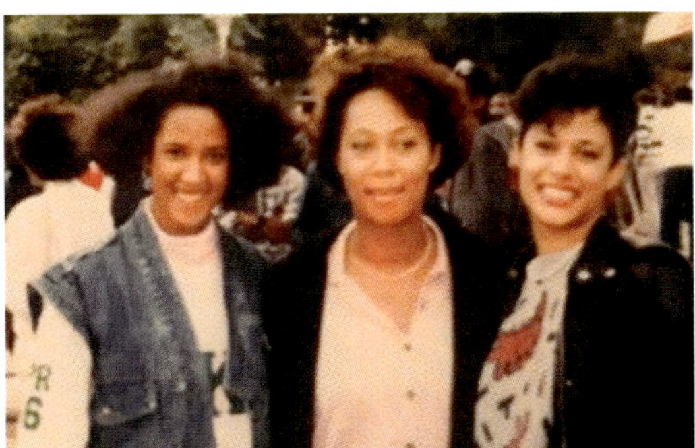

Above, clockwise:

KAMALA HARRIS and her line sisters on the yard at Howard University during the spring of 1986.

THE AKA SISTERS in full force in a vintage photograph.

THE AKA line sisters surround Kamala Harris at a convocation speaker reception in Cramton Auditorium at Howard University in 2014.

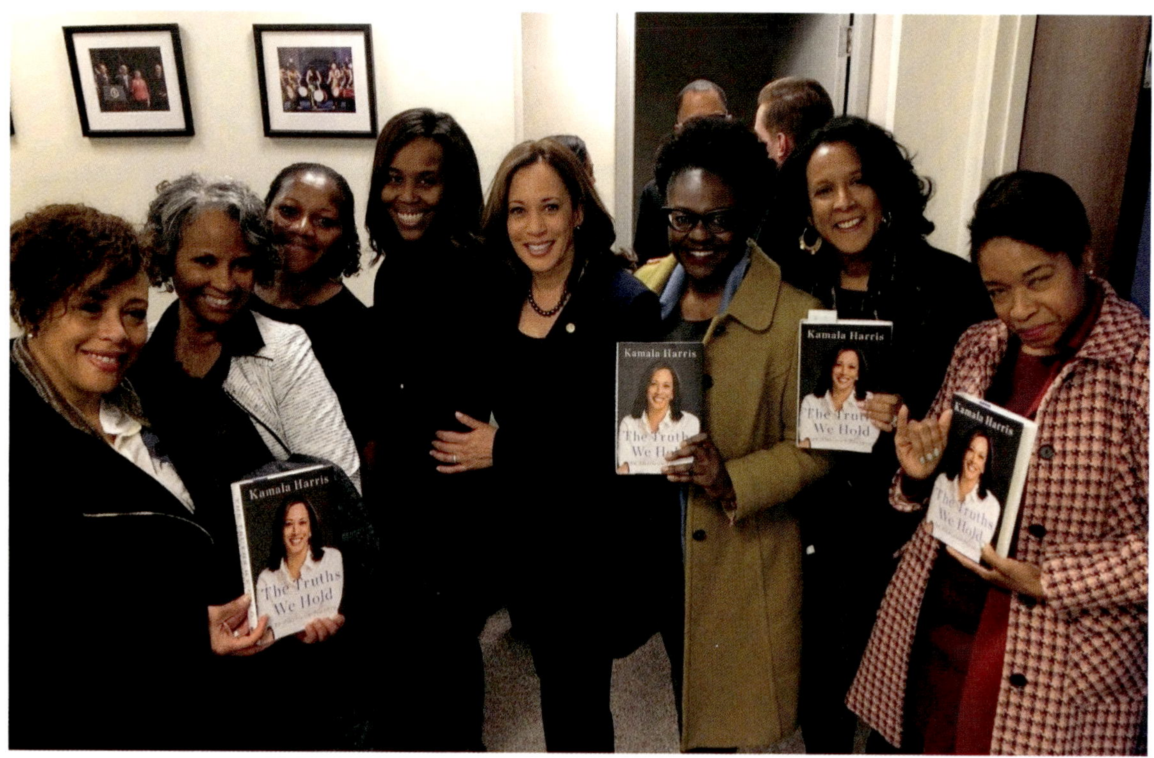

KAMALA HARRIS and her line sisters at a book event for her memoir, *The Truths We Hold*, at George Washington University in 2019.

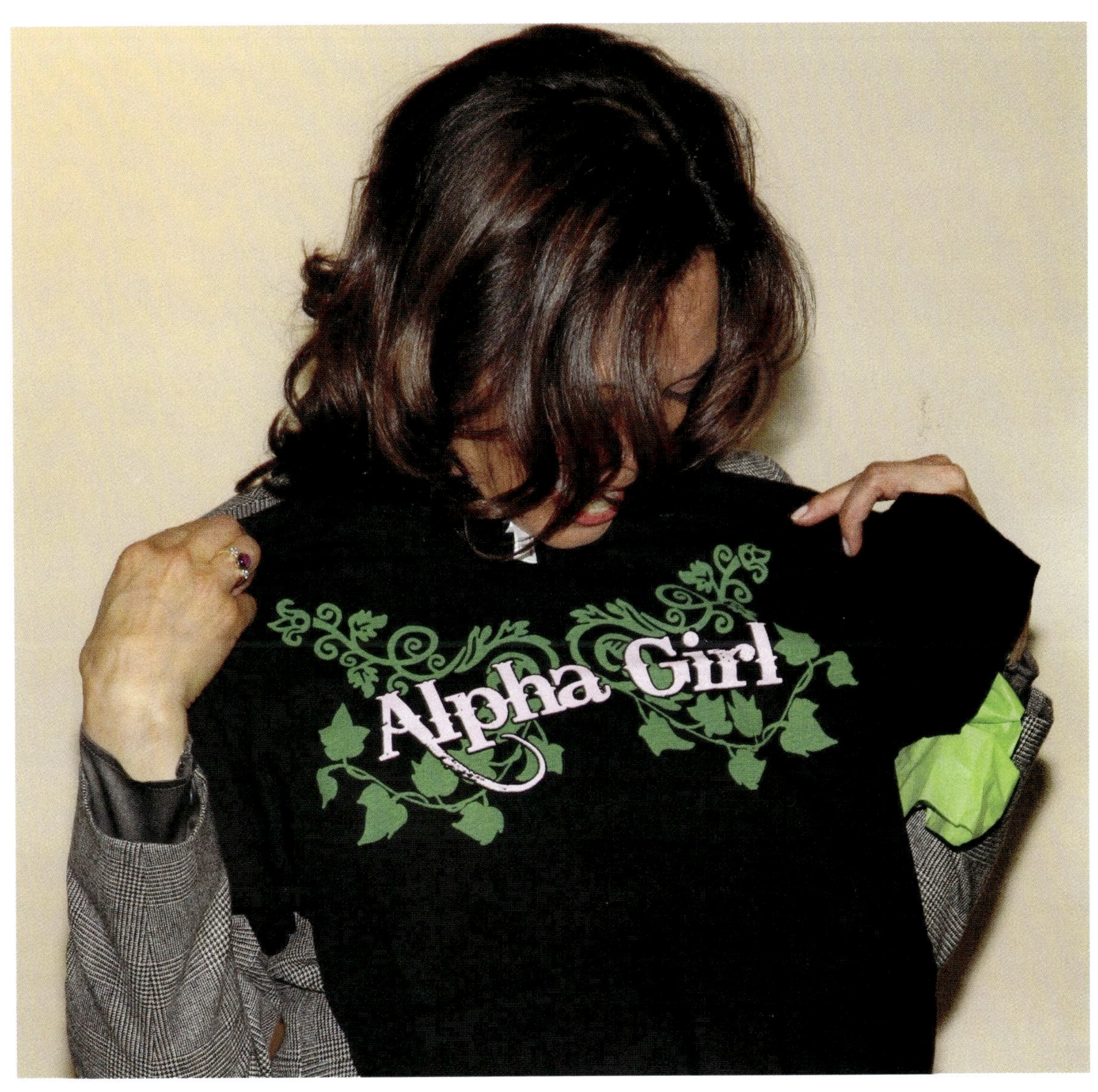

KAMALA HARRIS receiving a gift of an AKA T-shirt.

12

ARTISTIC EXPRESSION

"It's a no-brainer that if we want our children to thrive, we need to reinvest in America's public education system—including the arts."

—KAMALA HARRIS

Artists for Kamala is a collective of some of the most notable contemporary artists in America.

They include Simone Leigh, George Condo, Carrie Mae Weems, Annie Leibovitz, Hank Willis Thomas, Judy Chicago, Shepard Fairey, Glenn Ligon, Jeff Koons, and many others who committed to donating some of their work to support Harris's campaign. But artistic expression in politics extends to the button makers, the jacket makers, the T-shirt makers, the poster makers, and the action-figure makers, too.

The photos here are a sample platter of artistic expression.

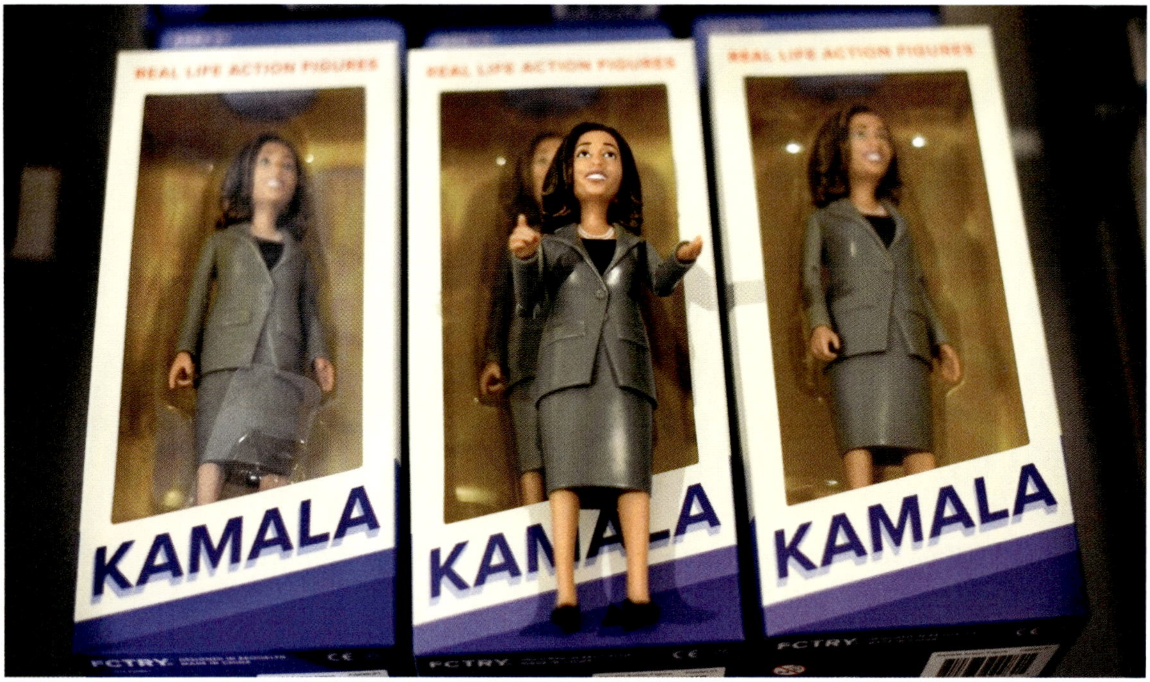

VICE PRESIDENT KAMALA HARRIS action figures for sale in a store in New Mexico.

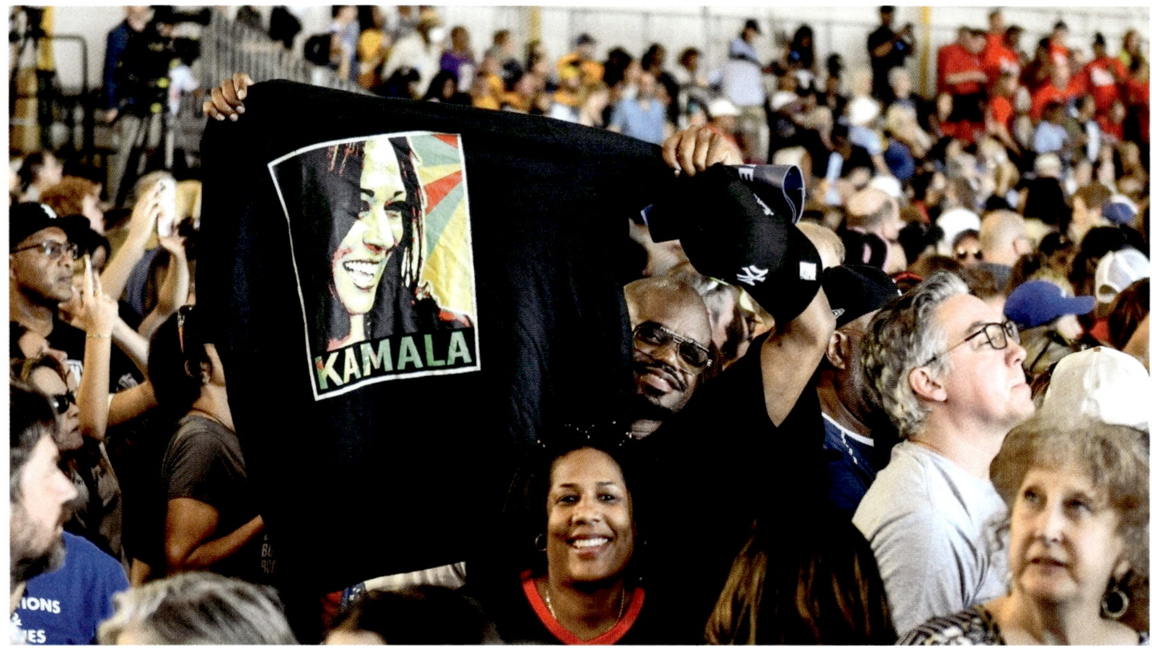

AN ATTENDEE holds up his Kamala Harris T-shirt as Vice President Harris and Governor Tim Walz hold a presidential campaign rally at Detroit Metropolitan Wayne County Airport in Romulus, Michigan, on August 7, 2024.

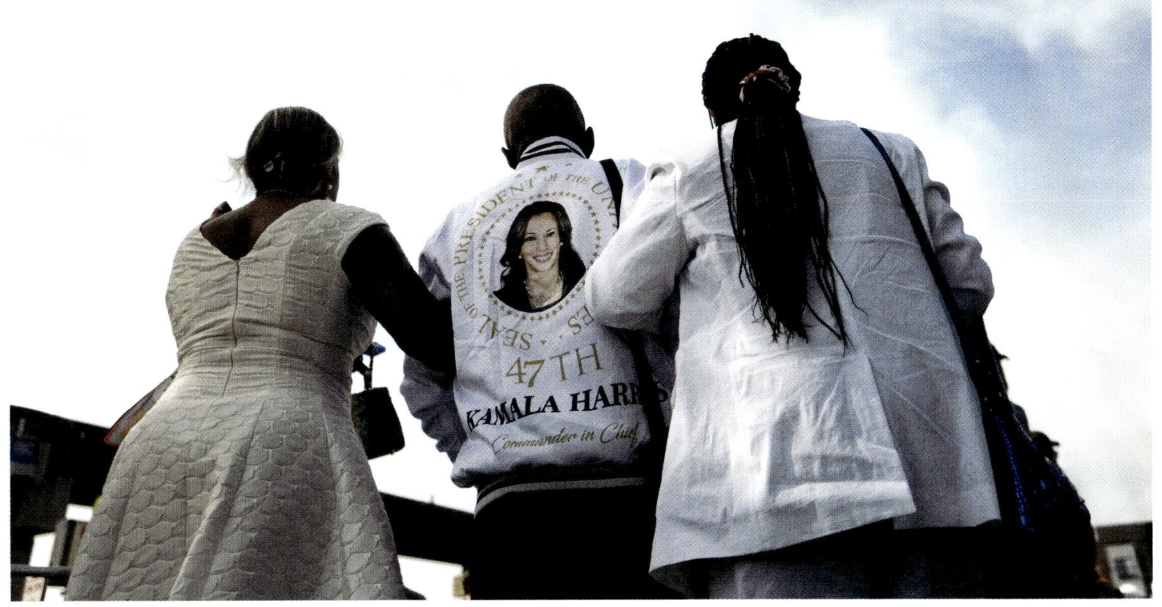

DELEGATE DANNY STONE of Georgia at the Democratic National Convention, rocking a Kamala Harris jacket.

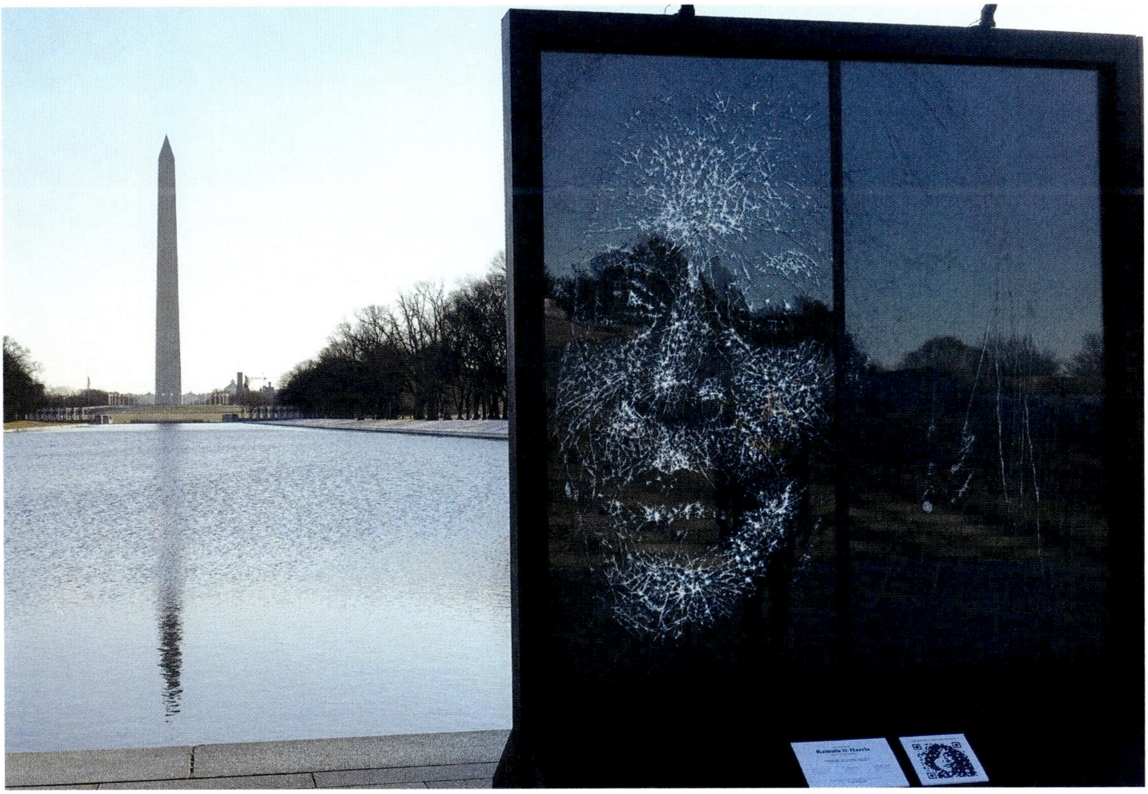

SIMON BERGER'S *Glass Ceiling Breaker*, based on Celeste Sloman's portrait of Vice President Kamala Harris, on the National Mall in Washington, DC, in 2021.

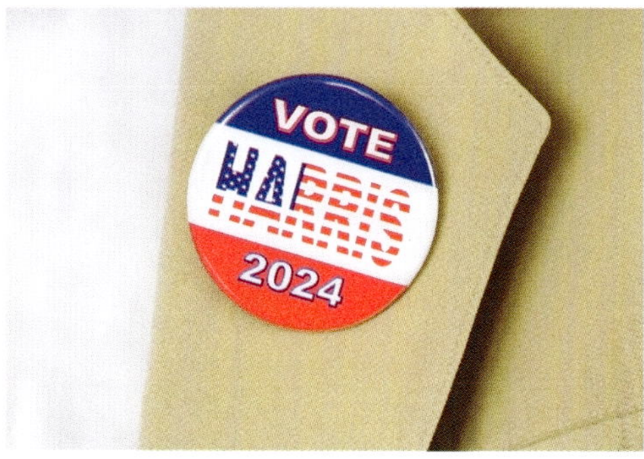

A CAMPAIGN button promoting Kamala Harris for president, shot in August 2024 in London.

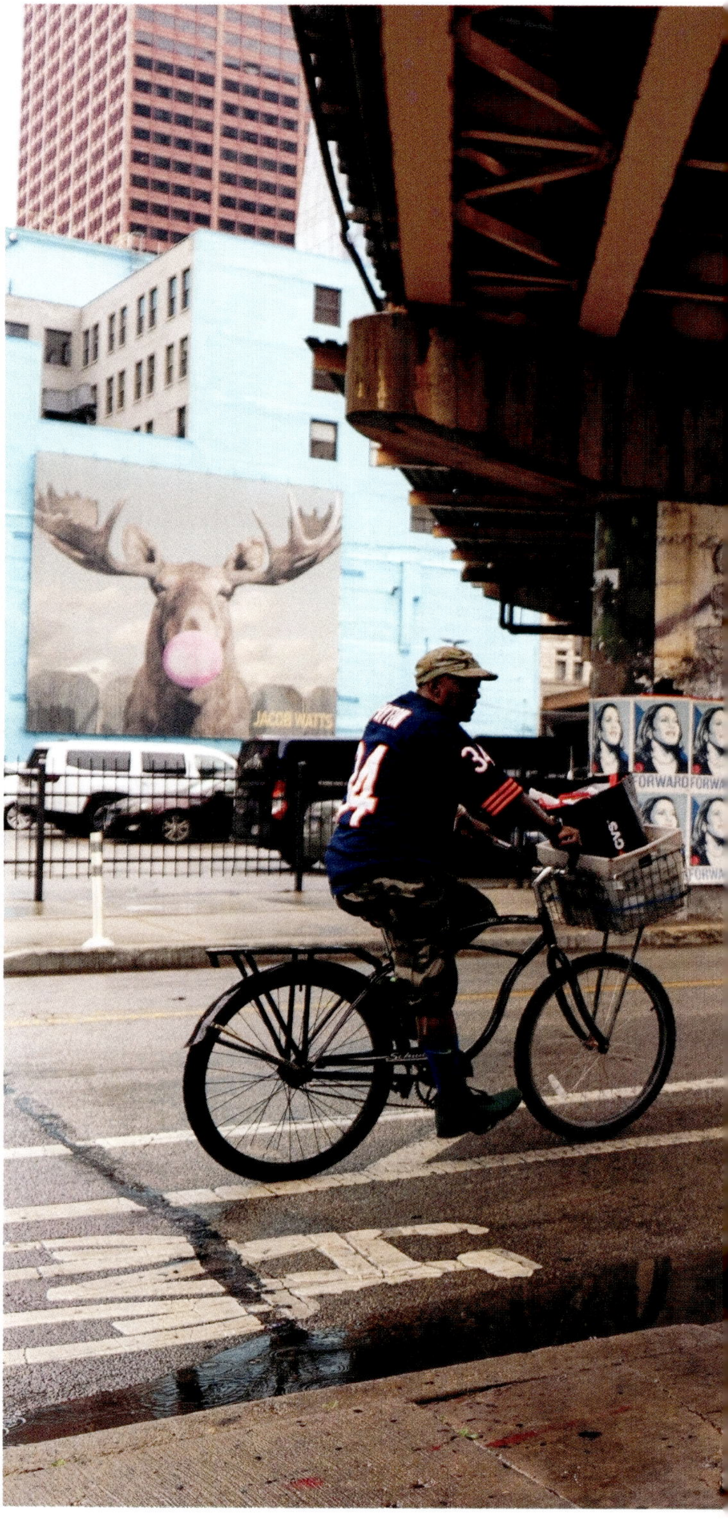

POSTERS OF Vice President Kamala Harris in the Loop neighborhood ahead of the Democratic National Convention in Chicago, August 15, 2024.

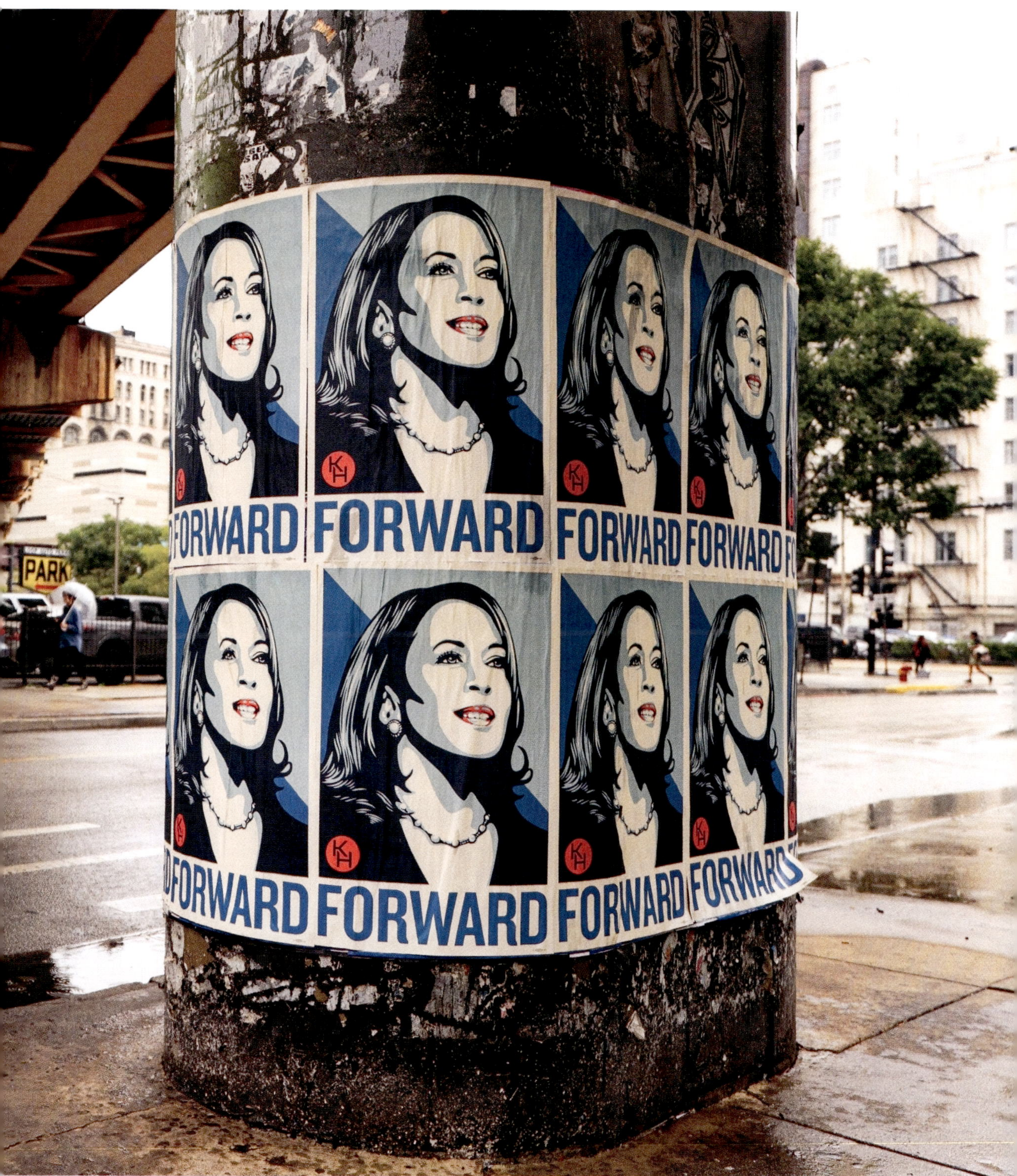
KH
FORWARD
KH
FORWARD
KH
FORWARD
KH
FORWARD
KH
FORWARD
KH
FORWARD
KH
FORWARD
KH
FORWARD
PARK

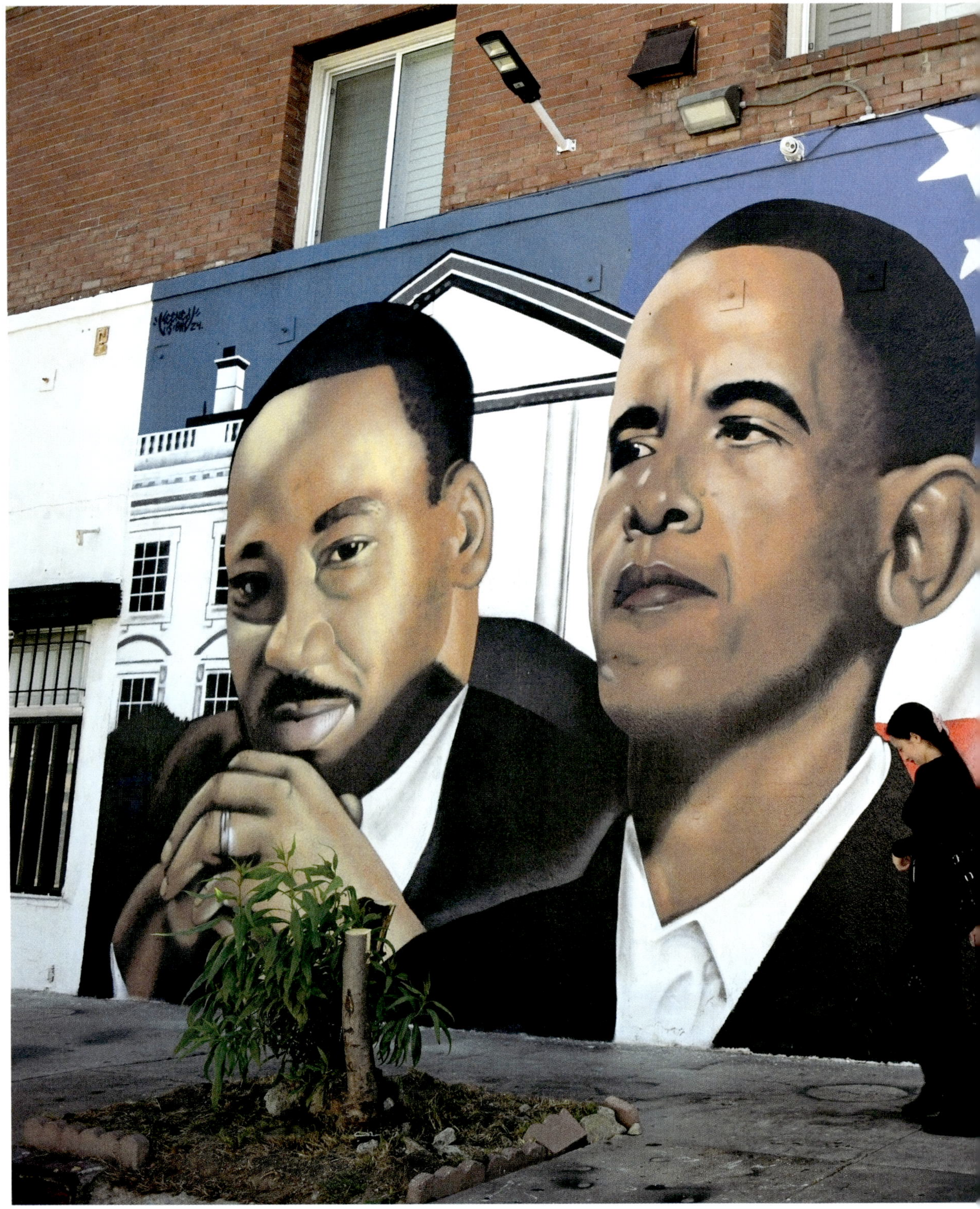

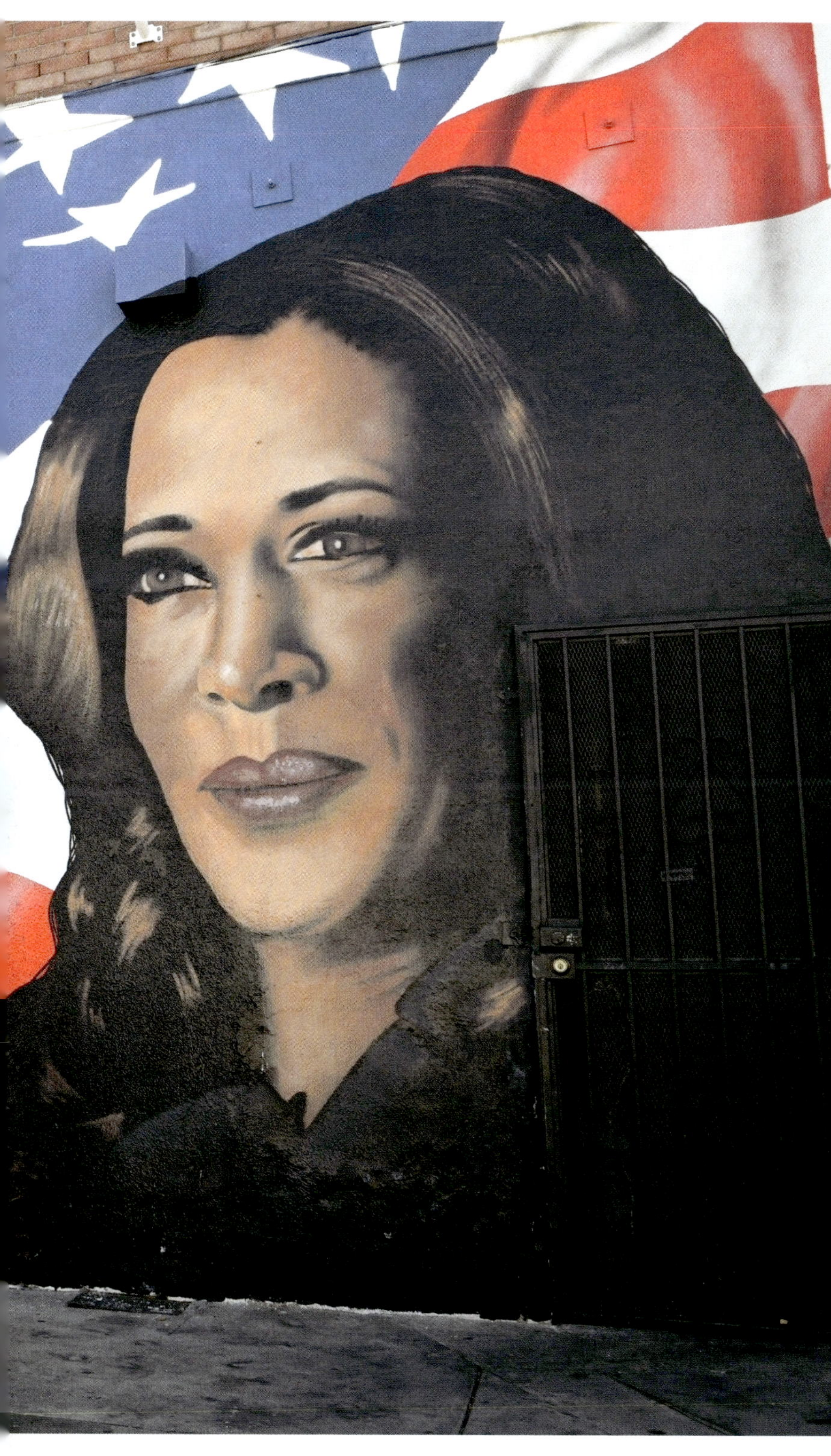

A WOMAN walks past a mural by artist 4eene Vision depicting Martin Luther King Jr., former president Barack Obama, and Vice President Harris in Los Angeles, on August 19, 2024.

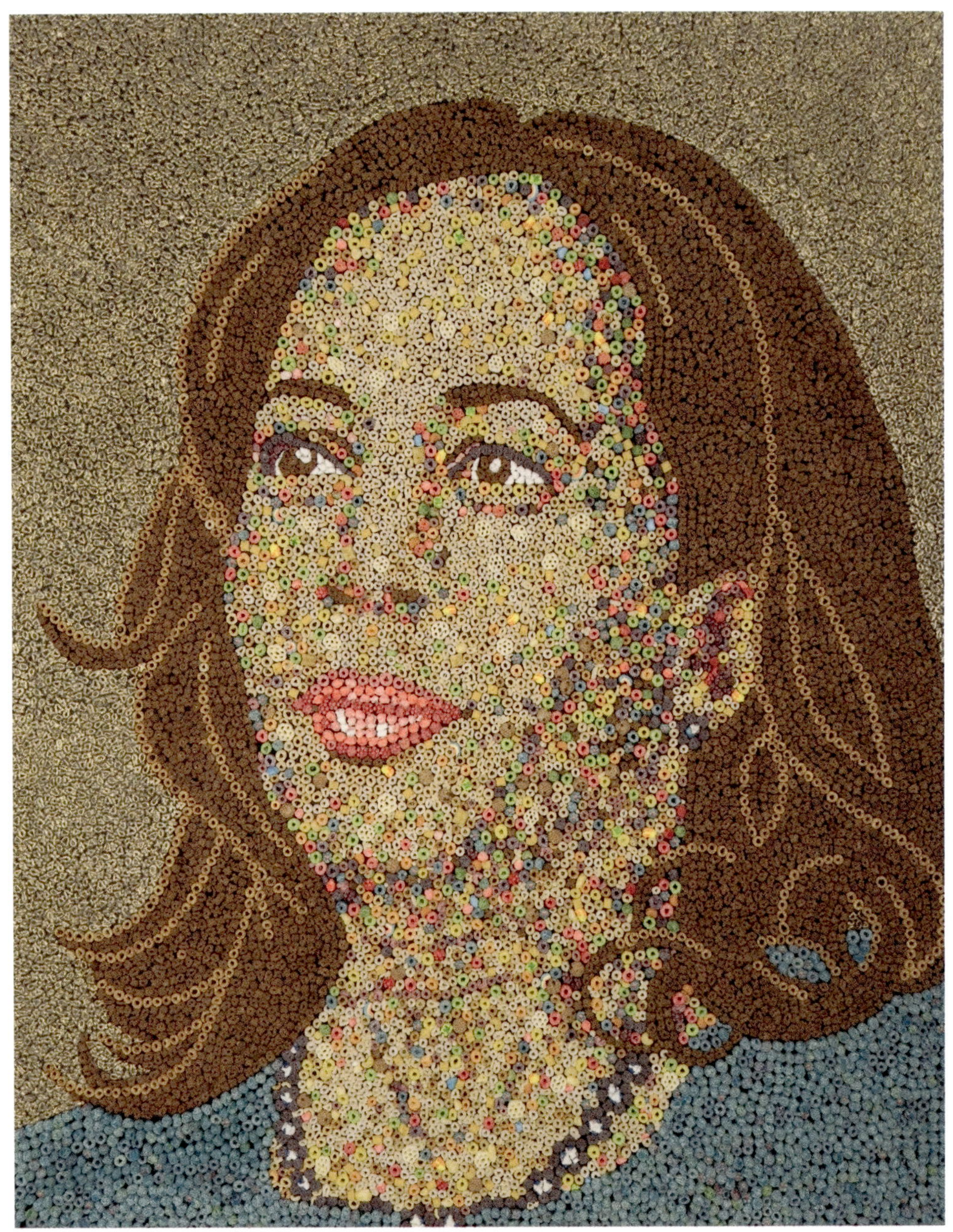

AN INNOVATIVE "cereal art" piece by artists Ryan Alexiev and Hank Willis Thomas. It's called *Breakfast of Champion (Kamala)*, 2024, mixed media.

Facing page:

RENDERED IN POWERFUL NEON at a reception in the arena on the final night of the DNC, in an image taken by Tonya Lewis Lee.

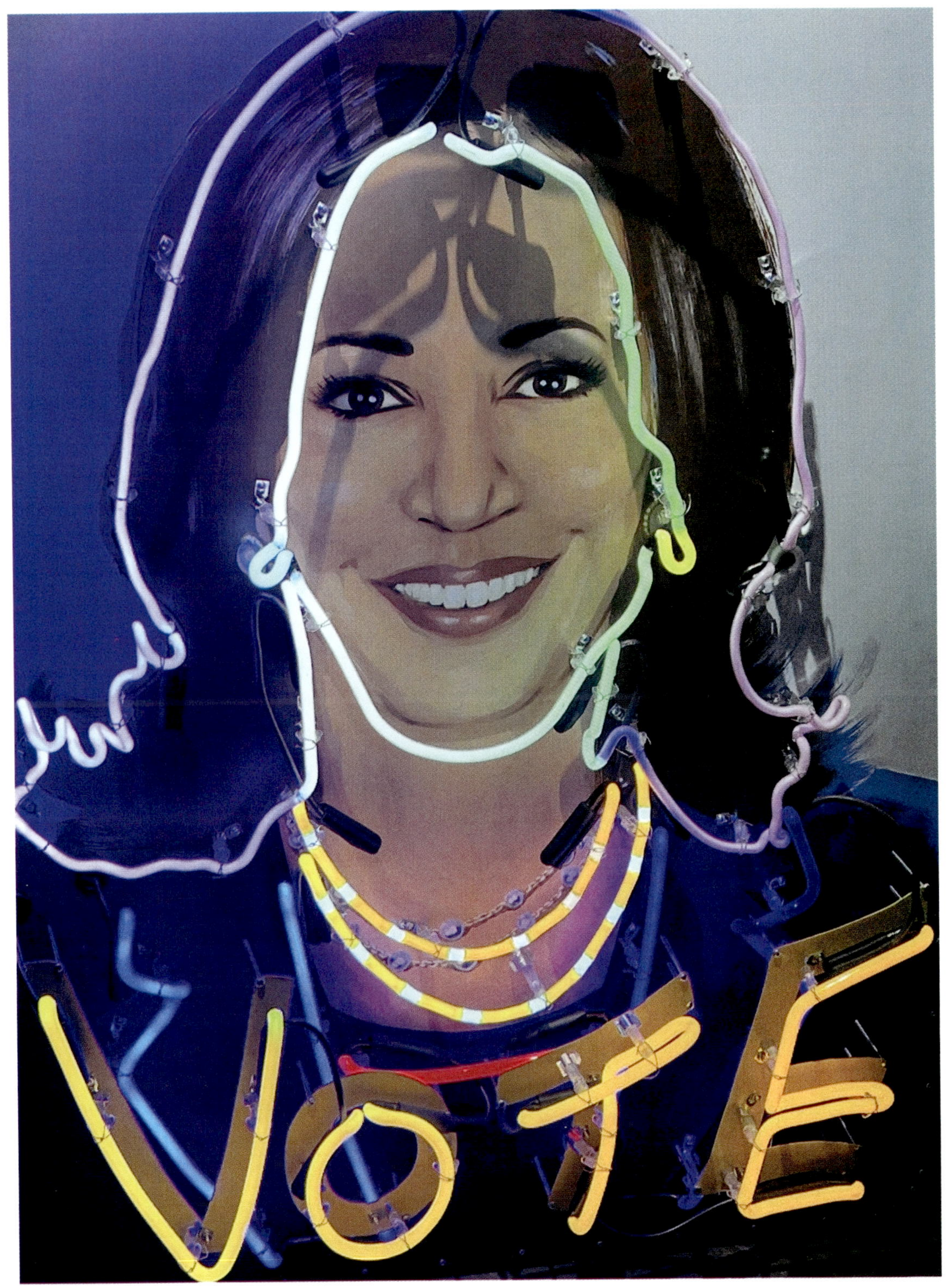
VOTE

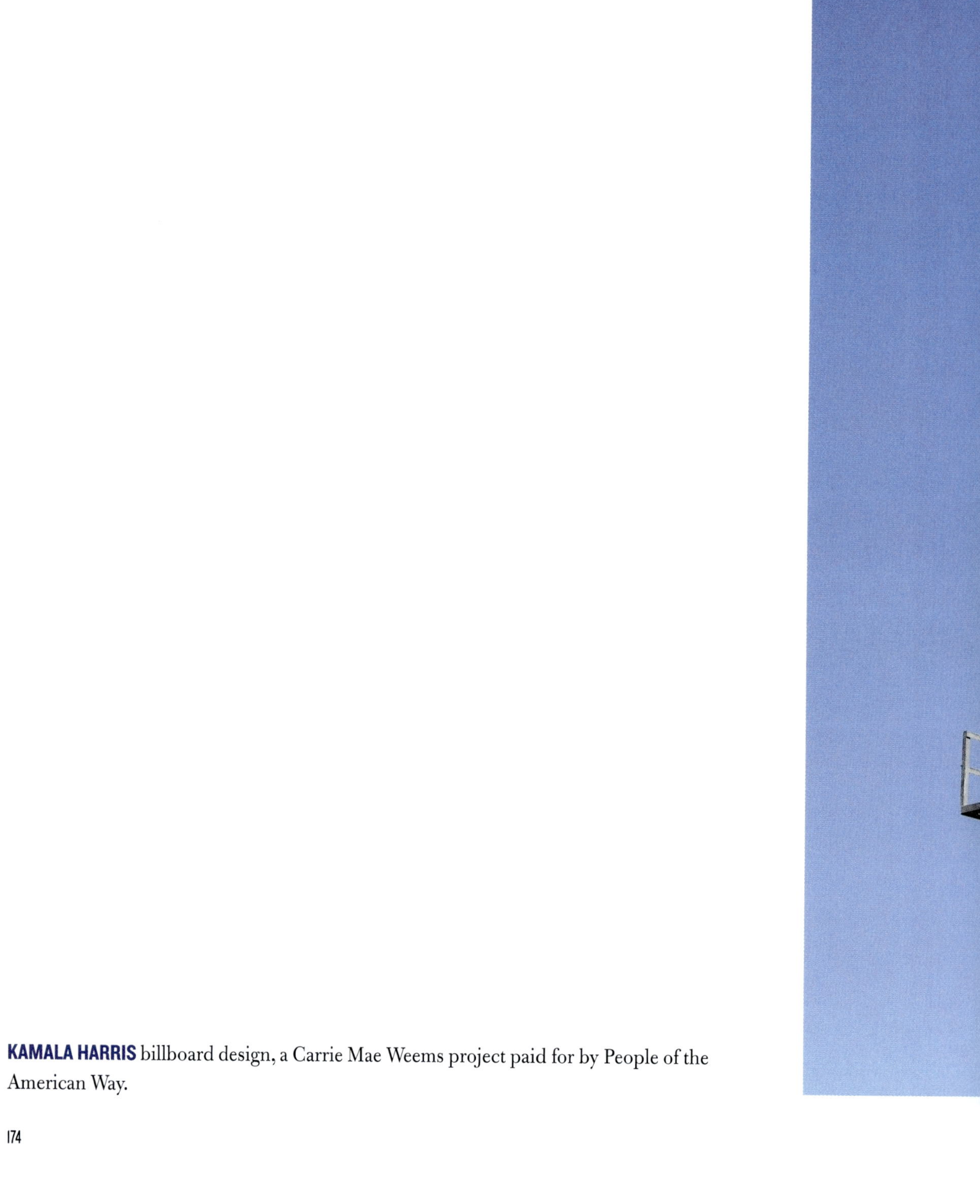

KAMALA HARRIS billboard design, a Carrie Mae Weems project paid for by People of the American Way.

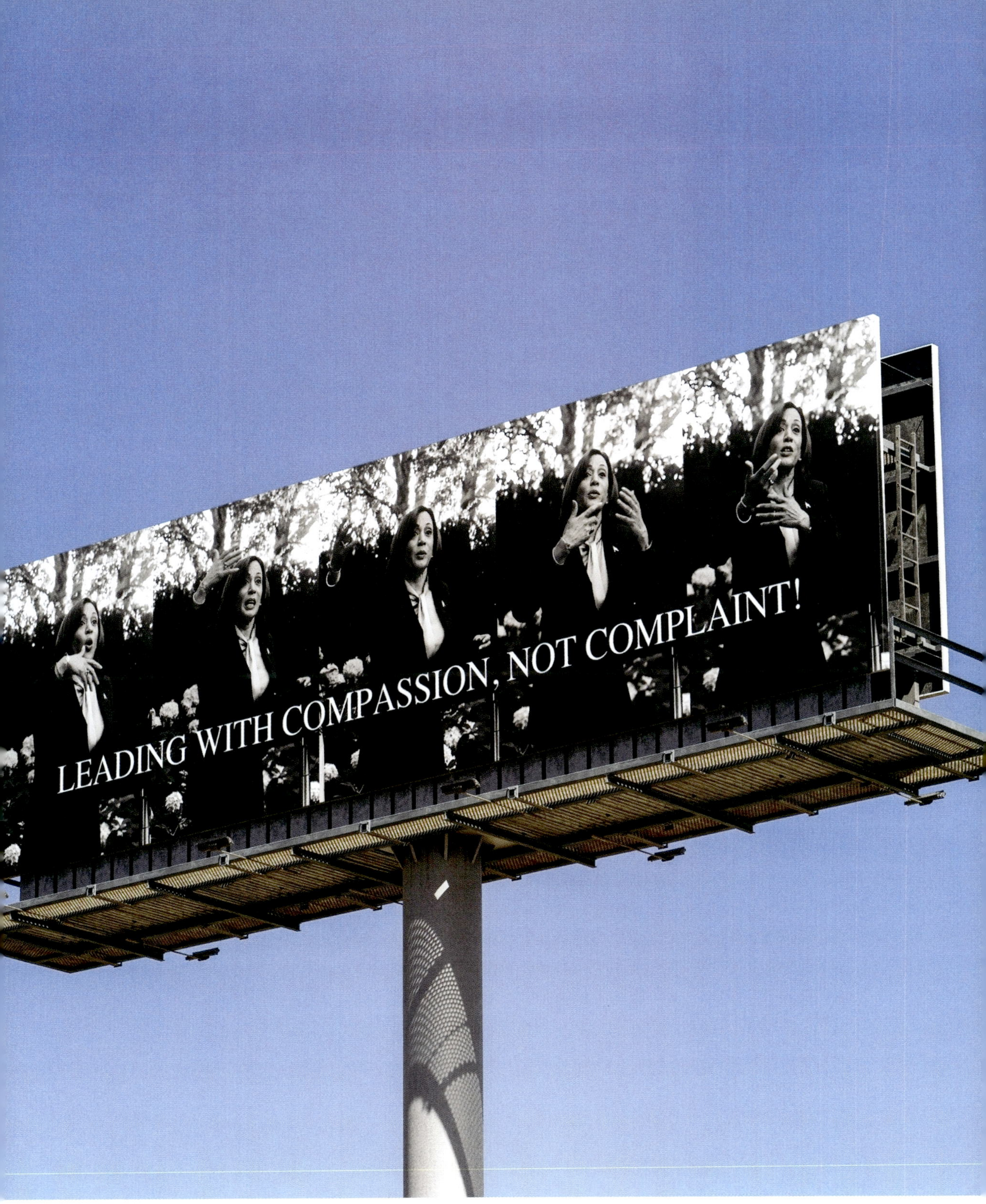
LEADING WITH COMPASSION, NOT COMPLAINT!

ACKNOWLEDGMENTS

We thank Dawn Davis, senior vice president of Simon & Schuster and publisher of 37 Ink, for this inspired idea and for bringing us together again for our second photo-book collaboration. Our agents, Faith Childs and Gail Ross, provided crucial support, and Gail Marshall was invaluable to us. The production team at Simon & Schuster worked gracefully under a tremendous deadline. We want to especially thank Maria Mendez for her extraordinary effort.

Special thanks to all of the photographers and photo agencies. We also thank Kuae Noel Kelch, Karen Hayes, Tonya Lewis Lee, Jasmine Scriven, Mecca Brooks, Christina Caputo, and Niki Kekos, and the artists who created work reflecting on this moment, such as Carrie Mae Weems, Hank Willis Thomas, and Shepard Fairey, among others.

Finally, and most important, we thank our families for their love: Kevin's wife, Donna Britt (who also lent an essential editing hand); and sons, Skye, Darrell, and Hamani; daughter-in-law, Angela; sister, Leisa; and Pop George Hill.

Deb's husband, Hank Thomas Sr., and family Rujeko, Leslie, Michael, Kalia, Masani, Medea, and Giovanni.

ILLUSTRATION CREDITS

Page xv: Robert Gauthier/Los Angeles Times via Getty Images
Page xvii: Pictorial Parade/Getty Images
Pages 4–6: Kamala Harris Campaign
Page 7: Pictorial Press/Alamy
Page 8: Kat Wade/San Francisco Chronicle via Getty Images
Page 9: HUM Images/Universal Images Group via Getty Images
Page 10: Pictorial Press Ltd / Alamy
Page 11: Gabrielle Lurie/The San Francisco Chronicle via Getty Images
Page 16: Bayeté Ross Smith
Page 17: Michael Maloney/San Francisco Chronicle/Polaris
Pages 18–19: Ralf-Finn Hestoft/Corbis via Getty Images
Page 20: Josh Edelson/AFP via Getty Images (top), David Paul Morris/Bloomberg via Getty Images (bottom)
Page 21: Genaro Molina/Los Angeles Times via Getty Images (top), Justin Sullivan/Getty Images (bottom)
Page 22: Tom Williams/CQ Roll Call/Getty
Page 23: Pictorial Press/Alamy
Page 24: Ronen Tivony/SOPA Images/LightRocket via Getty Images (top), Drew Angerer/Getty Images (bottom)
Page 25: Bill Clark/CQ-Roll Call, Inc via Getty Images
Page 26: Saul Loeb/AFP via Getty Images (top), Santiago Mejia/The San Francisco Chronicle via Getty Images (bottom)
Page 27: Jessica Christian/The San Francisco Chronicle via Getty Images
Page 32: Chip Somodevilla/Getty Images
Page 33 (clockwise from top): Adam Schultz/Official White House Photo, Pete Marovich/UPI via Alamy, Tom Williams/CQ Roll Call/POOL
Page 34: Robyn Twomey
Page 35: Adam Schultz/Official White House Photo
Pages 36–37: Bonnie Cash/UPI/Bloomberg via Getty Images
Pages 38–39: Adam Schultz/Official White House Photo
Pages 44–45: Photo by Calla Kessler
Pages 46–47: Drew Angerar/Getty Images
Page 48: Elijah Nouvelage/Reuters
Page 49: Sarah Silbiger/Getty Images
Page 50–51: Stefani Reynolds/Bloomberg via Getty Images

Page 56: Andrew Harnik/AFP via Getty Images
Page 57: Lawrence Jackson/White House Official Photo
Page 58: Drew Angerer/Getty Images (top), Chip Somodevilla/Getty Images (bottom)
Page 59: Lawrence Jackson/White House Photo/Alamy Live News
Page 60: Liu Jie/Xinhua/Alamy Live News
Page 61: Brett Coomer/Houston Chronicle via Getty Images
Pages 62–63: The Syndicate/Alamy
Page 64: Aaron Schwartz/Sipa USA/Alamy Live News (top), Olivier Douliery/AFP via Getty Images (bottom)
Page 65: Lawrence Jackson/White House Photo/Alamy Live News (top), Lawrence Jackson/Official White House Photo (bottom)
Page 66: Stephen Maturen/AFP via Getty Images (top), Photo by Noah Berger/UCSF (bottom)
Page 67: Daniel Acker/Bloomberg via Getty Images
Page 68: Nick Reynolds/Post & Courier
Page 69: Lawrence Jackson/Official White House Photo
Pages 70–71: Erin Scott/Official White House Photo
Pages 72–72: Michael M. Santiago/Getty Images
Pages 74–75: Michael Reynolds/EPA/Bloomberg via Getty Images
Page 80: Dominic Gwinn/Middle East Images/AFP via Getty Images (top), Anna Moneymaker/Getty Images (bottom)
Page 81: Christian Monterrosa/Bloomberg via Getty Images
Page 82: Amy Lemus/NurPhoto via Getty Images
Page 83: Maria Magdalena Campos-Pons (left), Courtesy of Roland S. Martin/Black Star Network (right)
Page 84–85: Hannah Beier/Bloomberg via Getty Images
Page 86: Peter Zay/Anadolu via Getty Images
Page 87 (all): Julia Beverly/Alamy Live News
Page 88: Chip Somodevilla/Getty Images
Page 89: Andrew Harnik/Getty Images (top), Tom Williams/CQ-Roll Call, Inc via Getty Images (bottom)
Page 90: Tom Williams/CQ-Roll Call, Inc via Getty Images
Page 91: Andrew Harnik/Getty Images (top), Chip Somodevilla/Getty Images (bottom)
Page 92 (top to bottom): Joe Raedle/Getty Images, Chip Somodevilla/Getty Images, David Paul Morris/Bloomberg via Getty Images
Page 93: Chip Somodevilla/Getty Images, Saul Loeb/AFP via Getty Images, Chip Somodevilla/Getty Images, Chip Somodevilla/Getty Images, Andrew Caballero-Reynolds/AFP via Getty Images
Pages 94–95: Kyle Mazza/Anadolu via Getty Images
Page 96–97: Al Drago/Bloomberg via Getty Images
Pages 98–99: Saul Loeb/AFP via Getty Images
Page 100: Doug Mills/The New York Times/Bloomberg via Getty Images
Page 101 (all): Saul Loeb/AFP via Getty Images
Page 106: Tyler Mitchell/Vogue
Page 107 (all): From TIME. ©2019 TIME USA LLC.. All rights reserved. Used under license.
Page 109: Richard B. Levine/Alamy
Page 110: Shiiko Alexander / Alamy Stock Photo
Page 111: Flo Ngala for Rolling Stone. May 22, 2022

Page 116: Polly Irungu/Official White House Photo
Page 117: Andrew Harnik/Getty Images
Page 118: Brett Coomer/Houston Chronicle via Getty Images (top), Lawrence Jackson/Official White House Photo (bottom)
Page 119: Gabrielle Lurie/The San Francisco Chronicle via Getty Images
Page 120: Alex Wong/Getty Images
Page 121: Kamil Krzaczynski /AFP via Getty Images
Page 126: Bill Ingalls/NASA via Getty Images
Page 127 (all): Courtesy of Nashormeh Lindo
Page 128: Nipah Dennis/AFP via Getty Images
Page 129: Courtesy of Vision to Learn Center
Page 130: Courtesy of Dawn Davis
Page 131: World Politics Archive (WPA) / Alamy Stock Photo
Page 132: Arun Sankar/AFP via Getty Images
Page 133: Jeremy Hogan/SOPA Images/LightRocket via Getty Images (top), Mandel Ngan/AFP via Getty Images (bottom)
Page 138: Lawrence Jackson/Official White House Photo
Page 139: Pictorial Press/Alamy
Page 140: Brian Snyder/Reuters
Page 141: Alex Wong/Getty Images
Page 142: Samuel Corum/Getty Images
Page 143: The Second Gentleman/Douglas Emhoff
Pages 144–145: Jack Kurtz/ZUMA Wire/Alamy Live News
Page 146: Celal Gunes/Anadolu Agency via Getty Images
Page 147: Bill Clark/CQ Roll Call via Getty Images
Pages 148–149: Lawrence Jackson/Official White House Photo
Pages 150–151: Mandel Ngan/AFP via Getty Images
Page 156 (all): Courtesy of Kuae Noel Kelch
Page 157 (all): Courtesy of Jill Louis
Page 158: Arturo Holmes/Getty Images for ESSENCE
Pages 159–161: Courtesy of Kuae Noel Kelch
Page 166: Shiiko Alexander / Alamy Stock Photo (top), Adam J. Dewey/Anadolu via Getty Images (bottom)
Page 167: Sheila Pree Bright (top), Shannon Finney/Getty Images for National Women's History Museum & Chief (bottom)
Page 168: Peter Dazeley/Getty Images
Page 169: Al Drago/Bloomberg via Getty Images
Pages 170–171: Agustin Paullier/AFP via Getty Images
Page 172: Courtesy of Ryan Alexiev and Hank Willis Thomas
Page 173: Photo by Tonya Lewis Lee
Pages 174–175: A Carrie Mae Weems Project Paid for by People For The American Way

ABOUT THE AUTHORS

DEBORAH WILLIS is a photo historian, photographer, and professor and chair of New York University's Tisch School of the Arts. A Guggenheim and MacArthur fellow, she coauthored the bestselling *Obama: The Historic Campaign in Photographs*. She lives in New York City.

KEVIN MERIDA is a contributing essayist to *The Washington Post* and the former executive editor of the *Los Angeles Times*. He coauthored the critically acclaimed *Supreme Discomfort: The Divided Soul of Clarence Thomas* and the bestselling *Obama: The Historic Campaign in Photographs*. He lives in Los Angeles.

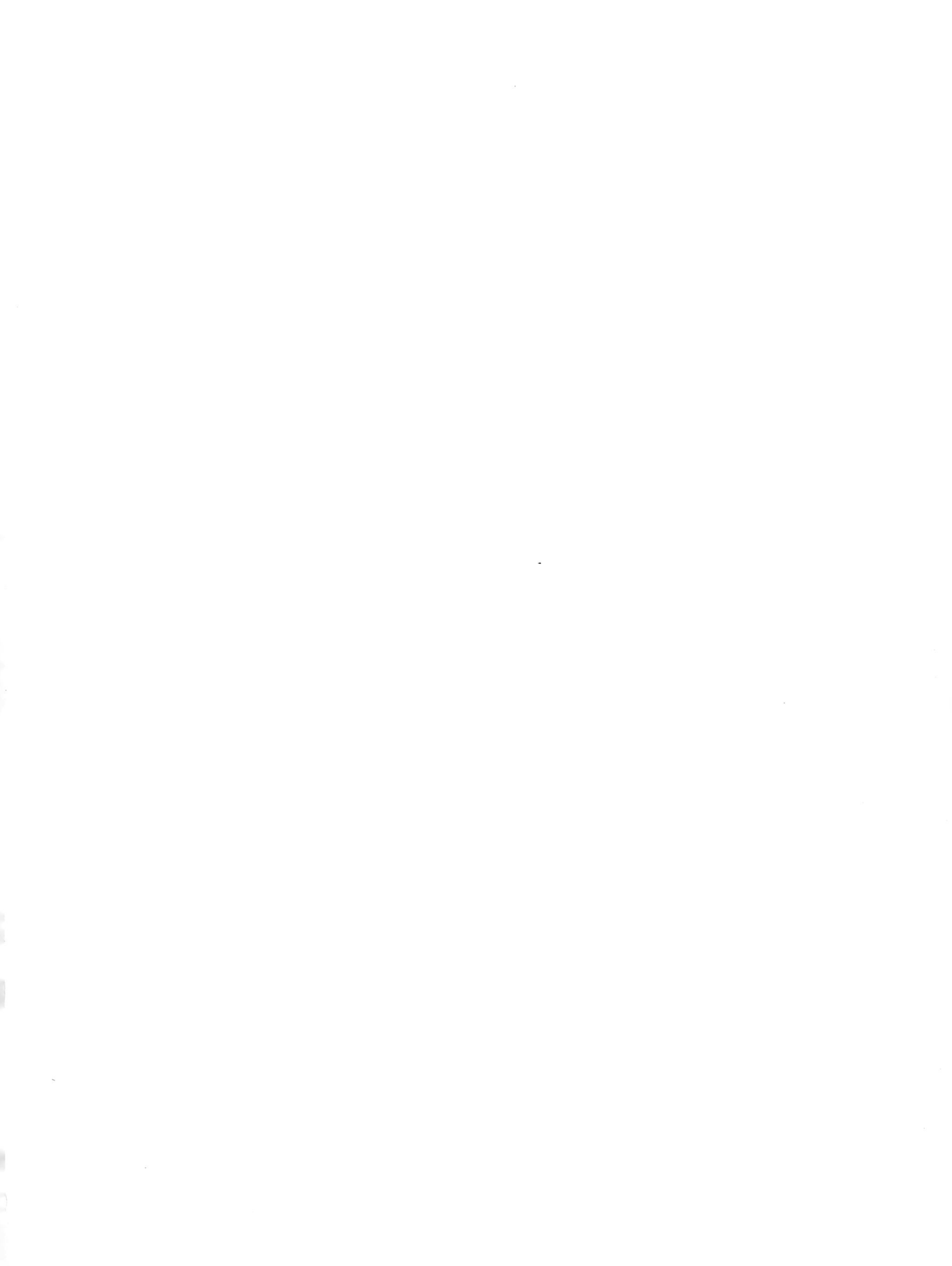